iPAQ™ FOR DUMMIES®

by Brian Underdahl

WILEY

Wiley Publishing, Inc.

iPAQ™ For Dummies®

Published by
Wiley Publishing, Inc.
111 River Street
Hoboken, NJ 07030-5774

WILEY

About the Author

Brian Underdahl is the best-selling author of over 70 books, numerous magazine articles, and dozens of Web pieces. He has appeared on a number of TV shows as an expert on computing and has taught many different computer courses.

Brian loves to play with the newest gadgets, and he gets a lot of enjoyment out of making computers easier to understand and use for people who don't have the time to wade through all the gory details on their own. When he isn't typing at the keyboard, you'll often find Brian preparing a gourmet meal at his home in the mountains above Reno, Nevada. His wife enjoys that part, too.

Author's Acknowledgments

I have to admit that it's a lot of fun seeing my name on the cover of a book. But it's probably a little unfair that only one name gets listed there because there are so many other people who helped make the book into a reality. To address this, I'd like to thank a whole bunch of people who made the book possible. They include:

Tiffany Franklin, Andy Cummings, Chris Morris, and a raft full of other great folks at Wiley Publishing.

Jim Kelly, my technical reviewer.

Monisha Khanna, ACD Systems; Dr. Cyrus Peikari, Airscanner; Mary Kelly, ALK; Melody Chalaban, Belkin; Bob Thomas, Bitstream; Chris Mossing, Cirond; Carrie Hall, Conduits; Sadie Pope, Crucial; Søren Peter Andersen, Danware; Caleb Mason, DeLorme; John Psuik, Developer One Software; Anna-Marie Claassen, D-Link; Janet Lill, Funk Software; Andrew Green, Griffin Mobile; Kathleen Gilpatrick, Handmark; Nita Miller, HP; Mark Perkins and Mike Matthews, iBIZ; Charles Gelinas, ICP Global Technologies; Ellen Craw, Ilium Software; Wasyl Dolgow, Inesoft; Darrell Musick, Innergy Power Corporation; Chris Repetto, Intuit; David Porfido, LandWare; Amanda Kuna, LifeView; Imani James, Marware; David Horwich, neohand; Mike Siris, Officeonthegogo; Ben Moore, Pacific Wireless; James Oyang, Pharos; Patrick Lin, Portable Innovation Technology; Bob Goligoski and Elias Castillo, SanDisk; Elaine Marshall and Jose Zavala, SimpleTech; Trisha Grahn King, SMC Networks; Tatia Meghdadi, Socket; Corey McLaughlin, Soft Pocket Solutions; John F.C. Cheong, Ph.D. and Abe Wu, Space Machine; Phil Weiler, Symantec; Marleen Winer, TeleType; Andrew Wong, Veo; Charles Oliva and Andrew Grosso, Vindigo; and Nicole Rund, Zagat.

I'm sure there are many others whose names I've misplaced in the confusion that passes for writing a book. For that I apologize.

Publisher's Acknowledgments

We're proud of this book; please send us your comments through our online registration form located at www.dummies.com/register/.

Some of the people who helped bring this book to market include the following:

Acquisitions, Editorial, and Media Development

Project Editor: Christopher Morris

Acquisitions Editor: Tiffany Franklin

Copy Editor: Virginia Sanders

Technical Editor: James F. Kelly

Editorial Manager: Kevin Kirschner

Media Development Supervisor: Richard Graves

Editorial Assistant: Amanda Foxworth

Cartoons: Rich Tennant (www.the5thwave.com)

Production

Project Coordinator: Courtney MacIntyre

Layout and Graphics: Andrea Dahl, Joyce Haughey, Barry Offringa, Heather Ryan, Jacque Schneider

Proofreaders: Andy Hollandbeck, Carl William Pierce, TECHBOOKS Production Services

Indexer: TECHBOOKS Production Services

Publishing and Editorial for Technology Dummies

    Richard Swadley, Vice President and Executive Group Publisher

    Andy Cummings, Vice President and Publisher

    Mary C. Corder, Editorial Director

Publishing for Consumer Dummies

    Diane Graves Steele, Vice President and Publisher

    Joyce Pepple, Acquisitions Director

Composition Services

    Gerry Fahey, Vice President of Production Services

    Debbie Stailey, Director of Composition Services

Contents at a Glance

Table of Contents

Introduction

Several different manufacturers make Pocket PCs, but none are as popular as the iPAQ. The iPAQ has the style, the power, and the features to make it the best PDA there is. That Hewlett-Packard is able to pack so much into such a convenient little package is a true marvel of modern engineering.

In this book, I cover hundreds of neat and fun ways to make use of your iPAQ. In reading this book, I hope you get lots of enjoyment and see just how much you really can do with your iPAQ!

About This Book

iPAQ For Dummies is a hands-on guide that uses real-world examples to show you just what you need to know about iPAQs and why you want to know it. You don't find a lot of hype or jargon. You do find useful information presented clearly and concisely.

iPAQ For Dummies is also a reference that you can use according to your own style. If you're already somewhat familiar with your iPAQ, you can skip around to find out about things that you're a little unsure of. If you're new to iPAQs, you may want to read the entire book. Either way, you're bound to find out lots of little things — and some very important and useful ones.

Finally, *iPAQ For Dummies* is primarily about the new iPAQ Windows Mobile 2003 systems. It can also be useful for owners of older iPAQs, of course, but the focus is on the newest models and the features that are unique to them.

Conventions Used in This Book

I use a few conventions in this book to make it easier for you to spot special information. Here are those conventions:

- New terms are identified by using *italic*.
- Web site addresses (URLs) are designated by using a `monospace font`.

✔ Any command that you enter at a command prompt is shown in bold and usually set on a separate line. Set-off text in italic represents a placeholder. For example, the text might read:

At the command prompt, enter the command in the following format:

ping *IPaddress*

The *IPaddress* part is the IP address of the remote computer that you want to query.

✔ Command arrows, which are typeset as ⇨, are used in a list of menus and options. For example, Tools⇨Options means to choose the Tools menu and then choose the Options command.

✔ Key combinations are shown with a plus sign, such as Ctrl+F2. This means that you should hold down the Ctrl key while you press the F2 key.

What You're Not to Read

If you're really looking for a book about how to miniaturize your desktop PC so that you can stuff it into your pocket, you can probably skip this entire book. Otherwise, you may want to read most of it — especially if you're interested in knowing why and not just how things work on your iPAQ. Still, I recognize that you may not want to waste any time on technical explanations. If so, you can skip the text next to the Technical Stuff icons. You can possibly skip a few other things, too, if you really want to. For example, you can certainly skip the chapter on choosing your iPAQ if you already own one of the newer models.

Foolish Assumptions

Making assumptions is always a gamble because they can quickly come back to haunt you. However, in writing this book I made some assumptions about you. This book is for you if:

✔ You have an iPAQ and want to know how to get the most from it.

✔ You don't have an iPAQ yet, but are wondering whether you should get one.

✔ You have a different type of PDA and are thinking of upgrading to an iPAQ.

✔ You have one of the original iPAQs, and you want to discover what's new and improved in the new iPAQs.

✔ You want to see how an iPAQ can make travel fun again.

✔ You want to find out if it really is possible to surf the Internet while you're sitting at that coffee shop.

✔ You're tired of lugging around a laptop and want to see how you can get real work done with an iPAQ.

✔ You want to complete your framed set of *The 5th Wave* cartoons.

How This Book Is Organized

iPAQ For Dummies has seven parts. Each part is self-contained, but you also find that the parts are somewhat interconnected. That way, you see the most useful information without a lot of boring repetition.

Part I: Introducing the iPAQ

Part I lays the foundation for getting to know your iPAQ. You discover how your iPAQ compares with other computers that you may have used in the past and you discover how to take advantage of the iPAQ's unique features. If you're still deciding which iPAQ best suits your needs, you get some help choosing the correct model. You find out how to use all the basic features of your iPAQ quickly and efficiently. Finally, you find out how to interact with your iPAQ, including how to make use of the great handwriting recognition software that's built into your system.

Part II: Personal Organization with Your iPAQ

Part II shows you how to use your iPAQ to help keep your personal life in order. You see how your iPAQ can keep track of your address book, act as your personal note taker, and help you manage your schedule no matter how hectic your life may seem.

Part III: Putting Your iPAQ to Work

Part III shows you how to use the powerful yet easy-to-use applications that are built into your iPAQ, the ones that set it apart from those other, less powerful palm-sized devices some people use. You see how to use Pocket Word to read, edit, and create Word documents. You discover how Pocket Excel gives you most of the power of your desktop PC's Excel program right in the palm of your hand. You see how Pocket Money, Pocket Quicken, and some other applications make it easy for you to track your expenses on the go.

Part IV: The iPAQ and the Internet

Part IV describes how you can use your iPAQ to access the Internet as well as how to connect directly to your network. Here you see just how convenient it is to be able to surf the Internet and handle your e-mail from wherever you happen to be. You see how you can make use of the exciting new wireless Internet options as well as the more familiar wired connections. You haven't surfed until you've done it on an iPAQ miles away from your desktop.

Part V: Multimedia Time

Part V shows you how to have some fun with your iPAQ. In this part, you see why an iPAQ can be a great musical companion, how you can read all sorts of the new electronic books on your iPAQ, how to make your iPAQ into the perfect partner for your digital camera, and why your iPAQ is the ultimate handheld game machine. In addition, you see that your iPAQ can even become a great tool for PowerPoint presentations with the right accessories.

Part VI: Working with iPAQ Add-Ons

Part VI shows you some of the many great ways to add even more utility to your iPAQ by adding new programs, and how your iPAQ can be a great traveling companion. You see where to find iPAQ programs, how to install them, and how to make the ones you want fit into the available space. You find out the essential information that you need to make traveling with your iPAQ a truly enjoyable experience.

Part VII: The Part of Tens

The Part of Tens provides information on some great ways to enhance your iPAQ by showing you the best iPAQ accessories. I included a chapter that shows you some of the best business-related iPAQ programs and a chapter on ways to enjoy your iPAQ. You see some great ways to get even more productivity from your iPAQ. I don't leave out those of you who just have to tinker and tweak, either. I even included a chapter that shows you some nifty utilities that let you really take control of your iPAQ.

Icons in This Book

iPAQ For Dummies includes icons that point out special information. Here are the icons that I use and what they mean:

 Technical Stuff is information for folks who want to know all the gory details. You can probably skip this stuff unless you really find it interesting.

 This icon is the one that can make you seem like a real iPAQ expert in no time. It highlights special tricks and shortcuts that make using iPAQ even easier. Don't miss any of these!

 Be careful when you see this icon. It points out an area where you want to be extra cautious so that you don't cause yourself problems. It also tells you how to avoid the problems.

 The Note icon steers you to additional information about iPAQs.

Where to Go from Here

You are about to find out just how much fun an iPAQ really can be. As you read through *iPAQ For Dummies,* you notice that I emphasize ways to really become more efficient and comfortable with using your iPAQ, but I guarantee that you can have fun doing so. Feel free to jump around, but I suggest that you start with Chapter 1 for a good introduction to your iPAQ.

Part I

Introducing the iPAQ

"Well, it's not as functional as my iPAQ, but the monitor is interesting."

In this part . . .

Find out how to get started with your iPAQ. In just a few short chapters, you can discover how to take advantage of the iPAQ's unique features. I help you choose the iPAQ that best suits your needs and show you basics of using your iPAQ. You see how to input information into your iPAQ, including how to use handwriting recognition so that you can write directly on your screen. Finally, I show you how to exchange data with your desktop PC.

Chapter 1

Getting to Know the iPAQ

. . . .

In This Chapter

▶ Understanding your iPAQ

▶ Finding out what's new in iPAQs

▶ Partnering with your desktop PC

▶ Putting multimedia in your pocket

▶ Using the iPAQ as your personal assistant

▶ Keeping in touch while on the go

▶ Reading eBooks

. . . .

*I*t's really pretty amazing that something as sleek and small as an iPAQ can be so useful and fun. The latest iPAQ models have the power to do all sorts of cool things such as making sure you never miss an important date, letting you find your way in strange places without having to ask for directions, or even responding to spoken commands. And they do it all in a stylish little package that easily fits into your pocket.

This chapter shows you a number of things that you can do with an iPAQ. If you don't have an iPAQ yet or if you have an older model iPAQ, you can discover just how great the newer models really are. Chapter 1 is, of course, just a quick overview, and I can't show you everything in just a few pages. But even in this limited space, you can get a feeling for why iPAQ fans don't want to be without their iPAQ.

Understanding Your iPAQ

So just what is an iPAQ, anyway? Is it a real PC, and does it really fit into a pocket? Do you look like a propeller-head as soon as you pull it out and start using it? Here are some basics about the iPAQ to answer some of these types of questions:

- ✔ An iPAQ is a Pocket PC — a real computer that's been shrunk down into a very small package. In fact, the smallest of the iPAQs (the h1900 line) is just about four and a half inches tall, two and a half inches wide, and about a half inch thick. The other iPAQ models are a bit larger, but still small enough to fit an average-sized pocket.

- ✔ Don't shove your iPAQ into your back jeans pocket. It makes an uncomfortable lump and it probably won't survive being sat upon — even if it really does fit into that pocket.

- ✔ iPAQs and Palm PCs use completely different *operating systems* (OS), meaning that they can't run each other's programs. Make certain any programs you buy specifically state that they are designed for the iPAQ (or the Pocket PC 2003).

- ✔ The iPAQ OS is technically a version of Windows called *Windows Mobile*, but this doesn't mean that you can run your favorite Windows-based programs on your iPAQ. You need special iPAQ versions of any programs that you want to run. Because the iPAQ OS is based on Windows, at least you won't have to learn new ways of doing things; most of what you know about using Windows-based programs still applies on your iPAQ. Figure 1-1 shows an example of the iPAQ screen when Pocket Excel has a document open.

- ✔ As for the question about whether you look like a propeller-head when you pull out your iPAQ, I don't really know. But maybe there are worse things in the world than having the coolest toy on the block!

Figure 1-1:
Your iPAQ runs special versions of some of your favorite Windows programs.

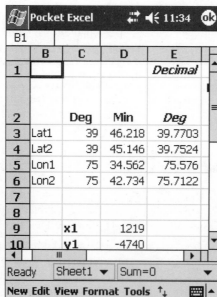

Finding some real power in your pocket

Sure, an iPAQ may seem like a cool toy, but can something that size *actually* be a powerful computer? Yes: It not only can but it is. Consider for just a moment how far PCs have advanced in just a few short years. Comparing an iPAQ with a desktop PC, here are some interesting points:

✔ The brain (okay, the *processor* for all you technical types) inside the iPAQ is functionally as powerful as the fastest desktop PC processors of two or three years ago.

✔ Your iPAQ has as much memory as most desktop systems of just a few years ago.

✔ An iPAQ is typically able to run for an entire workday on a single charge — all the more amazing when you consider that the battery is inside that pocket-sized package along with the processor, the memory, the display, and all the other components.

✔ iPAQs are ready to use immediately. Touch a button and you can instantly pick up right where you left off without waiting for the system to boot up (because it doesn't have to boot up the way your desktop PC does).

✔ The iPAQ runs special versions of programs you're already familiar with such as Word and Excel. You can even share your document files between your iPAQ and your desktop PC.

What's New in iPAQs?

As great as the first iPAQs were, the new iPAQ systems represent a big step forward in putting real computing power into your pocket. Here are some of the changes that you can find in the latest iPAQ systems:

✔ iPAQs are available in more sizes. In addition to the models like the h5550/5555, which are available in the original iPAQ dimensions, you can now buy iPAQs that are even smaller. A variety of sizes ensures that you have a better chance of finding exactly the one you want when you go shopping.

✔ The OS and built-in applications have once again been upgraded. It's true that all iPAQs have upgradeable flash memory and this means that both the iPAQ OS and the built-in applications can be upgraded, but the newer models already have the latest upgrades installed.

✔ All of the new iPAQ systems now use a *trans-reflective* display that can show 65,536 colors. This is a huge improvement over the displays on some earlier iPAQs because you can now view pictures in full color, and more importantly, you can now see the display quite well in bright sunlight! If you add a Global Positioning System (GPS) receiver to your iPAQ, you can easily see the display in your car or when you're out hiking.

✔ All iPAQs now have built-in expansion slots. Some even have a second memory expansion slot for CF (CompactFlash) memory cards in addition to the standard SD (Secure Digital) expansion slot. This second memory slot opens up a whole new world of possibilities because you can have all the advantages of expanded memory capabilities and still use a device such as a GPS receiver, a digital camera attachment, a Bluetooth card, a wireless network adapter, or whatever else you might want to add. For example, by adding a 256MB SD memory card, you can store your GPS receiver detailed maps that cover a large part of the country, or you can store a full-length movie that you can watch during a cross-country flight.

✔ The newer iPAQs come equipped with more base memory than their earlier iPAQ counterparts.

✔ Many iPAQ models include built-in Bluetooth, Wi-Fi, or both so that you can connect wirelessly. In fact, these new wireless communications capabilities are probably some of the most important changes you'll find in the new iPAQs because they open up so many important options for you. Figure 1-2 shows an example of how this capability allows you to browse the Internet on the go.

Figure 1-2:
You can browse the Internet wirelessly on many of the new iPAQs.

One problem you may encounter is deciding which iPAQ is the right one for you. Because all of the options are now so great, it's much harder making that choice. Now your choice is more likely to come down to some of the extras that a particular model offers rather than simply choosing the one with the best basic design. Some models offer more expansion possibilities than others, and some just seem to fit into an ordinary pocket a little better. Regardless of their differences, it's hard to go wrong, no matter which iPAQ you choose. Chapter 2 discusses the different iPAQ models so that you can choose the one that best suits your needs.

Although this book intentionally covers the latest iPAQ models, much of what you will find in these pages also applies to the older iPAQs. This is especially true if you obtain upgrade discs to update your existing iPAQ to the current software versions.

Your Desktop PC's Partner

Even though your iPAQ is a powerful computer on its own, thinking of your desktop PC and your iPAQ as partners is probably the best way to go. They make a great team, and both have features that complement the other. It's just a fact that some things you simply wouldn't want to do with one or the other. For example:

- ✔ Even though you can type on the onscreen keyboard or use the handwriting recognition feature to enter data into your iPAQ, you aren't likely to use either one when you type in your great novel. Your desktop PC keyboard works better when you need to enter lots of text. Sure, you can get a folding keyboard for your iPAQ, but somehow it's not quite the same thing.

- ✔ On the other hand, your desktop PC or even your notebook PC doesn't fit into a shirt pocket — no matter how big your shirts may be. When you're on the go, your iPAQ gives you access to your files in a package that's easy to carry along.

Figure 1-3 shows how to write notes directly on your iPAQ's screen. Of course, if your handwriting is as bad as mine, you may end up with some interesting results after you click the Recognize command.

What really makes the PC and iPAQ partnership work is that you can easily share files between the two. In fact, it's very easy to designate certain files (or even entire folders) that you want to *synchronize* between your iPAQ and desktop PC. Then, whenever you connect them, those files are automatically updated. So, if you add a new person to your iPAQ address list, that person is added to your desktop PC's address list without any further effort on your part. Of course, your address list is just one example. You can also synchronize your calendar, your résumé, or even your wine collection database. The possibilities are endless.

Figure 1-3:
You can
enter text by
using the
character
recognition
feature on
your iPAQ.

You can set up partnerships between your iPAQ and two different desktop PCs, making your iPAQ a great way to develop the same document on the PC in your office and the one in your home. Having said that, be sure to read the following paragraph. . . .

Even though you can partner your iPAQ with two desktop PCs, you can synchronize your e-mail with only one desktop PC. If you need to have the same e-mail messages on two different desktop PCs, you may want to configure the e-mail program on one of them to leave messages on the server, and then download those messages on the second PC later. Alternatively, you can connect directly to your mail server through your iPAQ without even bothering with your desktop system.

If you're a real iPAQ fanatic like me, it's possible to set up partnerships between any number of iPAQs and a single desktop system. You need to be aware of a few caveats, however. First, each iPAQ needs a unique name (you find more on this topic in Chapter 3), and second, only one iPAQ can connect at a time. Most iPAQ owners don't have to worry about this, of course, but it can get interesting connecting several different iPAQs to a single desktop system!

Putting Some Multimedia in Your Pocket

The next time you want to make other people jealous, just whip out your iPAQ and start using some of its multimedia capabilities. Because your iPAQ is a real computer that has both fantastic sound and video capabilities built-in, it's great at playing music and displaying color images, as well as letting you read your e-mail. You can't find many other devices that can do all that and still fit into your pocket!

Putting music in your pocket

You've probably seen those little pocket-sized gadgets that people use to download music from the Internet or audio CDs so they can carry their favorite music with them. What you may not realize is that your iPAQ not only serves the same function, but offers plenty of advantages over those single-purpose music players, too.

Music you download is usually stored in either an MP3 (MPEG version 3) or a WMA (Windows Media Audio) file. These are two different ways of compressing audio files so they don't take so much storage room. After you load either type of file into your iPAQ (or standalone music player), you can play back the music almost as if you were playing an audio CD. See Chapter 15 for more about using your iPAQ as a portable music player.

MP3 and WMA files don't sound quite as good as the originals because both types of compression are *lossy* — some of the audio signal data is tossed out, or lost, to make the files smaller. You probably won't notice much difference, though, because you most likely play the music back through a tiny set of earphones on your iPAQ or music player. Unless you're a musician, you may not even detect the lower quality if you play the music back through a high-end stereo system. The quality difference between the original and the compressed file isn't likely to be very significant in most listening environments.

When choosing the format for audio files for your iPAQ, choose WMA rather than MP3. WMA files can be as small as half the size of similar sounding MP3 files.

Putting images in your pocket

In addition to playing back your favorite music, you can also view images on the iPAQ screen. Of course, at 240 pixels wide by 320 pixels high, the iPAQ screen has just one-fourth the display capability of a plain old Video Graphics

Array (VGA) monitor, but the iPAQ does have to fit in your pocket, after all. (*Pixels* are picture elements — the number of dots that can appear on the screen per line.)

Even though the iPAQ screen has to be small enough to fit into your pocket, that doesn't mean that you have to get eyestrain from viewing the iPAQ's screen. In Chapter 4 you find out about a slick little clip-on magnifier that can really make your iPAQ screen much easier to read.

A lot has changed since the iPAQ was first introduced. At that time, a PowerPoint viewer wasn't available, and you couldn't show PowerPoint slide shows with your iPAQ. Now you have several different ways to show PowerPoint slide shows using an iPAQ. In fact, as you discover in Chapter 20, you can even connect your iPAQ to a video projector, a large screen TV, or a standard computer monitor so that the slide show can easily be seen by whatever size crowd you have assembled (and you're no longer limited to the 240 x 320 iPAQ screen resolution, either). It's hard to imagine a more convenient way to bring along a PowerPoint presentation than in your iPAQ.

The iPAQ as Your Personal Assistant

Just about everyone could use some help keeping track of schedules, contacts, and to-do lists. The first *PDAs* (Personal Digital Assistants) were created primarily to fulfill just this set of functions.

The iPAQ serves as a superb personal assistant. It's got a built-in calendar so that you can maintain your schedule. It's got a great contact manager so that you can always remember those important details — such as someone's birthday. It even has a task manager that helps you get your to-do list in order (even if it's still up to you to actually do the tasks).

Oh sure, you're probably saying something like, "I can do all that stuff with this little paper notebook I carry." But have you considered how much more convenient the iPAQ makes these tasks? Here are just a few ways the iPAQ beats out the little paper notebook method:

✔ The iPAQ always has a correct calendar for any date — whether it's next week, next year, or two years from now. You can easily schedule an appointment for any date and time you choose.

✔ Adding a new contact or changing someone's information is always easy in the iPAQ contact list. You don't have to worry about finding room on the right page because you can add as many new contacts as necessary and they always appear in just the right place.

✔ You can set a reminder so that your iPAQ automatically lets you know when you're supposed to do something. (Your paper notebook is perfectly happy to just sit there and let you forget about that important dinner date.)

✔ With the right software, you can even have your iPAQ read your appointments aloud so that you can hear your schedule. Try getting your paper notebook to match that!

Figure 1-4 shows an example of how you can keep track of your schedule by using your iPAQ.

Figure 1-4:
You can use your iPAQ to make certain you never miss an important date.

Keeping in Touch While on the Go

Do you ever experience e-mail withdrawal if you have to go without access to your messages for a few days (or even just a few hours if you're a *really* connected person)? With an iPAQ, you no longer have to do without e-mail, instant messaging, the Internet, or the latest beach-cam shot. Your iPAQ has the Pocket Internet Explorer and Pocket Inbox built right in, so you can access all of that from almost anywhere and at just about any time you like.

You have lots of options for connecting on the go — some may suit your needs better than others. For example, here are a few of the methods you may use to connect your iPAQ to the Internet:

- ✔ If you have access to a telephone line, you can use a modem that fits into the expansion slot on your iPAQ. This type of connection typically requires a CompactFlash (CF) type of modem, such as the Pretec Compact Modem (www.pretec.com) or the Socket 56K Modem CF Card (www.socketcom.com). Using this type of modem, you can access your regular Internet service provider (ISP), and unless you're making a toll call, you don't typically pay any extra for the service because you can use the same Internet account that you use on your desktop PC.

- ✔ If you live in selected areas, you may be able to access the Web using a wireless modem such as one of the Sierra Wireless units (www.SierraWireless.com). This type of access is generally more expensive and slower than wired access through a phone line, but you can't beat the convenience of accessing your e-mail or browsing the Web without having to look for a telephone jack.

- ✔ If you have a cell phone, you may be able to get an adapter that connects your iPAQ to your phone. If so, you can access the Internet either through your wireless phone service provider or by dialing in to your regular ISP. Of course, you use some of your airtime minutes whenever you connect. You also need to make certain that you get the correct adapter specific to the exact make and model of your cell phone.

- ✔ Finally, Wi-Fi *hotspots* (places where you can connect to the Internet on the go) are becoming very popular, and several iPAQ models have the required 802.11b Wi-Fi radios built-in. (You can also buy Wi-Fi adapters to fit any iPAQ model.) This is probably the best way to connect on the go because the same Wi-Fi signal can connect you to your wireless network in your home or office. In addition, Wi-Fi connections are far faster than any of the other options (and usually less expensive).

Chapter 12 is the place to look to find out everything you need to know about connecting your iPAQ on the go. There I discuss your hardware options as well as explain how to make it all work.

Unfortunately, I've found a couple downsides to browsing the Web on the relatively small iPAQ screen. For one thing, you have to spend so much time scrolling the display that browsing isn't always tons of fun. (However, I show you another option that may work better for you in Chapter 13.) For another, typing in Web site URLs on that tiny on-screen keyboard gets old pretty fast. Still, it's pretty cool to be able to whip out your iPAQ and get on the Web. Being able to send and receive e-mail wherever you are is pretty slick, too.

Reading eBooks

Just owning an iPAQ is a good indication that you're the type of person who likes to make the best use of your time. The iPAQ adds one more element that helps you to do even more — eBooks.

eBooks are electronic books that you can download into your iPAQ and read on the screen. At first glance, you may wonder just how readable a book on the iPAQ screen can be — even a small paperback book has larger pages. Surprisingly, though, the iPAQ makes eBooks very easy and enjoyable to read. For example, I have found that the downloadable *Rough Guides,* which are available for a number of major travel destinations, can make you a real expert on having a great time when you're traveling. You can find the *Rough Guides* at www.roughguides.com.

Among the things that make eBooks easy to read, none is quite as important as something called *ClearType Technology,* a method of making even small-sized text extremely easy to read. ClearType Technology works its magic by making very subtle changes in the way characters are displayed. In a sense, ClearType makes it seem like your iPAQ's screen has higher resolution than it actually does. Certain iPAQ models even allow you to adjust your ClearType settings for improved readability.

Of course, the backlighting on the iPAQ screen also contributes to improved readability, too. *Backlighting* is the light that makes the screen on your iPAQ bright — it's light that comes from behind the images on the screen. With backlighting, you don't need to hold a flashlight next to your ear as you read under the covers late at night (or whatever other dark place you prefer for reading scary stories).

A number of publishers and booksellers, including Amazon.com and Barnes & Noble, offer eBooks. Often you can download an eBook for free, but even when you have to pay for one, the cost is surprisingly low. With no printing, ware-housing, or stocking costs to jack up the price, eBooks can be a real bargain.

You can find a huge collection of downloadable eBooks in the Microsoft eBook Catalog at www.mslit.com. With a wireless Internet connection you can even download them directly to your iPAQ without first going through your desktop PC.

Chapter 2

Choosing Your iPAQ

*B*ack in the ancient times (a few years ago), choosing the right iPAQ model was pretty easy. Only a few choices existed, so if you wanted an iPAQ, you just bought whatever model was available at the time. In our more modern era, choosing your iPAQ is much more complicated because you have so many more options.

In this chapter, you see how the different iPAQ model lines compare with each other so that you can have an easier time deciding which iPAQ best fits your needs. You may be surprised to find out just how great a selection of options is available. These aren't your father's iPAQs!

Before we begin our look at the iPAQ model lines, it's important for you to keep in mind the fact that the available models can and do change often. This chapter represents a snapshot in time, and some new iPAQ choices may be available by the time you read this. But despite that, the information that you find here can help you to make a better decision as you choose your iPAQ.

Model Number Mayhem: Understanding the iPAQ Models

One of the biggest problems you face in selecting the best iPAQ to suit your needs is that so many different iPAQ models are available. To make matters worse, as Figure 2-1 shows, they don't really look all that different from each other, either.

h4150   h2215   h1935   h4350

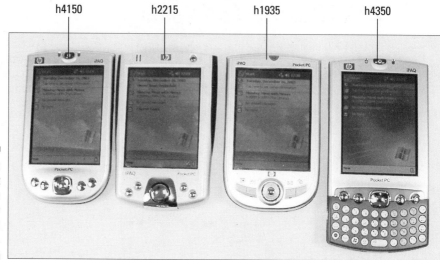

Figure 2-1:
The different
iPAQ models
look pretty
similar on
the surface.

Although the iPAQ models look pretty similar on the outside, a number of very important differences lurk on the inside, and these differences can ultimately help you choose your favorite iPAQ. The following sections provide more details about the current iPAQ model lines.

What's this 0/5 stuff?

When shopping for an iPAQ, you may have noticed that some identical iPAQ models sometimes have different model numbers. For example, take the h2210 and the h2215: If you compare the specifications of these two, they appear identical, and in reality, they are identical twins. So why, you ask, are there two different model numbers for the same device?

The answer to that question is pretty simple and maybe just a bit silly. Hewlett-Packard (HP) sells the iPAQs through dealers, but HP also sells them directly to end users (that's you and me) through their online store. The two model numbers make it possible for HP to sell "different" iPAQ models directly and through their dealers so that HP can claim that they aren't in competition with the independent dealers.

The bottom line: It doesn't matter if the final digit in the model number is a zero or a five. As long as the other three numbers match, it's the same iPAQ.

h1900 series highlights

The h1900 series is the smallest and least expensive of the current iPAQ models. But that doesn't mean that they aren't really iPAQs. They are, in fact, extremely well equipped — especially considering how little you have to spend for them. Check out Figure 2-2.

Here are the specifics of the h1900 model iPAQs:

- 3.5-inch trans-reflective, 65,536 color display
- Samsung 2410 processor (203 MHz or 266 MHz)
- Windows Mobile 2003 Professional
- 64MB RAM (short for random access memory)
- 4.46 x 2.75 x 0.5 inches in size
- 4.37 oz weight
- Multi-color notification light-emitting diode (LED) indicator
- Removable, rechargeable, 900 mAh Lithium-Ion battery with an estimated 8-hour usage
- Integrated SDIO slot that supports both SD and MMC cards — both memory and I/O
- Microphone, speaker, one 2.5 mm headphone jack, MP3 stereo (through audio jack)
- A suite of applications in addition to those standard in Windows Mobile 2003 Professional

The two current h1900 model iPAQs aren't completely identical, however. The h1940/1945 has integrated Bluetooth and a slightly faster processor than does the h1930/1935. Of these two features, the integrated Bluetooth proves far more important to most iPAQ owners.

The headphone jack on the h1900 series iPAQ models is 2.5 mm rather than the more common 3.5 mm size. If you want to listen to stereo music on your h1900 series iPAQ, make certain that you buy headphones with a 2.5 mm plug. This only applies to h1900 series models; the other iPAQ series models include the more conventional 3.5 mm headphone jack.

h2200 series highlights

The next step up from the h1900 series iPAQs is the h2200 series. (See Figure 2-3.) They cost a little more and are a bit larger, but they also pack considerable power into that slightly larger package.

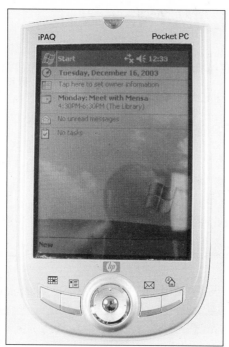

Figure 2-2:
The h1935
iPAQ.

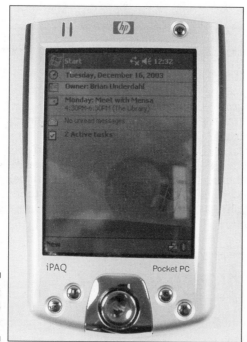

Figure 2-3:
The h2215
iPAQ.

Here are the specifics of the h2200 model iPAQs:

- ✔ 3.5-inch trans-reflective, 65,536 color display
- ✔ 400 MHz Intel XScale processor
- ✔ Windows Mobile 2003 Premium
- ✔ 64MB RAM
- ✔ 4.54 x 3.00 x 0.61 inches in size
- ✔ 5.1 oz weight
- ✔ Integrated Bluetooth
- ✔ Multi-color notification LED indicator
- ✔ Removable, rechargeable, 900 mAh Lithium-Ion battery with an estimated 12-hour usage
- ✔ Integrated SDIO slot that supports both SD and MMC cards — both memory and I/O
- ✔ Integrated CompactFlash Type I/II slot (Type II slots are capable of holding thicker adapter cards than Type I)
- ✔ Microphone, speaker, one 3.5 mm headphone jack, MP3 stereo (through audio jack)
- ✔ A suite of applications in addition to those standard in Windows Mobile 2003 Premium including Nevo Universal Remote Control

The two built-in expansion slots are one of the most important upgrades in the h2200 series compared to the h1900 series. With both slots, you get many more expansion options.

h4100 series highlights

The newest iPAQ models are currently those in the h4100 (and closely related h4300) series. These iPAQs are clearly aimed at people who want just about everything, but don't want to give up an extremely compact package to get it. Take a look at Figure 2-4.

Here's what you can find in the h4100 model iPAQs:

- ✔ 3.5-inch trans-reflective, 65,536 color display
- ✔ 400 MHz Intel XScale processor
- ✔ Windows Mobile 2003 Premium
- ✔ 64MB RAM

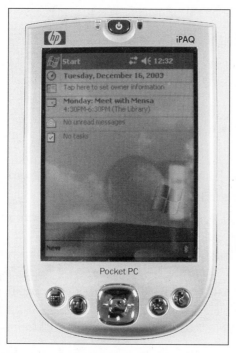

Figure 2-4:
The h4150
iPAQ.

✔ 4.47 x 2.78 x 0.51 inches in size

✔ 4.67 oz weight

✔ Integrated Bluetooth

✔ Integrated Wi-Fi (802.11b)

✔ Multi-color notification LED indicator

✔ Removable, rechargeable, 1000 mAh Lithium-Ion battery

✔ Integrated SDIO slot that supports both SD and MMC cards — both memory and I/O

✔ Microphone, speaker, one 3.5 mm headphone jack, MP3 stereo (through audio jack)

✔ A suite of applications in addition to those standard in Windows Mobile 2003 Premium

The h4300 models (see Figure 4-5) also include a small, thumb-operated keyboard below the screen (which adds some additional height and weight, of course).

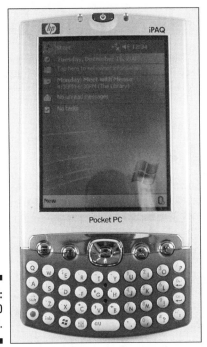

Figure 2-5:
The h4350
iPAQ.

The h4100 series iPAQs are virtually the same size as the h1900 series, but include both Bluetooth and Wi-Fi capabilities built-in. This series does not include the CF expansion slot that you find in the h2200 series, but with both wireless communications options built-in, you may not miss it.

End of an era: the h5500 series

The h5500 series (and closely related h5100 series) are the big boys when it comes to iPAQ models. This is the only iPAQ line that can accept the traditional iPAQ expansion sleeves (big, bulky things that slide onto the back of the older iPAQs — but you could argue that the other iPAQs probably don't need that capability because they have so many features built in). As it happens, they also represent the end of an era — HP has decided to stop producing these pocket-stretchers.

Deciding Which iPAQ Is Right for You

Now that you have a better idea of how the different iPAQ models stack up, you should have an easier time deciding which iPAQ is right for you. In the following sections, I show you several different factors that you may want to consider in making your choice.

What kind of iPAQ user are you?

When you get right down to it, knowing what kind of iPAQ user you're likely to be is one of the most important pieces of information in the whole process of choosing the right iPAQ. Consider the following points:

✔ If you primarily intend to use your iPAQ to manage your schedule and contacts, any of the models can do the job. You may as well buy one of the h1900 iPAQs and save your money for other things.

✔ If you would like to use your iPAQ to help you navigate, you want to consider your options in Global Positioning System (GPS) receivers. Currently GPS receivers come in the following styles:

- Those that plug into the sync jack on the bottom of the iPAQ
- Those that plug into a CF expansion slot
- Those that communicate with your iPAQ via Bluetooth

Of these options, the Bluetooth method is by far the most convenient. Still, this means that any iPAQ can connect to a GPS receiver as long as you buy one to fit your iPAQ. See Chapter 19 for more information on GPS receivers.

✔ If you're one of those people who is always on the go and can't stand being away from your e-mail, you definitely want to consider one of the iPAQs with built-in Wi-Fi capabilities. See Chapter 12 for more information on this subject.

It's pretty clear that knowing what you want to do with your iPAQ helps you choose the correct one for you. But keep in mind that you may discover a whole lot of really cool new ways to use your iPAQ as you read this book. If so, you may want to choose an iPAQ that has the capability to grow with your needs.

Built-in capabilities

The various iPAQ models all are extremely capable Pocket PCs. Each of the current models has at least 64MB of RAM. Every iPAQ now boasts an Secure Digital Input/Output (SDIO) expansion slot so you can easily add memory or certain Input/Output (IO) cards like the SanDisk SD Wi-Fi card shown in an h1935 in Figure 2-6.

But even with these similarities, take some time to consider how the models differ. For example, only the h2200 series models have two expansion slots built-in. A single slot generally limits your expansion options, because most expansion cards don't offer memory in addition to other capabilities. (SanDisk does offer a version of the SD Wi-Fi card that also has 256MB of memory). This means that if you want to use a device that plugs into the expansion slot on your iPAQ, you must give up the ability to add extra memory. Unfortunately, this can somewhat limit the iPAQ's capabilities.

Figure 2-6:
The SanDisk
SD Wi-Fi
card enables
any iPAQ
model to
connect
wirelessly.

Earlier, I mention that built-in Bluetooth can be a very important feature when choosing your iPAQ. Essentially, the built-in Bluetooth capabilities in some iPAQ models allow you to use Bluetooth-enabled devices without filling up the iPAQ's expansion slot. This is especially handy if you want to use your iPAQ for GPS navigation, because you can then add a high-capacity SD memory card so that you have plenty of room for detailed maps.

Always be sure to check out what type of expansion slot is required before you buy any add-ons for your iPAQ. Some devices are offered in more than one format, but most are not. Unfortunately, you simply can't ever use an add-on device that fails to match the built-in capabilities of your particular iPAQ model.

Size differences

Size really does matter — at least in choosing your iPAQ. And in this case, smaller is generally better. But now that Hewlett-Packard (HP) has dropped the larger format iPAQs, you really don't have to give size too much thought, because any of the current iPAQ models is truly small enough to fit in your pocket.

How much smaller are the new iPAQs compared to the older models? Here's a rough estimate:

- ✔ The new iPAQs are about 20 percent smaller in every dimension. This makes quite a difference in how well your iPAQ fits into an ordinary pocket.
- ✔ The overall volume of the new series of iPAQs is only a little more than half the size of the original iPAQs.
- ✔ The newer iPAQs are only about 60 percent as heavy as the older models.

Chapter 3

Understanding the iPAQ Basics

*E*ven though the iPAQ is Windows-powered, you find lots of obvious differences between using an iPAQ and a desktop PC. (I use the term *Windows-powered* here because your iPAQ uses a version of Microsoft Windows — but probably not the version you've used in the past.) One of the most glaring differences strikes most iPAQ users the first time they want to enter information: "Where's my keyboard?" After you get over the fact that your iPAQ doesn't have some standard PC features (like a keyboard), you most likely start to wonder just how you actually use the darn thing. Well, never fear: This chapter offers all the tools that you need to become comfortable with using an iPAQ.

(Although this chapter does cover the basics of using an iPAQ, I hold off on most of the details about the on-screen keyboard and handwriting recognition until Chapter 4. Those topics really do deserve a chapter all to themselves.)

Even though an iPAQ (the h4350) with an actual built-in keyboard is now available, all the information in this chapter applies to that model, too.

Using the Touch Screen

Okay, because the typical iPAQ doesn't have a keyboard, just how do you interact with it? Those four or five buttons certainly don't seem to hold much promise, do they?

The answer is right in front of you — the iPAQ's screen. Every iPAQ uses a *touch screen* — a screen that recognizes when and where you touch the screen with your finger or the stylus. Figure 3-1 shows several different items to give you a better idea of how this works.

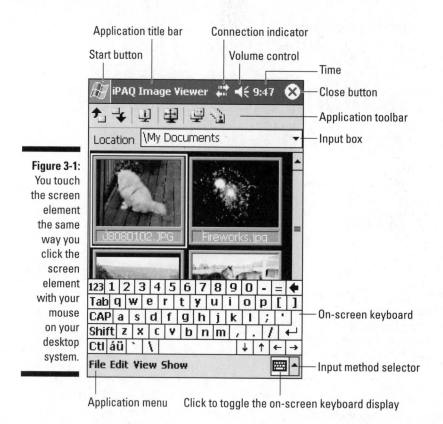

Application title bar

Connection indicator

Start button

Volume control

Time

Close button

Application toolbar

Input box

Figure 3-1:
You touch
the screen
element
the same
way you
click the
screen
element
with your
mouse
on your
desktop
system.

On-screen keyboard

Input method selector

Application menu

Click to toggle the on-screen keyboard display

The figure shows several different areas where you touch the screen in order to use your iPAQ. Following are some typical things you may find.

The iPAQ Start button

The Windows flag emblem in the upper-left corner of the iPAQ screen is the Start button. Clicking this button works very much like the Start button on a desktop PC — it displays the Start menu — but the following list explores some important differences:

- ✔ The iPAQ Start button drops down the Start menu from the top rather than zooming it up from the bottom. This design strategy is intended to keep you from covering up the Start menu with your hand. In truth, though, your Start menu probably fills up most of the screen's height anyway, so the location doesn't really matter.

✔ The top row of the Start menu displays the iPAQ equivalent of the Quick Launch toolbar, which normally appears next to your desktop Start button. The iPAQ Quick Launch toolbar is a little different, though, because it changes to show the programs you use the most.

✔ Many (but not all) of your iPAQ applications appear on the main Start menu, which can be a little confusing if a program you want to run doesn't appear on the iPAQ Start menu. The solution is simple — select the Programs item in the lower half of the Start menu to open the Programs folder. You can start your program from that folder by clicking the program's icon.

The iPAQ program menus

Because the iPAQ Start button is at the top, the program menus are now at the bottom of the screen. (I guess that means it's okay for your hand to cover up a program menu but not to cover up the Start menu.)

iPAQ program menus work just like the menus on your desktop PC. You *tap* — the iPAQ way of saying *click* — a menu to open the menu, and then tap the menu selection you want to open. In Figure 3-2, I've tapped on the iPAQ Image Viewer File menu to open that menu.

Figure 3-2:
Tap a program menu to open the menu so that you can select commands.

Items that are grayed-out on the iPAQ program menus are currently unavailable — just like on your desktop PC.

If you accidentally open the wrong menu, you can close the menu by tapping outside the menu. This first tap outside the menu closes only the open menu, so you need to tap again if you want to open a different menu.

Using your stylus

By now you've probably figured out that the iPAQ screen is too small to tap accurately with your fingers. Sure, sometimes you may get away with pointing your finger in just the right place, but your luck won't last. Tapping with your fingers is an exercise in frustration — especially when you start trying to type on the on-screen keyboard.

Every iPAQ comes with a *stylus* — a small, plastic, pen-like device that you use to tap on or to write on your screen. Unlike a pen, though, the stylus doesn't contain any ink, so it won't leave permanent marks on your screen.

It's a good idea to buy at least one replacement stylus for your iPAQ. You won't, of course, give too much thought to buying one until you lose the stylus that came with your iPAQ (or, if you absent mindedly use it as a toothpick and chew off the end of it). One excellent alternative I like is the Belkin LaserWright 3-in-1 Stylus: It combines a stylus, a fine-point ballpoint pen, and a laser pointer in a compact package. (Check out the Web site at www.belkin.com.)

Never use a pen or any sort of metal pointer on your iPAQ screen. Doing so quickly does permanent damage to the screen, and it's virtually certain that this type of damage is explicitly excluded from your warranty.

The three basic stylus actions you use are as follows:

- ✓ **Tap:** To lightly touch the on-screen item you want to select or open. Lift the stylus after you tap the item. This tap action is the equivalent of clicking an item on your desktop PC using the left mouse button. (In fact, I use both *click* and *tap* interchangeably in this book.)

- ✓ **Drag:** To place the point of the stylus on an item on-screen and then drag the stylus across the screen without lifting the pointer until you have completed the selection. This action works just like holding down the Shift key while you drag your desktop PC mouse with the left mouse button held down.

> ✔ **Tap-and-hold:** To hold the stylus pointer on an item for a short time until a context menu pops up, essentially the same as right-clicking your desktop PC mouse. When you tap-and-hold, a series of red dots appears around the stylus pointer to let you know that the context menu will soon pop up.

Practice using your stylus to make certain that you understand just how long the difference in time is between the tap and tap-and-hold actions.

Protecting your screen

No, this section isn't about keeping your iPAQ safe from diseases. It's about keeping your iPAQ healthy and in good condition.

If the idea of tapping and dragging a metal pointer across your iPAQ screen doesn't bother you, go ahead and pull out your pen and have a go at it. If you'd rather protect the screen from damage, I've got another tip for you — buy some screen protectors for your iPAQ. *Screen protectors* are simply plastic overlays that fit on top of your iPAQ screen to protect it from scratches. If you don't use screen protectors, you have a 100 percent chance of scratching your screen — and probably a lot faster than you can imagine. Better safe than sorry!

Belkin also offers some excellent screen protectors for the iPAQ. Look for the Belkin ClearScreen Overlay for Hewlett-Packard iPAQ Series.

Navigating on Your iPAQ

In this section, I don't tell you how to find your way on the high seas (or the low plains) by using your iPAQ. For that information, you need to turn to Chapter 19. Rather, here I help you to find your way around the screen and the file system inside your iPAQ.

Without a keyboard or a mouse, navigating on an iPAQ seems difficult at best. The reality is far better, though. After you get used to using the stylus and the buttons on the front of your iPAQ, you can easily go anywhere you want.

Opening your Start menu

The Start menu is the one item that ultimately gives you access to everything on your iPAQ. Through this menu, you can open any program, access any file, or adjust any of the settings that control how your iPAQ functions.

Because the Start menu is so vital, it's also easy to find. Just look for that Windows flag in the upper-left corner and give it a tap to open the Start menu.

Do you notice how the positions of the Start button and the menu bar sometimes seem to swap places? This swapping can happen when you run an older Windows CE-based program — one designed for Windows CE 2.*x*. (*Windows CE* is the official name of the iPAQ's operating system.) If the button and the bar switch on your iPAQ, don't worry. The change is temporary and things move back where they belong when you run a newer iPAQ program.

Figure 3-3 shows a typical example of an iPAQ Start menu. Your Start menu may be a little different, especially if you have installed additional programs on your iPAQ.

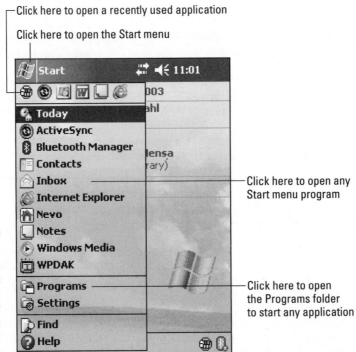

Figure 3-3:
Open
the Start
menu to
access your
programs
and files.

If you don't see the Start button when you first turn on your iPAQ, you may need to press one of the buttons on the front of the unit to display the Today screen. Your iPAQ can be set up to show the owner's information screen when it is first powered on, and this screen may not show the Start button.

When the Start menu is open, you can click one of the icons in the top row of the menu to quickly open one of the six most recently used applications. You can also click one of the items further down on the menu, or you can click the Programs folder to gain access to any of your installed programs. The sections "Finding your stuff" and "Adjusting your Settings," found later in this chapter, show you how to use the Settings and Find options.

Exploring your iPAQ

One of the most useful items on the Start menu is the Programs folder. Opening this folder is the key to running any installed program or locating any file. Figure 3-4 shows the Programs folder on an iPAQ where I've installed a number of third-party programs.

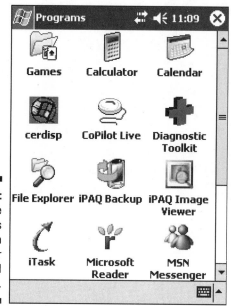

Figure 3-4: Open the Programs folder to run any of your installed programs.

As Figure 3-4 shows, a few additional program icons aren't currently visible. Some are sitting off-screen below the visible icons, and some are contained in folders, such as the Games folder. To view these additional icons, use the scrollbar along the right edge of the screen or click the folder icon to open the folder.

Using scrollbars on the iPAQ screen can be a little tricky. Make certain that you place the stylus pointer tip just to the left of the right edge of the screen and somewhere near the middle of the scrollbar slider. Then, drag the slider up or down as needed. You can also click the up or down arrows at the ends of the scrollbar, but it's really easy to select an icon instead of hitting the arrow in the right place.

Opening the File Explorer

You open a program or folder by clicking it with the stylus. To open the File Explorer, click the File Explorer icon (refer to Figure 3-4), and then the My Documents folder opens, as shown in Figure 3-5.

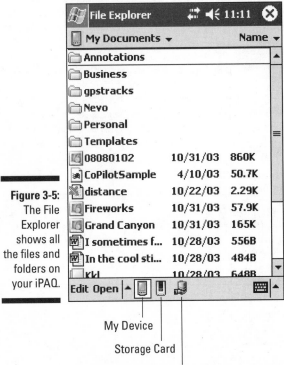

Figure 3-5: The File Explorer shows all the files and folders on your iPAQ.

My Device

Storage Card

Network Shares (for browsing your network)

Just as in recent versions of desktop Windows, the File Explorer on an iPAQ first displays the My Documents folder (more than a mere coincidence). The My Documents folder is one of the most important folders on your iPAQ. Many iPAQ applications find only documents that are in the My Documents folder. If you place document files anywhere else, you have to navigate with the File Explorer, find the document file, and then click to open it in the application.

If you add a memory card to your iPAQ so that you can store additional files, make certain that you create a My Documents folder on the memory card. If you store your documents, music, pictures, and so on in this folder, your iPAQ applications can locate those files without additional fuss and bother on your part.

Navigating your files and folders

Click a file or folder to open it. If you click a file, your iPAQ first tries to open the application that is *associated* with the type of file you clicked. For example, if you click a Word document, the document opens in Pocket Word because the Word application is associated with the Word document. Sometimes, though, no application is associated with a file type, and your iPAQ isn't able to open the file. This usually happens when you click a file other than one of the document file types. You can simply ignore files that aren't associated with applications — they may actually be necessary to the operation of various programs on your iPAQ, but may not be intended to be opened by you. Whatever you do, don't delete or move files that you can't open, because this could prevent you from using some of the applications that are installed on your iPAQ.

When you open a folder, you can then view any files or subfolders that the folder contains. In some cases, you may end up several levels deep into the file system before you realize that you wish you'd left a trail of breadcrumbs to help you find your way back. Fortunately, navigating back up the folder tree is easy, even if the method doesn't seem obvious at first. Figure 3-6 gives you the clue.

Figure 3-6:
Click the folder name in the second row to display the navigation list.

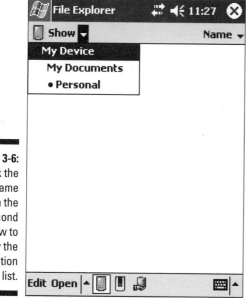

Just below the Start button is a row that normally shows the name of the current folder and the sort method used to display the items in the folder. In Figure 3-6, I selected Personal to drop down the navigation list. Select one of the folder names in the list to move back up the folder tree to the folder that you clicked.

When you select the folder name to drop down the navigation list, the folder name drops down to the bottom of the list, and the word *Show* appears where the folder name was, which tells you that selecting one of the folder names in the navigation list shows you the contents of that folder.

You can also use the My Device, Storage Card, or Network Shares icons in the menu bar to quickly navigate through the file system. You may need to set up a special user account to access shared network folders.

To create a new folder, choose Edit⇨New Folder from the menu bar at the bottom of the File Explorer window. Use the on-screen keyboard to type in a new name for the folder, and then press the Enter key. (The Enter key is indicated by a bent arrow that looks like the one on your desktop PC's Enter key.)

Working with your files

In addition to simply opening a file on your iPAQ, you can perform many of the same file management functions that you do on your desktop PC. The trick is to know how to access these functions. On your desktop PC, you can open a context-sensitive menu by right-clicking a file. On the iPAQ, you do the same by using the tap-and-hold method. That is, rather than a quick tap, press lightly with the stylus and don't let up until the menu pops up, as Figure 3-7 shows. (It wasn't possible to show this in the figure, but as you hold the stylus down, a ring of red dots appears around the stylus's screen position to indicate that you have activated the tap-and-hold menu.)

Before deleting files from your iPAQ, you may want to back them up on your desktop system. You find out more about backing up (and synchronizing) files in Chapter 5, but for now it's important to remember that backing up and synchronizing aren't the same thing. Synchronizing does copy certain files between your iPAQ and your desktop PC, but doesn't protect those files from being lost if they're accidentally deleted in either place. If you delete a synchronized file from your iPAQ, that file is also deleted from your desktop system the next time you synchronize files — unless you move the file out of the Pocket_PC My Documents folder on your desktop system *before* you allow the files to synchronize. In reality, synchronizing makes certain that the same versions of certain files you've selected are on your iPAQ and your desktop PC, and that anything you do to those files on either PC will also be done to the same files on the other PC.

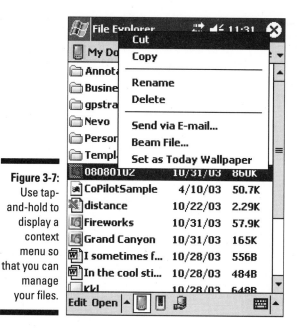

Figure 3-7:
Use tap-and-hold to display a context menu so that you can manage your files.

Finding your stuff

As small as your iPAQ is, it's still large enough to have plenty of hiding places for your files. And just like on your desktop PC, the files you need the most are the ones you probably can't find when you really need them. But those files can't hide forever — especially when you know the secret to finding them.

To find those errant files, click the Start button and choose Find to display the Find program. If you know the name of the file, click the down arrow to the right of the Find drop-down list box and use the on-screen keyboard to enter the name. If you want to look for files by type rather than by name, make certain that the Find drop-down list box contains ⟨ . . . ⟩ so that any filename can be found. The ⟨ . . . ⟩ simply means that you aren't specifying a filename — it's the equivalent of *.* on your desktop PC. Be sure to delete any name that is currently showing in the Find drop-down list box so that ⟨ . . . ⟩ appears if you want to find all files of a specific type.

To specify the type of file that you want to find, click the down arrow next to the Type drop-down list box, as shown in Figure 3-8. Select the type of file you want and then click Go to begin the search.

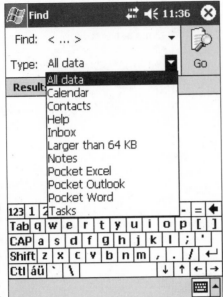

Figure 3-8:
Choose the
type of file
before you
click Go.

Switching between programs

Your iPAQ can do quite a few different things at the same time. You don't have
to close Pocket Word in order to work on a Pocket Excel worksheet, nor do you
have to close Internet Explorer in order to read your e-mail. But you do need to
be able to switch between different programs easily if you want to make effective use of several different iPAQ capabilities this way.

If you're accustomed to using Windows on your desktop PC, you know that
you can keep several programs open and switch between them with a variety
of techniques. Two of the most common ways to switch are by clicking a program's Taskbar button or by pressing Alt+Tab to use the Task Switcher. If you
decide to try these techniques on your iPAQ, though, you're immediately
faced with a couple of problems:

✔ To save precious screen real estate, the iPAQ doesn't have a Taskbar
running along the bottom of the screen. This pretty much cuts out the
click-a-program's-Taskbar-button option, doesn't it?

✔ Pressing Alt+Tab is also kind of hard when you don't have a keyboard.
(And don't even think about trying to do this using the on-screen
keyboard — it simply won't work.)

Looks like you need a different method to switch between running programs on your iPAQ. You can switch to a different program by choosing it from the Start menu or by selecting it from the set of icons at the top of the Start menu.

You may expect that choosing a program from the Start menu or the Home menu runs the risk of starting a second copy of a program that's already running. However, the iPAQ's operating system prevents this. Only one copy of any particular program can run at any time, and only one document can be open in a program. You cannot, for example, have two different documents open in Pocket Word at the same time — although you can have a Pocket Word document open and a Note document open at the same time.

Depending on the iPAQ model you have, you may have an additional way to switch between open applications. Figure 3-9 shows the iTask Task Switcher program that's available on certain iPAQ models. (You find it in the Programs folder if your model has it.) When you open iTask, simply tap the application that you want to switch to in the pop-up list.

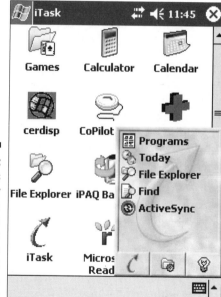

Figure 3-9:
iTask makes it easy to switch between applications on some iPAQ models.

Closing programs

By now, you're probably getting the idea that you have to do a few things a little differently on your iPAQ than what you're used to on your desktop system. It should come as no surprise, then, that closing iPAQ programs is just a little different, too.

On a desktop PC, you have several ways to close a program you no longer need. You can usually choose File➪Exit (or something similar) from the program's main menu. You can click the Close button in the upper-right corner of the program's window. You can even press Alt+F4 when the program is in the active window. Well, guess what? None of these options work in most iPAQ programs. (It's almost as though you're never supposed to close a program once you've opened it.)

As I show you in the preceding section, you can have several iPAQ programs open at the same time, which reduces the need to close programs. It doesn't, however, eliminate this need. Depending on the programs that are running in your iPAQ, you may need to close some programs so that you can run other ones.

Okay, if you *really* want to get picky about it, your iPAQ is supposed to be able to unload programs from memory if necessary, which is the real reason why it's often so difficult to close iPAQ programs. Your iPAQ is supposed to do it automatically, without your intervention. You know what? I still like to be able to control that myself.

So how do you close an iPAQ program? You click the Start button and choose Settings. Click the System tab and then the Memory icon. Then, click the Running Programs tab, as shown in Figure 3-10, and select the programs you want to close. Click the Stop button to close the selected programs or the Stop All button to shut down all running programs. Click OK to close the memory configuration utility.

Figure 3-10:
You can close programs by using the Running Programs tab of the memory configuration utility.

Starting with Today

Your iPAQ is the perfect assistant. Not only does it perfectly keep track of your schedule, but also quite happily gives you timely reminders without nagging. If only humans were as easy to get along with!

The Today screen on your iPAQ shows all of your essential daily information in one place. You see the current date and time, who owns the iPAQ (handy when everyone just has to see that neat little gadget so that you can be sure to get it back), any appointments on your schedule, the status of your incoming and outgoing messages, and all of those tasks you need to get around to doing one of these days.

You can select any of your Today screen items to open the item for whatever reason — to modify the item, for example. You can also choose New from the menu bar and then choose the type of new item to create.

Along the right edge of the menu bar, you see several icons, such as Bluetooth and your task switcher. The number of icons varies depending on the current status of your iPAQ, but you can click on any of the icons to access the associated settings.

To set up your iPAQ for a different time zone — handy for when you're traveling — tap-and-hold the date near the top of the Today screen. See the section "Setting the date and time," later in this chapter, for more information.

Adjusting Your Settings

People often adjust some of the settings on their desktop PCs, so wanting to play around a little with the settings on your iPAQ is only natural. And, of course, your iPAQ has a different set of options than those in your desktop system. The next few sections discuss the most common settings.

Changing your screen settings

Adjusting the screen settings on your iPAQ is easy because you have only two screen-related settings to adjust: the brightness of the backlighting and the amount of inactive time before the screen dims. Well, you *might* consider one other setting to be screen-related — alignment. But because I consider the alignment setting to be more closely related to improving the accuracy of character recognition, I show you more about that one in Chapter 4.

If you want to play around with color schemes and background images, see the next section, "Using themes," for more information.

You can access a couple of different screen settings. You may need to use more than one of the following to get the exact combination that you like:

- ✔ **Backlight brightness:** To adjust the backlight brightness, tap the Start button and choose Settings, click the System tab, and tap the Backlight icon. Then, tap the Brightness tab. Drag the sliders to adjust the brightness. You can set different levels for times when your iPAQ is running on batteries or when it is plugged in.

- ✔ **Inactive time:** To set the amount of inactive time before the backlight dims, tap the Start button and choose Settings, and then click either the Battery Power or External Power tab — depending on which setting you wish to adjust. Select the time from the drop-down box, and make certain the check box is selected. Keeping the time quite short before the backlight dims is usually best, because this greatly improves the length of time that you can use your iPAQ between battery charges.

If you select the Turn On Backlight When a Button Is Pressed or the Screen Is Tapped check box, the backlight automatically returns to your desired setting as soon as you tap the screen or press one of the buttons on the front of your iPAQ.

If you're going to be using your iPAQ outdoors in bright sunlight, remember that all the iPAQs have a reflective display that's quite visible even with the backlight turned completely off. This setting helps you to extend your iPAQ's battery life to the maximum.

Using themes

If you are one of those people who really wants your iPAQ to reflect your own personality, you're going to love the way that you can use *themes* on your iPAQ. Themes enable you to display background images on the Today screen, to choose which items appear on the Today screen, and even to choose different colors for the various screen elements.

Applying new themes

Your iPAQ comes with at least one theme that you can use in place of the standard theme. It's really easy to apply a different theme. All you need to do is to tap the Start button, choose Settings, and then tap the Today icon on the Personal tab. As Figure 3-11 shows, you can then select a theme from the list. When you tap OK, the theme is applied.

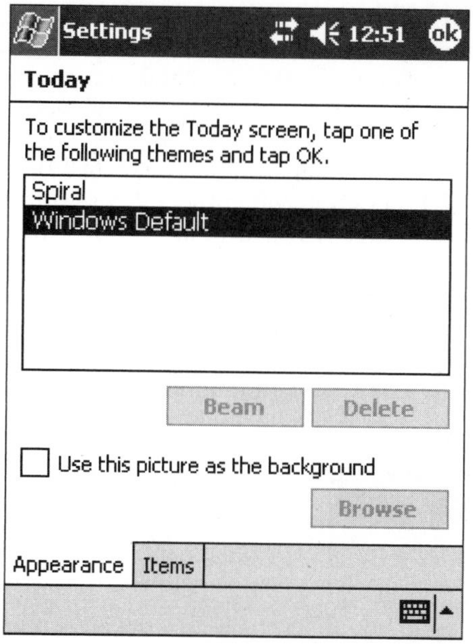

Figure 3-11:
You can
choose a
theme to
change the
appearance
of the Today
screen.

Downloading themes

Because custom themes can be so much fun to use, lots of people have created themes that you can download and use on your iPAQ. Most of these
themes are free, so try out a bunch of them to find the one you like the best.

Quite a few different sites offer you themes to download. Probably the best
place to start is the Windows Mobile Example Today Themes site at www.
microsoft.com/windowsmobile/resources/downloads/pocketpc/
themes.mspx.

After you've downloaded some themes to try out, copy them to the Pocket_PC
My Documents folder. After you synchronize your iPAQ, the new themes will
appear in the themes list (refer to Figure 3-11).

Creating your own themes

Even though all sorts of custom themes are available for download, sometimes you can have more fun creating your own. The following are a couple of
ways to do so:

✔ Select the Use This Picture as the Background check box on the
   Appearance tab when you are choosing a theme. Then, tap the Browse
   button and select the picture you want to use.

✔ Click the Items tab and then select the items you want to appear on the Today screen. Deselect any items you don't want. You can also use the Move Up, Move Down, and Options buttons to make some additional modifications.

The Theme Generator power toy that Microsoft had available for download in the past is not supposed to be compatible with any of the newer iPAQ models running Windows Mobile 2003 or later. If you attempt to create a theme using the Theme Generator, the program generates the theme but refuses to send it to your iPAQ. However, you can copy the theme file (it has a .tsk extension) from your desktop PC to the My Documents folder on your iPAQ and then use the theme as described earlier in this section. Figure 3-12 shows an example of a theme I created with a digital image of a hummingbird at a feeder.

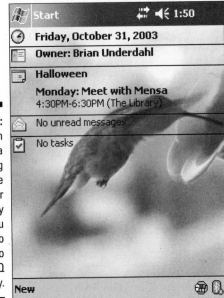

Figure 3-12: You can create a theme using the Theme Generator power toy but you have to copy it to your iPAQ manually.

Adjusting your security

One of the great things about an iPAQ is that it's small enough to fit into a pocket. Unfortunately, this also makes an iPAQ an attractive target for thieves or even people who simply can't resist playing around with that neat-looking gadget.

I can't do much about preventing theft except warn you to be careful about leaving your iPAQ where someone could grab it. However, I can at least show you how to prevent some bozo from accessing your data. That way, if nothing else, you have the satisfaction of knowing that no thief can make use of your personal information or files.

Enabling a password

Setting up security on your iPAQ means creating a password that must be entered whenever the unit is turned on. Without the correct password, no one can access your files or use your iPAQ.

Don't depend too heavily on the simple 4 digit password option — especially if you tend to keep very sensitive files on your iPAQ. These passwords consist of just four numeric digits, and someone who really wants in could discover your password just by being persistent. Sure, it may take a person several hours, but if your information is valuable enough, a thief or a snoop may decide it's worth the effort.

To set a password, choose Start⇨Settings. On the Personal tab, click the Password icon. Select the Prompt If Device Unused For check box. Next, choose the type of password you want to use, and then use the on-screen keypad (which appears if you selected the Simple 4 Digit Password option) or the on-screen keyboard (which appears if you selected the Strong Alphanumeric Password option) to enter a password code, as shown in Figure 3-13. Be sure to also tap the Hint tab and set up a clue to remind you in case you forget your password!

Figure 3-13:
Enable password protection to make it harder for people to snoop on your iPAQ.

If you don't want to have to enter the password every time you turn on your iPAQ, select the Prompt If Device Unused For option. Then enter the length of time that you want to wait before a password is required. For example, in Figure 3-13, the time interval is 1 hour. If you turn on your iPAQ when it has been suspended for less than 1 hour, you don't need to enter the password.

What to do when you forget your password

If you set a password and then forget what it is (or if someone else sets a password on your iPAQ just to be mean), you'd better hope that you can guess the correct password. If this doesn't work, you're in big trouble!

Yes, an easy way to bypass (and remove) the password does exist, but you pay a heavy price if you use it. To forcibly remove the password so you can again use your iPAQ, you must restore your iPAQ to the factory default settings. In doing so you remove all of your data, any files you've created, and any special settings you've applied. In other words, your iPAQ is wiped clean of anything you've done.

If you've tried everything else and are so desperate that you feel you *must* start fresh, here is the procedure you use to remove the password:

1. **Remove your iPAQ from the cradle, making sure that it's running on the internal battery power.**

2. **Use the stylus to press down the recessed reset button on the back or side of the iPAQ.**

3. **While the reset button is held down, press the On/Off button.**

4. **Release the reset button.**

When you press the On/Off button again, your iPAQ turns on and all your files are gone. To avoid repeating this major disaster in the future, you may want to refer to Chapter 5 to see how to back up your iPAQ files on your desktop PC.

Setting the date and time

What good would an assistant be if it didn't know the correct date and time? If you want to be on time to your meetings and appointments, knowing the date and time is certainly important.

In most cases, you don't really need to adjust the date and time on your iPAQ, because every time your iPAQ and your desktop PC synchronize, your iPAQ asks your desktop system for the correct time. Synchronizing the date and time makes it possible for the two of them to always know which files are newer, and to make certain they don't overwrite newer data with older information.

Still, you can set the date and time on your iPAQ if necessary. More importantly, you can choose a different time zone so that you're always on schedule even when you're traveling.

Even if you don't travel with your iPAQ, you can make good use of the time zone feature. Set the visiting time zone for the location of a business partner or relative in a city in another time zone and you can quickly see the current time at their location simply by opening the Clock Settings screen.

To access the Clock Settings screen, tap-and-hold the date in the Today screen. You can also display this screen by clicking the Start button, choosing Settings, and then clicking the Clock icon on the System tab. Figure 3-14 shows the Clock Settings screen.

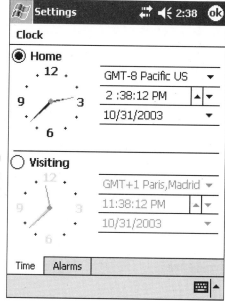

Figure 3-14: Set your location and time zone by using the Clock Settings screen.

After the Clock Settings screen is open, make your selections by using the drop-down boxes. You can also click the Alarms tab if you want your iPAQ to chirp at you at some specified time.

If you choose a time zone that's different from the one set on your desktop PC, your iPAQ still synchronizes the time with your desktop system, but the times are offset by the differences between the selected time zones.

Changing memory settings

Mark Twain once said, "This memory of ours stores up a perfect record of the most useless facts and anecdotes and experiences." In the case of the iPAQ, the memory stores even more than that — it's the best place to store files when you don't have disk drives or other offline storage.

Your iPAQ normally manages its own memory automatically. It shifts the balance between storage and program memory as needed (see Figure 3-15). Sometimes, though, you may want to give your iPAQ just a bit of extra help.

Storage memory is that portion of the total memory in which your data and document files are stored. *Program memory* is the portion of memory in which your programs are run. If necessary, you can drag the memory slider left or right to change the balance between the available storage and program areas. You may, for example, need to make just a bit more space to temporarily store a document that's too large to fit into the remaining storage memory.

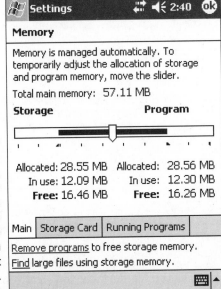

Figure 3-15: iPAQ memory represents a delicate balance between different needs.

Your iPAQ has two types of memory. *RAM* (random access memory) is the memory in which you can store data or programs that you download. This is also in which programs are run. *ROM* (read-only memory) is the memory in which your iPAQ's operating system and built-in programs like Pocket Word are stored. All the iPAQs use a special type of ROM known as *Flash ROM,* which can be updated by special programs. Normally you cannot add anything to Flash ROM on your own, but as you can see in Chapter 5, you can make use of Flash ROM to store certain types of backup information.

Aside from making temporary changes to the way memory is allocated between storage and programs, you can make a few other adjustments to free up more memory for other uses:

- ✔ When you click the Running Programs tab, you can choose to stop one or more of the currently running programs. Doing so frees program memory. Freeing up program memory allows your iPAQ to shift the balance between the two, and gives you a bit more memory to play around with when you want to manually allocate more memory for storage.

- ✔ If you click the Remove Programs link, you can choose to uninstall some of the extra programs you may have added to your iPAQ, freeing up storage memory (and maybe some program memory if you remove a program that is currently running). In Chapter 18, I show you how to manage your add-on programs.

- ✔ The ultimate way to free up memory in your iPAQ is to add a storage card — such as the SanDisk Secure Digital (SD) memory cards. Adding a storage card enables you to place programs, documents, and even music files into your iPAQ without using up precious built-in memory. Chapter 18 also tells you more about adding a storage card.

You can always reinstall programs from your desktop PC even if you temporarily remove them from storage memory to free up some space in your iPAQ. Just make certain that you don't remove them from your desktop system when you remove them from your iPAQ.

Setting your preferences

In addition to the options already mentioned in this chapter, you can adjust several other settings to suit your own personal preferences. Most of these settings are available through the Settings option on the Start menu. Here is a sampling of some of the adjustable preferences that you may find useful:

- ✔ **Buttons:** This option lets you to specify what the buttons on the front of your iPAQ do. You can, for example, specify that one of those buttons opens the Media Player if you like to use your iPAQ as a personal music player.

- ✔ **Menus:** This option enables you to add or remove items from your Start menu, giving you quick access to the programs you use most often and reducing the clutter by removing programs you seldom use.

- ✔ **Owner Information:** Use this option to change your personal information — such as your address and phone number if you move.

- ✔ **Sounds & Notifications:** This option lets you control the volume of audio alerts and to choose which sounds are played to signal events.

- ✔ **Regional Settings:** Move to this option on the System tab to configure your iPAQ for a different country.

Feel free to play around with the options — you can always change back if you don't like the effect created by a setting.

Chapter 4

Entering Information into Your iPAQ

Soon after you first get your iPAQ, you're probably hit with an interesting revelation — the darn thing doesn't have a keyboard! Looks like tapping out an e-mail message on this thing is going to be a whole lot of fun, doesn't it? (Well, okay, so one iPAQ model does have a tiny little keyboard, but it's still not common for most iPAQs.)

Things aren't always quite what they seem at first glance. Getting information into your iPAQ is one of those things that's probably somewhat different than what you expect, but in many ways it's much easier than you may realize. You may just need to adjust your thinking a little before you start having fun.

Handwriting and Your iPAQ

An iPAQ is about the same size as a small pocket-sized notepad. If you use a notepad, you certainly know that the most natural way to put information down in the notepad is simply to pull out a pen or pencil and start writing. You probably hold the notepad in one hand, and write with the other. It turns out this is also one of the best ways to enter information into your iPAQ, too.

Earlier generations of handheld PDAs (Personal Digital Assistants) touted their ability to recognize handwriting, but before the PDA got the raw power that's built into the iPAQ, this recognition capability was pretty much a joke. In fact, a whole series of Doonesbury comic strips once made fun of just how bad handwriting recognition was on the Apple Newton. Fortunately, things have improved tremendously on the iPAQ.

Understanding the options

Handwriting recognition on an iPAQ is pretty advanced. Unless you're one of those doctors with handwriting that no one can read, you probably find that your iPAQ does a pretty good job of deciphering your chicken scratchings — especially if you choose the correct handwriting option to match your style (and maybe practice just a little).

You can choose from the following three different methods of writing on your iPAQ's screen.

- ✔ **Transcriber:** Allows you to write pretty much like you would in a paper notebook.

- ✔ **Letter Recognizer:** Provides better accuracy than the Transcriber at the expense of input speed.

- ✔ **Block Recognizer:** A simpler version of the Letter Recognizer. The inclusion of Block Recognizer is intended to make life easier for users who move from a Palm PC to an iPAQ.

See the following sections for more detail on these iPAQ writing methods.

Using the Transcriber

When you use the Transcriber, you write complete words directly on your iPAQ's screen. The Transcriber accepts printing, cursive writing, or any combination of the two.

The Transcriber has an easier time figuring out where words begin and end when you use cursive writing because you typically write an entire word in one continuous motion.

Figure 4-1 shows how the Transcriber works. You write a complete word and then when you lift the stylus, the Transcriber does its best to understand what you wrote and to convert it into text. In Figure 4-1, I've written *Hello* and the Transcriber correctly converted it into text. I then wrote *world* and the Transcriber hasn't yet made the conversion into text.

Figure 4-1:
When you use the Transcriber, your writing is converted into text one word at a time.

As you complete each word, the Transcriber does the conversion into text. If you continue to add text, your note scrolls up as necessary.

If the Transcriber stops doing an automatic handwriting-into-text conversion, tap the hand icon just to the left of the input method selector at the lower-right corner of the screen. When this icon has a white background, the conversion happens automatically as soon as you complete each word. When this icon has a gray background, you can choose Tools⇨Recognize to tell the Transcriber to convert the handwriting into text.

Transcriber also uses a series of *gestures* to enable you to enter things (like pressing the Enter key by dragging straight down and then making a 90 degree turn and dragging to the left) or to make a quick correction by simply writing a specific character without having to stop and find the key. When you select Transcriber as your input option, the first screen you see as Transcriber opens shows you how to enter these special gestures. The Transcriber Help file shows a bunch more special gestures — most of which you probably won't use often enough to remember.

The Transcriber is supposed to respond to a series of gestures that indicate certain keystrokes and actions such as the Enter key, the Tab key, Undo, Copy, Paste, and so on. For example, a motion that first moves down and then left is supposed to be recognized as pressing the Enter key. Whether the Transcriber actually recognizes each gesture depends pretty heavily on how accurate you are at remembering and executing the correct stylus motions. If you really want to know the set of gestures you can make on your iPAQ, tap the question mark icon on the iconbar to open the Transcriber Help file. Then, tap Microsoft Transcriber Gestures. Remember, though, that you must use the stylus to enter any gestures — not one of your fingers.

To enable the Transcriber, click the up arrow in the lower-right corner of the screen and select Transcriber. You can also choose Options at the top of the menu that pops up from the up arrow to adjust the Transcriber's settings. When the Settings screen opens, click the Options button to choose from several settings:

- ✔ On the General tab, select the Sound On check box to enable sound effects. You may want to turn this one off if you need to work silently.

- ✔ Select the Show Intro Screen check box to redisplay the introductory screen so that you can again see the hints about how to create the special gestures. This is only necessary if you deselected the option to show the introductory screen when it was displayed.

- ✔ Select the Show Iconbar check box to display a set of tools that works with the Transcriber. For example, one tool pops up a small keyboard that makes it easier to enter symbols such as parentheses and brackets. Another tool adjusts the angle at which you write on the screen so that you can write diagonally or even vertically if that's more comfortable for you. These tools make it easier to enter unusual characters, but they also eat up some of your screen space.

- ✔ If you have trouble seeing what you're writing, use the Color and Width options to select settings that are easier to see.

- ✔ Move to the Recognizer tab and select the Add Space After check box to have the Transcriber automatically add spaces between words. In this mode, you don't have to enter a special gesture whenever you finish a word.

- ✔ If you want to enter individual characters rather than complete words, select the Separate Letters Mode check box. Using this option may help if you have really sloppy handwriting and the Transcriber is making a lot of mistakes reading your writing.

   Don't select the Add Space After option if you select the Separate Letters Mode check box — if you do, you get a space after each letter.

- ✔ Use the Speed of Recognition vs. Quality slider to improve either the speed or the accuracy of handwriting recognition. This is one of those delicate balancing acts where you have to decide the best setting based on how accurately the Transcriber understands your handwriting.

- ✔ Finally, use the Recognition Start Time slider to make certain that you have enough time to cross your t's and dot your i's. A shorter delay improves the speed of recognition, but may reduce the overall accuracy.

When the Transcriber's iconbar is showing, you can click the fourth icon from the left (a cursive letter *a*) to display the Letter Shapes screen. On this screen, you can specify how you tend to write each character. If you say that you never use a certain shape when writing a character, the Transcriber doesn't waste time trying to translate that shape into the specified character. This can improve handwriting recognition speed, but may also lead to the Transcriber making more errors. You just have to experiment to see what works best for you.

If you want to adjust the angle at which you can write on the screen, tap the arrow at the left end of the iconbar. Continue tapping the arrow until it points upwards at the angle you prefer. You probably have to play around with this setting to find the angle that works the best for you.

Using character recognition

If you happen to be one of those people whose handwriting is really bad — if most of the time, even *you* aren't sure what you wrote — the Transcriber may not be such a hot idea. Spending half your time correcting transcription mistakes probably isn't the best way to get much done.

Just because the Transcriber doesn't work too well for you doesn't mean you have to give up on handwriting recognition, though. Your iPAQ has two other options for understanding your handwriting — the Letter Recognizer and the Block Recognizer.

Using the Letter Recognizer

Because it works one character at a time, the Letter Recognizer can be a better choice than the Transcriber when it comes to understanding your handwriting. It also uses specific areas near the bottom of the screen for different types of characters, so Letter Recognizer has less guessing to do than the Transcriber. With no ambiguity about where one character ends and the next one begins, it can be far easier to translate even sloppy handwriting into text. Figure 4-2 shows the Letter Recognizer in action. In the figure, I just completed the letter *r* but haven't lifted the stylus so the Letter Recognizer hasn't translated the character yet.

Another feature that helps the Letter Recognizer work is that it uses three distinct areas to separate your input of capital letters, lowercase letters, and numbers (plus one area where you can select special characters). Sure, it's more work for you because you have to select the correct area to enter different types of characters. But because this cuts down the number of possibilities that the Letter Recognizer considers, it tends to improve the accuracy. Of course, if your handwriting is *really* bad, even this may not be enough. (But in that case, you're probably one of those people who gets lots of calls from pharmacists asking what that prescription says, so you're used to no one being able to read your writing, anyway.)

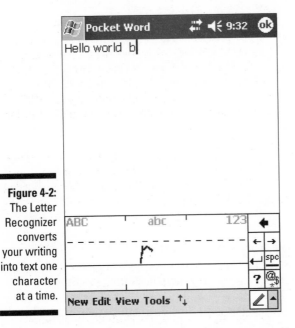

Figure 4-2:
The Letter
Recognizer
converts
your writing
into text one
character
at a time.

The Letter Recognizer claims the bottom third of your iPAQ's screen and is divided into the following five areas:

- ✔ The left section (under ABC) is the area where you enter letters when you want to enter capital letters. You can enter letters as upper- or lowercase — they appear as uppercase in the document.

- ✔ The second section (under abc) is the area for entering lowercase letters. Here, too, you can use upper- or lowercase, and the letters appear as lowercase in the document.

- ✔ The third section (under 123) is where you enter numbers and symbols.

- ✔ You can enter spaces or delete characters by using the area below the solid line.

- ✔ The right-most section has seven blocks that you can tap for special purposes. The fat left arrow at the top is the one that you use the most — it's the backspace, which wipes out characters that weren't recognized correctly. Below it are arrows to move one place left or right; the Enter key and the spacebar; and in the bottom row a help button and a button to make entering special characters easier.

Writing on the iPAQ

Do you want to feel like a kid again? If so, discovering how to write on your iPAQ may be just the ticket. Remember how frustrating it was when you drew a picture and your kindergarten teacher didn't see what you knew was in the picture? At first, it may seem like you've gone back to those days, but with just a little practice, you can make yourself understood by your iPAQ. Unfortunately, writing on an iPAQ won't make you into a better artist, but hey, you can't have everything!

You've probably noticed that two horizontal lines divide the Letter Recognizer's input area (see Figure 4-2). The upper line is a dashed line and the lower one is solid. Sort of reminds you of that lined paper you had back in grade school, doesn't it? Actually, the lines in the Letter Recognizer do serve the same purpose as those on that lined paper — they exist to show you where to write:

✔ The solid line is where the base of all of your characters should rest.

✔ The dashed line is where the top of most lowercase characters should end. Uppercase characters should have the dashed line right about in their middle.

✔ Descenders (such as *j*) and ascenders (such as *t*) should cross below the solid line or above the dashed line, respectively.

One of the hardest things to figure out about writing on your iPAQ's screen is creating an entire character in a single motion. In most cases lifting the stylus off the screen signals the end of a character — even if you weren't done with it. When you realize the importance of keeping the stylus on the screen until you're done, you find that the character recognition accuracy goes way up.

Don't waste your time trying to go back and add more to a character you've already drawn. Just wait to see if it's recognized correctly, and if not, click the backspace arrow. Try again, but this time, use a single motion to enter the entire character.

If you are having trouble with the Letter Recognizer not understanding certain characters, tap the Help button — the button with the question mark. Then, click the Demo button and tap the character on the on-screen keyboard to see a couple of examples of how to write the character. Figure 4-3 shows how the letter *y* appears after the demo finishes drawing it two different ways.

What Figure 4-3 can't show you is that the demo slowly draws the character so that you can see the best way to write it. You may find that it helps to watch the demo several times to see the correct method of drawing some of the more difficult characters. You can also tap additional characters to continue the demo with those characters.

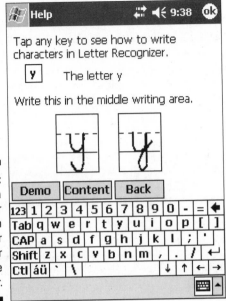

Tap any key to see how to write characters in Letter Recognizer.

y The letter y

Write this in the middle writing area.

Figure 4-3:
Click a character to watch the proper motions for drawing the character.

If the on-screen keyboard disappears after you've seen a demo, tap the Demo button to make it return. The keyboard then remains visible until you click OK.

Improving accuracy

Okay, so maybe it isn't just your handwriting. If you've looked at the character input demos and have practiced until your hand is sore, but the Letter Recognizer still doesn't understand your handwriting, it's possible that it really isn't your fault. It might just be that your iPAQ needs a bit of a tune up in the form of a screen alignment.

Aligning your iPAQ's screen can also improve the accuracy of how well the unit responds to clicking on-screen items such as characters on the on-screen keyboard.

Aligning your screen takes just a minute or so. To align, follow these steps:

1. **Click the Start button and choose Settings.**

2. **Tap the System tab.**

3. **Click the Screen icon and then the Align Screen button.**

4. **When the large plus sign (+) appears in the middle of your screen, press the stylus firmly into the middle of the plus sign. Press the middle of each new plus sign that appears near the corners of the screen.**

5. **When the alignment is finished, click OK.**

Too bad you can't align your car's front end so quickly and easily!

Using the Block Recognizer

The Block Recognizer is somewhat similar to the Letter Recognizer, but unless you're used to using a Palm PC, you probably won't find the Block Recognizer to be nearly as convenient. The reason for this is simple — the Block Recognizer emulates the Graffiti handwriting recognition found on Palms.

For a better idea just how different the Block Recognizer is, take a look at Figure 4-4. In the figure, I've run the demo to see how to enter the letter *q* using the Block Recognizer. If you compare this figure with Figure 4-3, it's easy to see that the Letter Recognizer is probably going to be a whole lot easier for most people to use.

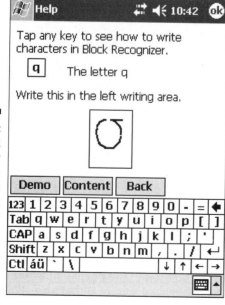

Figure 4-4:
The Block Recognizer uses the same strokes that are used for handwriting recognition on Palm PCs.

Using the Soft Keyboard

If your handwriting skills are really rusty or if you maybe just prefer typing, your iPAQ includes an on-screen keyboard that is sometimes referred to as the *soft keyboard* because it's created by software rather than out of various bits and pieces of plastic and metal. The on-screen keyboard is pretty darn small, though, so you can forget any notions about touch-typing on that thing.

Using the on-screen keyboard is easy but rather slow. Tapping out your several-hundred-page novel one key at a time with that little stylus won't win you too many awards for being the world's fastest writer. Still, for short notes and the like, it isn't too much of an ordeal to use the on-screen keyboard.

Typing on your screen

The on-screen keyboard works pretty much like an old-fashioned typewriter. You stab at each key to enter a character and then move on to the next one. If you want to type an uppercase character, tap the Shift key and then the character that you want. The keyboard returns to lowercase after you tap the character. To keep the keyboard in uppercase mode, tap the CAP key instead of the Shift key.

To move the insertion point, use the movement keys at the right edge of the lower row of the keyboard. You may find it easier to simply tap in the text with your stylus to move the insertion point.

If you need to enter accented characters, tap the second key from the left in the bottom row — the key with áü on the face. This shifts the keyboard so it shows accented characters. You can click the same key again to return to normal characters.

Some shortcuts to speed your typing

With a keyboard as small and awkward to use as the on-screen keyboard, you can probably use some help by way of typing shortcuts. As Figure 4-5 shows, the on-screen keyboard does its best to try and help you out by suggesting words that seem to match what you're typing. If the correct word appears in the pop-up list, tap that word to enter it into the document without having to finish typing the word out. One really cool feature is that your iPAQ remembers words you enter often — such as your name — so that they are added to the list of suggestions. Then, when you start typing the same word in the future, you can select the word instead of having to retype it each time.

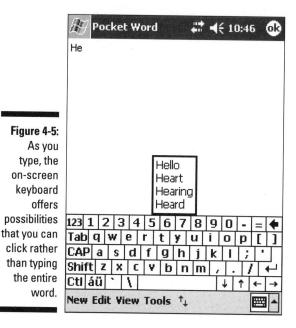

Figure 4-5:
As you type, the on-screen keyboard offers possibilities that you can click rather than typing the entire word.

To control how your iPAQ suggests words as you type, tap the input selector (the up arrow at the lower-right corner of the screen) and select Options at the top of the menu. Then, click the Word Completion tab, as shown in Figure 4-6.

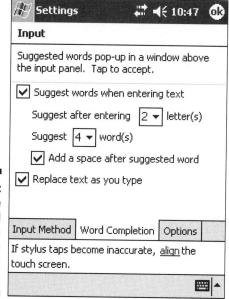

Figure 4-6:
Customize your Word Completion settings to make typing easier.

In the Suggest drop-down box, select 4 as the number of words to suggest; your iPAQ now offers four alternatives rather than just one possibility, and you're more likely to be able to select the word you want.

If you want to enter a bunch of numbers, don't waste your time with the number keys in the top row of the keyboard. Click the 123 key in the upper-left corner to change the keyboard into a numeric keypad for faster entries. Tap the 123 key again to return to the standard keyboard.

You can also use some of the Control key shortcuts you're used to from your desktop PC. For example, take a look at the following list:

- ✔ Tap Ctl and then A to select all text.
- ✔ Tap Ctl and then C to copy the text.
- ✔ Tap Ctl and then X to cut the selected text.
- ✔ Tap Ctl and then V to paste the text you copied.
- ✔ Tap Ctl and then Z to undo.
- ✔ Tap Ctl and then Q to close the current application.
- ✔ Tap Ctl and then N to begin a new document.

Using Other Ways to Input Info

Time to face the facts — if you need to enter a lot of information into a document, there's just no substitute for a real keyboard. But just because your iPAQ doesn't come with a keyboard doesn't mean that all is lost. You have several ways to add a real keyboard to your iPAQ, and each offers certain advantages. The following sections look at how they can make your life a little easier.

Belkin Wireless PDA Keyboard

If you can't even stand the idea of trying to type with the on-screen keyboard on your iPAQ, you may want to consider another option — a folding keyboard such as the one made by Belkin (www.belkin.com), shown in Figure 4-7. One of the excellent features of the Belkin Wireless PDA Keyboard is that it works with virtually any PDA because it connects wirelessly using infrared signals.

Figure 4-7:
The Belkin
Wireless
PDA
Keyboard
is a great
addition to
your iPAQ.

Folding keyboards are the ultimate space saver. They fold into a compact package that's just a bit larger than the iPAQ itself. To use a Belkin Wireless PDA folding keyboard, unfold it, set it on a hard flat surface, and place your iPAQ into the stand. Then you simply begin typing.

The Belkin Wireless PDA Keyboard works best with iPAQ models that have their IrDA port on the top rather than on the side. Although you can use this keyboard with the h1900 series iPAQ, you have to put up with placing your iPAQ on its side in order to properly line up the IrDA ports on your iPAQ and on the keyboard. Although the Belkin keyboard driver software offers a landscape option, I've found that attempting to use this option locks up my iPAQ h1935, and only a hard reset (which wipes out all of the data on the iPAQ) allows me to use the iPAQ again.

Because a folding keyboard folds, it's not very adept at sitting on your lap as you type. You really need to find a place for the folding keyboard that helps keep the keyboard flat as you type.

Using a Seiko SmartPad2 with your iPAQ

The Seiko SmartPad2 can function as a keyboard, but it's really much more than just another way to type on your iPAQ. Unlike a portable keyboard, the Seiko SmartPad lets you draw on a pad of ordinary paper (with a special pen) and then automatically transfers your drawing to your iPAQ using the infrared port.

In addition to being a really cool way to draw on your iPAQ, the Seiko SmartPad2 is a leather portfolio with room for your cell phone, business cards, and your iPAQ. In addition, you can find a touch-sensitive keyboard under the paper notepad, and its larger size makes typing far easier than using the on-screen keyboard.

You use an included program, InkNote Manager, to organize the notes you create with the Seiko SmartPad. You can send notes as e-mail messages and save them in several different formats. To discover more about the Seiko SmartPad, visit the Seiko Instruments Web site (www.siibusinessproducts. com).

You may also want to check out the Seiko InkLink Handwriting system. This unit functions similarly to the SmartPad2, but rather than being permanently installed in a leather portfolio, the Seiko InkLink Handwriting system clips onto an ordinary legal pad.

Seeing your screen Magnifico

If you haven't already noticed the following fact, I really hate to be the one who has to tell you this: The screen on an iPAQ is pretty small. This may seem exceptionally harsh to you if you're the sort of person whose arms don't seem to be able to hold the newspaper quite far enough away. If this phenomenon is happening to you, it may be time to check out the Magnifico, a Portable PDA Screen Magnifier, shown in Figure 4-8. The Magnifico has a two-power magnifying lens that sits in front of your iPAQ to make the screen far easier to read. It's especially useful when combined with a folding keyboard.

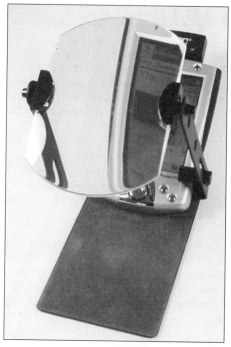

Figure 4-8:
The
Magnifico
makes your
iPAQ screen
easier
to read.

The Magnifico comes in clip-on and standalone versions. You can find out more about the different Magnifico versions at the Officeonthegogo Web site (www.officeonthegogo.com).

A slick alternative stylus

If you have ever lost a PDA stylus, you know what a pain it can be when you reach for the stylus and find an empty slot. That's one reason I like to always have an alternative stylus available. It's even better if you have an alternative stylus that serves more than one function.

My favorite alternative stylus is the Belkin LaserWright 3-in-1 Stylus because it combines a pen, a stylus, and a laser pointer in an ordinary-sized ballpoint pen case. The laser pointer is especially handy when you're giving a presentation: You can read your notes from the iPAQ and use the laser pointer to highlight on-screen information without having to switch between a stylus and a laser pointer.

Printing from Your iPAQ

It's only natural to expect that you might want to print whatever data you've spent so much time and effort putting into your iPAQ, right? Well, even though this seems like a logical expectation, there's just one little problem — none of the programs on your iPAQ has a Print command. In fact, no matter how much you look for a way to print your documents directly from your iPAQ, you just won't find it!

The basic idea behind this lack of native printing ability on the iPAQ is that you're expected to print stuff from your desktop system. But what if your desktop PC isn't handy and you just have to print out a document? After all, the idea behind having an iPAQ is that you can carry your computing power along in your pocket wherever you go.

Fortunately, the solution to the printing problem is both simple and free. All you need to do is to visit the HP Mobile Printing Web site and download the free HP Mobile Printing for Pocket PC utility. After you have installed this program, you can use Bluetooth, IrDA, or network connections to print your documents. To download the utility, visit `www.hp.com/go/pocketpcprint_software`.

After you install the HP Mobile Printing for Pocket PC utility, use your stylus to press the Reset button on your iPAQ. This step is necessary to complete the software installation.

Chapter 5

Keeping It in Sync

. . . .

In This Chapter

▶ Getting to know synchronization

▶ Exchanging data with your desktop PC

▶ Backing up your iPAQ

. . . .

The iPAQ is the perfect companion for a desktop PC. They can share information seamlessly, allowing you to work on either machine and still be assured of having the most up-to-date data that's available. When you're in the office, you probably opt for the large screen and comfortable keyboard on your desktop system. On the go, you most likely prefer the small, convenient size of your iPAQ. There's no reason why you can't enjoy the best features of both systems and still be on top of your world.

Sure, you can have just an iPAQ and no desktop PC, but somehow that seems a bit like Laurel without Hardy, apple pie without ice cream, or maybe even pancakes without syrup. Something is missing when one of the two partners isn't there.

To make the partnership work, your iPAQ and your desktop PC must exchange data automatically. The mechanism that makes this work is *synchronization*. In this chapter, I show you how to make synchronization work for you.

Understanding Synchronization

Synchronization can be defined as harmonization, organization, management, or unification. These are some pretty fancy ways of saying that you want the same information to exist in more than one place, and that you want that information to be the same in all of those places. From a practical standpoint, what this means in terms of your iPAQ is that you want to share certain files with your desktop PC, and that you want to be able to work on those files on whichever PC happens to be handy.

Hard resets cause sync problems

If you ever need to perform a *hard reset* (which is wiping out everything in your iPAQ's memory by holding down the Reset button with the stylus while you turn on the power and wait for a few seconds) on your iPAQ, you soon discover that ActiveSync no longer allows you to synchronize your iPAQ with your desktop PC. The reason for this is that you can only have one device that uses a specific name, and after a hard reset on your iPAQ, your desktop PC no longer recognizes your iPAQ by that name. (After a hard reset, the iPAQ's assigned name is deleted from its memory, but that name is still the only name by which the iPAQ is recognized by your desktop PC.) To correct the problem, you can either give your iPAQ a new name or you can use the

Delete Partnership command on the ActiveSync File menu to remove the existing partnership settings. After you have done so, you then have to create a new partnership. If you have backed up your iPAQ as described later in this chapter in the section "Backing Up Your iPAQ Files," you can then restore any missing files to your iPAQ.

A hard reset is seldom necessary and should be avoided if at all possible. Sometimes, however, you may need to do a hard reset if your iPAQ is so locked up that a soft reset (pressing the reset button with the tip of the stylus) doesn't cure the problem. You perform a hard reset by holding down the power button while pressing the reset button.

Why synchronization is important

For just a moment, I'd like you to imagine a scenario that probably isn't too unusual. Suppose that you keep all your personal address book listings in a small paper notebook. Now, imagine that someone else in your house has an address book, too. Nothing at all unusual there, right? Okay, so you're talking with Aunt Dee and you find out that your cousin Paige has just moved. You write down the new information in your address book and you're all set. But what about that other address book? Shouldn't it also be updated with the corrected information? Of course it should. The problem is that there's probably no formal system set up so that whenever someone gets new information he or she automatically shares it with everyone else in the house.

Okay, so that example is pretty obvious. Here's another example that may not seem quite so self-evident. Suppose you write a report on your desktop PC and then copy that report to your iPAQ so that you can easily take the report along to a meeting. Just before you leave for the meeting, someone phones you to tell you that one of the names in your report is wrong — it's Jim Johnson, not Jim Jensen, who's getting that big promotion. You quickly open your word processor and fix the error in your report, but because you're in such a hurry, you forget to copy the corrected report to your iPAQ. When you arrive at the meeting and begin your presentation, do you remember that whenever the report says Jim Jensen it really should say Jim Johnson? Or do you make the announcement that you're promoting the wrong guy?

These two examples are but a small sampling of the reasons why you need to synchronize information. Fortunately, synchronizing data files between your iPAQ and your desktop PC is a snap. And when you do synchronize, you don't have to worry about not having the correct information at your fingertips, whether your fingertips are on your iPAQ or desktop PC.

Setting up partnerships

You use a program called ActiveSync to synchronize the information between your iPAQ and your desktop PC. ActiveSync synchronizes information by creating a partnership between your iPAQ and your desktop PC. This partnership has the following characteristics:

- ✔ Whenever your iPAQ and desktop PC are synchronized, changes to the files you've specified are updated in both directions. This simply means that changes on your desktop PC appear on your iPAQ, and changes on your iPAQ also appear on your desktop PC.

- ✔ You can choose the types of items that each partnership synchronizes. If you set up partnerships between your iPAQ and two different desktop PCs, you synchronize the same set of files with each desktop PC.

If you set up partnerships between your iPAQ and two different desktop PCs, you can specify *only one* of those partnerships for sharing e-mail messages.

- ✔ In most cases, the partnership specifies that the synchronization happens automatically whenever the iPAQ and desktop PC connect, but you can control exactly how each partnership synchronizes its files.

- ✔ Your desktop PC can have partnerships with more than one iPAQ, but the default settings share the same set of files between your desktop PC and all of the iPAQs. You can change this by creating unique iPAQ identities, as I explain later in the section "Creating unique iPAQ identities."

Creating basic partnerships

Creating a basic partnership is one of those tasks that sounds much harder than it really is. All you have to do is insert a CD-ROM, click a few buttons, and you're done. Here's the rundown:

1. **Before you connect your iPAQ to your desktop PC, get out the HP iPAQ Pocket PC Companion CD-ROM that came with your iPAQ and insert it into your desktop PC's CD-ROM drive.**

2. **If the setup program doesn't start automatically, click the Start button on your desktop PC and choose Run.**

   The Run dialog box appears.

3. In the Open text box, enter *x*:\setup.exe **(where *x* is the drive letter for your CD-ROM drive). Click OK to run the setup program.**

4. **Click the Next button that appears in the first screen. (It's the blue button.)**

5. **Click Start Here.**

6. **Select Install Outlook 2002 and then select ActiveSync 3.7.**

7. **Connect your iPAQ to your desktop PC.**

   In most cases, you do this by turning on the iPAQ and popping it into the cradle (after you've plugged in the cables, of course). If you have an iPAQ model that does not use a cradle, plug the cable into the bottom of your iPAQ.

8. **When the setup program asks if you want to establish a partnership between your iPAQ and your desktop PC, select the Create a Partnership radio button, and then click the Next button.**

9. **Keep on clicking the buttons until the setup program concludes.**

   Basically, you just click OK to accept the default installation options for everything that remains.

Setting up the ActiveSync options

When ActiveSync is first installed, it's set up to synchronize lots of different types of items. A number of these are probably things that you don't really want synchronized, if for no better reason than the amount of time it takes for ActiveSync to check the status of items that you don't use. Rather than continue to be frustrated every time you pop your iPAQ into the cradle, you can change the ActiveSync settings.

To configure ActiveSync to work the way you want, follow these steps:

1. **If ActiveSync hasn't popped up into view on your desktop PC, click the ActiveSync icon in the system tray and choose Open Microsoft ActiveSync from the pop-up menu.**

2. **Choose Tools⊅Options (or click the Options button) to display the Options dialog box (see Figure 5-1).**

   You use this dialog box to control how ActiveSync works.

3. **Go down the list of items and select those that you want to synchronize or deselect those that you don't want to synchronize.**

   For example, if you don't want to share your favorite Web pages with your iPAQ, deselect Favorites. You can always change your mind later if you want to add or remove some items from the synchronization list.

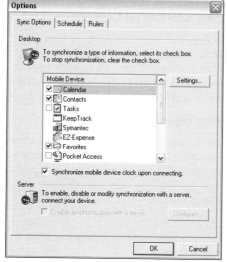

Figure 5-1:
Open the
Options
dialog box
to choose
your
ActiveSync
settings.

4. To modify an item for even more precise control, highlight the item and click the Settings button.

Figure 5-2 shows the settings that you can choose for synchronizing your Calendar. Other types of items do, of course, have other options. Click OK when you are finished making changes.

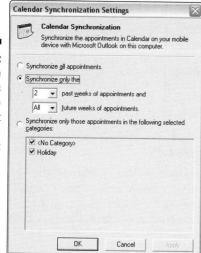

Figure 5-2:
Use the
Settings
button to
make it
possible
to exert
even more
precise
control over
items such
as your
Calendar.

5. **Before you leave the Sync Options tab completely, make certain the Synchronize Mobile Device Clock upon Connecting check box is selected.**

   This ensures that your iPAQ and your desktop PC always agree on the correct date and time. That they agree on this is very important; otherwise, an older file may overwrite a newer one because ActiveSync isn't able to determine which file is the newest.

6. **Click the Schedule tab (see Figure 5-3).**

   Choose the options that you prefer. The default setting in the Desktop schedule section, Continuously, is the safest option because it ensures that your files are always up-to-date at the moment you pop the iPAQ out of the cradle and into your pocket. You can also choose options for synchronizing with a server and for when you are connected via a wireless connection.

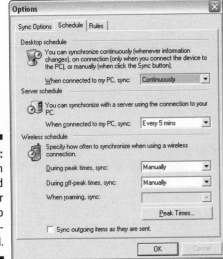

Figure 5-3: Select when you would like your files to be synchronized.

7. **Click the Rules tab (see Figure 5-4).**

   Here you can decide the rules for how the synchronization is performed. The best advice here is this: Don't tinker around too much. The default settings shown in the figure really do work the best in most instances. Messing around with the conversion settings is also just asking for trouble.

8. **Click OK to close the dialog box.**

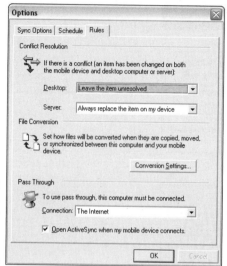

Figure 5-4:
Choose your
synchroniza-
tion rules.

Creating unique iPAQ identities

One aspect of the iPAQ affects almost everyone who spends a few minutes playing around with one — before long, you want one of your own. This isn't much of a problem unless several people in your family all decide they want their own iPAQ, and you all share a desktop PC. If that's the case, you need to create separate identities for each iPAQ.

Be sure to create the unique iPAQ identity *before* you create a partnership with your desktop PC. You can't create a partnership with the same name as an existing partnership.

To create a unique iPAQ identity, follow these steps:

1. **On your iPAQ, click the Start button and choose Settings.**

2. **Tap the System tab in the Settings screen.**

3. **Click the About icon to display the About screen in the Settings screen.**

4. **Click the Device ID tab (see Figure 5-5).**

5. **Enter a name for your iPAQ in the Device Name field.**

   Keeping Pocket_PC as a part of the name is best because ActiveSync creates a folder in your desktop PC's My Documents folder using this name, and then places a shortcut to the folder on the desktop.

6. **Click OK when you're finished.**

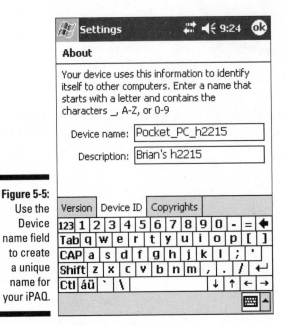

Figure 5-5:
Use the
Device
name field
to create
a unique
name for
your iPAQ.

Because ActiveSync uses the iPAQ's name when creating the synchronization folder on your desktop PC, only those files that are in the folder that's associated with a particular iPAQ are synchronized (if you have selected the ActiveSync option to synchronize files). Because of this, you may need to move files manually from the existing synchronization folder to the new one if you change the device name *after* you've already set up a partnership with your desktop system.

Exchanging Data

If your iPAQ and your desktop PC are going to be partners, they need to be able to share your data. You wouldn't want to have to retype everything just because you wanted to use it on both computers. I show you how to share information between these systems.

Using ActiveSync

You've already seen that you use ActiveSync to create a partnership between your iPAQ and your desktop PC. Earlier in this chapter, in the section "Understanding Synchronization," I also cover how you can control which types of information are shared. But just how does this data-exchange process really work? Here are some important details:

✔ iPAQs lack one of the important pieces of hardware that you find on every modern desktop PC — a hard drive. This is an important difference for reasons that you may not realize. In terms of sharing data, the lack of a hard drive is important because your iPAQ stores data differently than your desktop PC does. In fact, your iPAQ stores much information in a format that your desktop PC simply cannot use.

✔ Because of the differences between the ways your iPAQ and your desktop PC store information, you can't just copy most files between the two systems. Rather, the files must be converted from one format to the other as they are transferred. Likewise, they must be converted in the other direction if you transfer them back.

✔ ActiveSync automatically handles the format conversions as it transfers files, which is one reason why it can take a few minutes to move files between your iPAQ and your desktop PC.

✔ Remember that ActiveSync can convert only *data* files. You can't convert your desktop PC programs to run on your iPAQ (or the other way around, for that matter).

Synchronizing your contacts with Outlook

Most iPAQ users probably want to keep their contact list available on their iPAQ. Because of this, sharing address book information is one of those tasks that is virtually transparent. If you make any modifications in your Outlook Contacts folder on your desktop PC, those same changes appear in your iPAQ's Contacts list the next time you synchronize your iPAQ and your desktop PC — assuming that you've specified that you want your contacts synchronized, of course. And any changes that you make in your iPAQ's Contacts list also appear in your desktop Outlook Contacts folder.

If you don't have Outlook installed on your desktop PC, or if your version of Outlook is an older one, you can install Outlook 2002 from the HP iPAQ Pocket PC Companion CD-ROM.

Figure 5-6 shows a contact record that I've entered into Outlook on my desktop PC. When I click the Save and Close button, this record is added to the Outlook Contacts folder.

Next, I place my iPAQ in the cradle and wait for ActiveSync to do its thing. If the only change is in one contact record, the synchronization may even go so fast that you won't notice anything happening. But if you open the Contacts application on your iPAQ by tapping the Start button and choosing Contacts from the Start menu or by tapping the Start button and choosing Programs⇨ Contacts and look for the new record, it's there, as shown in Figure 5-7.

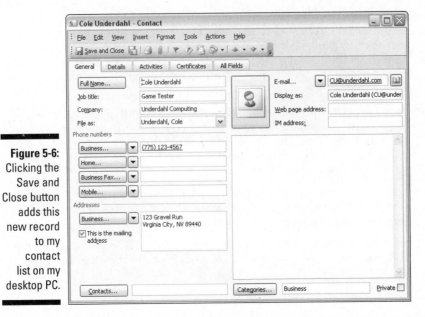

Figure 5-6:
Clicking the
Save and
Close button
adds this
new record
to my
contact
list on my
desktop PC.

ActiveSync handles the synchronization of every Outlook-related item as transparently as it does your contact list. So transparently, in fact, that the same appointments appear on both your iPAQ and your desktop PC.

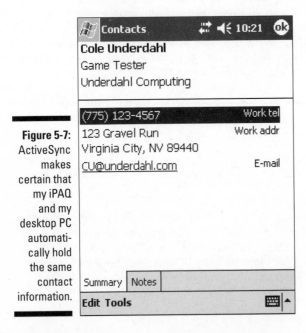

Figure 5-7:
ActiveSync
makes
certain that
my iPAQ
and my
desktop PC
automati-
cally hold
the same
contact
information.

Sharing data with other types of applications

You use a slightly different method of sharing other, non-Outlook types of data between your iPAQ and your desktop PC. For this, ActiveSync uses a special folder on your desktop PC and automatically synchronizes the contents of that folder with the My Documents folder on your iPAQ.

When you create a partnership between your iPAQ and your desktop PC, ActiveSync creates a new folder on your desktop PC. This folder appears as a subfolder in your My Documents folder. The folder is named with the device ID of your iPAQ and the words *My Documents* added on the end. Your iPAQ uses the device ID "Pocket_PC" by default, so most likely the synchronization folder is `My Documents\Pocket_PC My Documents`.

If you add a memory storage card to your iPAQ, you have to create a My Documents folder on the storage card and use it to store your files in order for most iPAQ applications to find the files on the storage card. This does not mean, however, that ActiveSync synchronizes the files on the storage card with your desktop PC. Indeed, when synchronizing files, ActiveSync simply ignores any files that are stored only on the storage card. However, as I discuss later in this chapter (in the section "Exploring Your iPAQ Files"), you can set ActiveSync to explore the storage card.

If you select the ActiveSync option to synchronize files, any files that you place in the Pocket_PC My Documents folder on your desktop PC automatically convert and copy to your iPAQ. Likewise, any new or changed documents in the My Documents folder on your iPAQ are converted and copied to your desktop PC. Limits to this do exist, however. If a file is too large for the storage space on your iPAQ, it won't be copied to your iPAQ. Also, if ActiveSync is unable to determine the type of the file, it may be copied without any translation. That is, the file is simply copied without trying to make it compatible with your iPAQ. You may or may not be able to use the file on your iPAQ — depending on how lucky you are that day.

Optional sync cables

If you carry your iPAQ between a couple of different locations and sync it with more than one PC, you have probably noticed that you end up carrying around a whole bunch of stuff — cables, power supply, and maybe the cradle — just so that you can share your files and keep your iPAQ charged up. To make matters worse, if you've been following this routine for any length of time, you've probably lost (or at least misplaced) one or more of those necessary bits from time to time. If so, you're going to really love the two products that I found to reduce this clutter. Both are inexpensive but essential items for any iPAQ user.

The first is the iBIZ USB Charging/HotSync Kit. This is nothing more than a simple cable, one end of which plugs into the port on the bottom of your iPAQ, and the other into a USB port on your desktop or laptop PC. But unlike the standard sync cable that came with your iPAQ, this cable also charges your iPAQ without requiring an external power supply. As long as your USB port is powered (virtually all are), the USB port supplies the power to charge your iPAQ. So instead of a cable, power supply and cradle, your traveling pack is cut down to a single cable. You can find out more about this cable at the iBIZ Web site (www.ibizpda.com/pda_accessories/pda_chargers.html).

Belkin makes a similar cable that they call the USB Sync Charger. The Belkin unit functions just like the iBIZ cable, but Belkin also throws in a cigarette lighter adapter so that you can charge your iPAQ in your car when no USB port is available. You can find out more about the Belkin products at their Web site (catalog.belkin.com/IWCatSectionView.process?IWAction= Load&Merchant_Id=&Section_Id=1979).

External memory card readers

Every current iPAQ model comes with an expansion slot that accepts Secure Digital (SD) and the similar MultiMedia Card (MMC) memory cards. Most desktop and laptop PCs lack any means of reading or writing directly to these memory cards. This normally isn't a problem because you can simply transfer files between your iPAQ and your desktop PC with ActiveSync. Even so, accessing those memory cards directly is a whole lot more convenient.

As I mention earlier in this chapter, many files need to be converted from one format to another when they're transferred between your iPAQ and your desktop system. While this is not true of all files, you should be aware that accessing memory cards by using a card reader does not engage ActiveSync, so those files that do need conversion won't be useable if you transfer them with the card reader.

One reason that you might want to use a card reader to transfer large files that don't need conversion is that iPAQs use the USB 1.1 standard rather than the newer and much faster USB 2.0 standard. The card readers that I mention in the following two sections both use USB 2.0, and this allows them to transfer files in a tiny fraction of the time required to move them through the standard iPAQ USB sync cable.

Crucial SD Card Reader

If you want a card reader that's extremely portable, you may want to consider getting the Crucial Hi-Speed USB SD/MMC Card Reader (www.crucial.com). This tiny unit can plug directly into a USB port or, if your USB ports are hidden on the back of your PC, you can use the included USB cable. This card reader is designed specifically for SD memory cards and is barely larger than matchbook.

'Disk 6-in-1 Card Reader

re a gadget freak like me, you probably have a number of different that use memory cards. Between iPAQs, digital cameras, video cam- ' the like, you may have a collection of memory cards in several dif- mats. If so, there's nothing quite so convenient as a card reader like ImageMate 6 in 1 Reader/Writer (www.sandisk.com). With it you rite to SD, MMC, Memory Stick, SmartMedia (SM), and rlash (CF) Type I/II cards. Not only that, but this handy device ws you to transfer files directly between the different memory card for- mats — awfully handy when you want to move digital images from your camera into your iPAQ, for example.

The SanDisk ImageMate 6 in 1 Reader/Writer is somewhat larger than the Crucial Hi-Speed USB SD/MMC Card Reader because it has four slots to accommodate the different memory card formats. Even so, the SanDisk unit is only about the size of your iPAQ.

Backing Up Your iPAQ Files

Synchronizing your files is a great way to keep your iPAQ and your desktop PC working together, but synchronization has one big problem — it doesn't protect you from losing important data. It's easy to become confused by the process of synchronizing your files and think that somehow having the same files on both your iPAQ and your desktop PC is the same as having a backup of your iPAQ files. Unfortunately, synchronization doesn't protect you because of the following reasons:

✔ If you delete a synchronized file from either your iPAQ or your desktop PC, that file is also deleted from its partner the next time you synchro- nize your files. If you think you'll remember to copy the file to some- place else before synchronization and thereby protect it, good luck! Murphy's Law will make certain that you pop that iPAQ into the cradle without remembering to make your copy.

✔ If you have to do a hard reset on your iPAQ because of a system prob- lem, any files on your iPAQ will be lost. Isn't it a good bet that this will happen just *before* you were going to synchronize your files?

✔ If a synchronized file somehow becomes corrupted on either your iPAQ or on your desktop PC, you can't complete the synchronization until that file is deleted. And of course, the corrupt file will almost certainly be one that you've spent hours on, or one that you can't easily re-create.

Doing a backup

When you back up the files from your iPAQ, all your data files, any programs you've installed, and any settings that you've adjusted on your iPAQ are saved in a file on your desktop PC's hard drive, which essentially protects the entire investment of time that you've placed in your iPAQ.

The backup/restore procedure that I describe here works with all iPAQ models. Later, in the section "Using flash memory for backup," I describe another option that's available on some iPAQs.

You can choose from two different types of backups:

✔ **Full:** A full backup saves everything on your iPAQ that can be backed up. Full backups take a little longer and use more disk space on your desktop PC, but because everything is backed up in one file, you don't have to worry about where your backed up data may be.

✔ **Incremental:** An incremental backup saves only items that are new or have been changed since the last backup. Incremental backups are usually somewhat faster than full backups, and they generally take less disk space. Of course, this can vary according to how much you've done with your iPAQ since the last backup.

Allow plenty of time for a full backup to finish. Depending on the method that you use to connect your iPAQ to your desktop PC and the size of the backup, the entire process can take anywhere from a few minutes to over an hour.

To back up your iPAQ files on your desktop PC, follow these steps:

1. **Make certain that your iPAQ is connected to your desktop PC.**

   This usually means placing it in the synchronization cradle, but you should determine your own appropriate method.

2. **Open ActiveSync on your desktop system by clicking the ActiveSync icon in the System Tray and choosing Open Microsoft ActiveSync from the pop-up menu.**

   You can skip this step if the ActiveSync window is already open on your desktop.

3. **Choose Tools⇨Backup/Restore to display the Backup/Restore dialog box (see Figure 5-8).**

4. **Select the radio button for the backup method that you prefer.**

   The first time that you do a backup, both options function the same way.

5. **If you want to keep more than one full backup, click the Change button and specify the name for the backup file in the File name text box.**

If you use the default name, new full backups overwrite older ones that use the same name.

6. Click the Back Up Now button to begin the backup.

After you click the Back Up Now button, you must leave your iPAQ alone and connected to your desktop PC until the backup is completed. If you remove your iPAQ from the cradle before the backup finishes, you run a high risk of corrupting the backup file.

7. Click OK to complete the backup after you see the message telling you that it is finished.

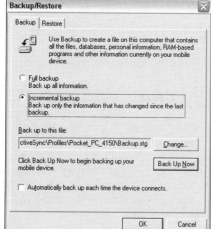

Figure 5-8:
Use
Backup/
Restore to
protect
the files on
your iPAQ.

Restoring from your backup

Restoring your files from an existing backup replaces the files that are currently on your iPAQ with the files from the backup. If you've made changes on your iPAQ since that backup, those changes will be lost after the restore.

Restoring your iPAQ files is even easier than backing them up. Here's what you do:

1. Make certain that your iPAQ is connected to your desktop PC, and then open ActiveSync (if it isn't already open) by clicking the ActiveSync icon in the System Tray and choosing Open Microsoft ActiveSync from the pop-up menu.

2. Choose Tools⇨Backup/Restore to display the Backup/Restore dialog box.

3. Click the Restore tab.

4. **Click the Restore Now button to display the Proceed With Restore dialog box.**

5. **Click the Restore button to confirm that you do indeed want to begin the restore.**

   You can't cancel this after the restore has begun, so don't click this button unless you're absolutely sure that you're ready to restore.

6. **Wait until the restore finishes (you see a message telling you it is done) and click OK.**

   Restoring takes about as long as backing up.

When you finish the restore, you're prompted to remove your iPAQ from the cradle, reset it, and then return it to the cradle. You may then be asked how to resolve a number of items that need synchronization. If so, choose the option that best suits your needs and complete the task.

An alternative to backup and restore

If you don't care for the all-or-nothing approach that a backup and restore offers, you may be interested in my more unofficial way to protect your iPAQ data files. This alternate method isn't a complete replacement for backup and restore because it protects only the files from your iPAQ's My Documents folder. However, it does offer certain advantages over backup and restore. For one thing, my unofficial method doesn't carry quite the same risk of undoing changes you've made on your iPAQ.

So what's this unofficial method, you ask? Why, it's so simple, you'll probably wonder why you didn't think of it first. When you have important files in your `C:\My Documents\Pocket_PC My Documents` folder, make a copy of them someplace else. Create an iPAQ Backups folder somewhere on your hard disk or copy the files to another computer or to removable storage like a CD-R disc or Zip drive.

If you do use this method, remember that you're responsible for making certain that you don't accidentally overwrite newer files in your `C:\My Documents\Pocket_PC My Documents` folder with ones from your backup folder. Your desktop PC warns you if you try to do this by displaying a dialog box in which you have to confirm what you really want to do, but you're the one who is clicking that mouse!

Using flash memory for backup

Depending on the model of iPAQ that you have, you may have another backup alternative that doesn't depend on your desktop PC. This option is especially attractive because you can use it at any time to protect your important document files from accidental deletion, even if you don't have immediate access to your desktop system.

Certain iPAQ models enable you to store some of your important files in *non-volatile memory.* This is also known as *Flash ROM* (although technically speaking, it isn't actually read-only memory). Essentially, this feature uses whatever space is left over in your iPAQ's *flash memory* — the place where the Windows Mobile operating system and the permanently installed programs are located. Files that you store in flash memory are protected from being accidentally deleted.

You can tell if this option is available on your iPAQ by looking for the iPAQ Backup application in your iPAQ's Programs folder. Figure 5-9 shows how the iPAQ Backup program appears when you are ready to begin your backup.

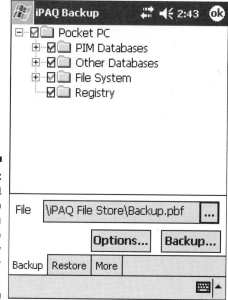

Figure 5-9:
iPAQ
Backup
enables you
to backup
files directly
on your
iPAQ.

Using the iPAQ Backup program is very similar to using the ActiveSync Backup procedure, so I don't go through the steps here. Keep in mind, however, that flash memory has very limited room, so you should set the options to conserve as much space as possible.

Exploring Your iPAQ Files

Even though your iPAQ includes File Explorer, a program that works much like Windows Explorer does on your desktop PC, managing the files on your iPAQ can be a little difficult. Somehow it just seems a little difficult exploring with a stylus. Wouldn't you like to be able to root around in the iPAQ files the same way that you do on your desktop PC?

Well, I've got good news for you: ActiveSync enables you to explore your iPAQ in your old familiar Windows Explorer on your desktop PC. Figure 5-10 shows an example of browsing the files and folders on a typical iPAQ.

To explore your iPAQ's files and folders, click the Explore button in ActiveSync. This opens a Windows Explorer view of your iPAQ.

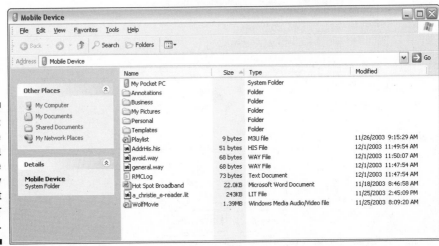

Figure 5-10: Browse your iPAQ files the easy way by doing it from your desktop PC.

Although you can explore your iPAQ's files and folders from your desktop PC, you need to remember a few things:

- If you delete files from your iPAQ, they are completely erased. The iPAQ has no Recycle Bin. If you aren't sure whether you need a file, make a backup on your desktop PC before you erase the file from your iPAQ.

- You can't open iPAQ files or run iPAQ applications from your desktop PC. If you try to open a file, a message box appears and tells you the file's properties.

- If you copy a file between your desktop PC and your iPAQ in either direction, ActiveSync checks to see if the file must be converted to a different format. If ActiveSync offers to make a conversion, allow it to do so — otherwise, the file may not be usable on the system to which it was copied.

- To see the contents of a storage card, you must first open the My Pocket PC folder. You then see the card listed as a folder named SD Card (or CF Card on some iPAQs) under the My Pocket PC folder.

- One of the easiest ways to create new folders — like the My Documents folder on a storage card — is through ActiveSync and Windows Explorer.

Part II

Personal Organization with Your iPAQ

The 5th Wave — By Rich Tennant

"OKAY—ANTIDOTE, ANTIDOTE, WHAT WOULD AN ANTIDOTE ICON LOOK LIKE? YOU KNOW, I STILL HAVEN'T GOT THIS DESKTOP THE WAY I WANT IT."

In this part . . .

Your iPAQ can help keep your personal life in order. It can keep track of your address book, help you manage your schedule, and act as your personal note taker. In this part, you see how to do all this and even how you can talk to your iPAQ without feeling silly.

Chapter 6

Keeping Your Address Book

. . . .

. . . .

The first hand-held computer-like devices filled an interesting niche. They weren't very powerful. They didn't have much memory. They couldn't perform a broad range of tasks. But they did make an excellent replacement for those pocket-sized paper address books that most people kept.

The iPAQ, of course, is quite powerful, has lots of memory, and can be called upon to handle many different types of tasks. In spite of all this, some people don't realize just how great the iPAQ is at replacing those handwritten address books. After you start keeping your address book in your iPAQ, you may never have an excuse for misplacing someone's phone number again.

What You Can Do with Your Address Book

One key to getting the most out of an innovative product like an iPAQ is to think outside the box. That is, you have to stop thinking about limits and start thinking wildly. It's hard to do that sometimes — especially when you're stuck in the rut of comparing a new product with whatever it replaced. Imagine just how little advancement there might have been in personal transportation if the early automobile manufacturers had thought of cars only in terms of a replacement for a horse. You probably wouldn't have climate control in your new car, for one thing. Only when you realize that a car can enclose you in a mobile, weather-tight cabin can you even begin to think about heating and cooling the air around the passengers.

The same thing applies to thinking about how your iPAQ's address book (which is called Contacts) can replace your little black book. You need to remember that the same old limitations that prevented you from doing things with your paper address book don't apply. You need to use your imagination to think about ways that your iPAQ address book can be useful.

Your address book as an address book

Okay, so maybe using your iPAQ's address book as an address book doesn't sound all that unusual. But consider this — when was the last time you tried to keep a hand-written address book up-do-date? Comparing the two, the iPAQ's address book has lots of advantages:

- Your iPAQ address book never runs out of room for another Johnson, Olson, or Smith. Try that with your paper notebook — especially if your family's name happens to be Johnson, Olson, or Smith!

- You don't have to worry about old iPAQ address book entries getting too faded or smudged to read.

- If someone you know happens to be like certain relatives of mine, you don't fill up your entire iPAQ address book changing that person's address listing every few months. (Yes, maybe you'd just give up on the friend or relative if you were using a paper notebook, but with the iPAQ address book, you still need only one record no matter how many times someone moves.)

- Because your iPAQ can easily exchange address book information with your desktop PC, having several copies of your address book that are all up-to-date is far easier. If something happens to one copy, you still have at least one more copy to bail you out. If you lose your little black book, you may lose your only copy. (Then how would you get a date for Saturday night?)

- Because you can use a password to restrict access to your iPAQ, you can make certain that no one else can snoop through the listings in your iPAQ address book. Your snoopy boss won't have any way to know that you've been in contact with that executive recruiter. See Chapter 3 for information about using a password to control access to the information that you have stored on your iPAQ.

- Because your iPAQ's screen has a backlight, you can look up phone numbers and make calls late at night without turning on a light — a definite advantage if all you can find is some broken-down phone booth when you're lost out in the boondocks. To discover how to control the backlight on your iPAQ, see the section on screen settings in Chapter 3.

- Finally, if you add the voice recognition software that I mention in the section "Using Voice Recognition to Manage Your Contacts" later in this chapter, you can amaze everyone by simply talking to your iPAQ to tell it whose record you want to see!

Your address book as an organizer

Some people are *really* well-organized. They're the ones whose sock drawer has dividers and a specific place for each pair of socks. Most of us are far less organized, but almost anyone can benefit from a certain amount of neatness and advance planning — as long as you don't get too obsessed with it, that is.

If you've used a paper notebook to keep your address book in the past, you're used to having a certain amount of organization. But the static nature of things written down on paper can also limit you to a rather narrow range of possibilities to organize your little black book. Consider the following options, some of which you may not have realized would be practical or even possible:

- When you add people to your iPAQ address book, you can assign them to categories. Some people may belong in the Personal category, some in Business, and some may be members of my favorite organization, Wombat Lovers Anonymous. Because your iPAQ address book gives you the option of limiting the view to display only people who are in a specific category, just one iPAQ address book can serve the function of a whole series of different paper notebooks.

- You can add people to more than one category in your iPAQ address book, so you need to record their information in only one place even if they fit several categories. If their address or phone number changes, you have to make the correction just one time to have it correct in every category that they belong to.

- Because you can easily create as many new categories as you like, creating special categories for one-time use is an easy task. You can, for example, create a category that includes all the members of your book club. Then, you can create a special category for members of the book club who want to be notified about book signings in your area by your favorite author. This enables you to first show just the book club members, and then easily add the author's fans to the special category. When you hear about a last-minute local appearance by the author, you don't have to waste time trying to remember who wants to know about it — your iPAQ address book can tell you in a flash.

Your address book as an electronic business card

I bet you don't have your own contact information listed in your address book — why would you? Well, for one very good reason — so that you can easily exchange your information in the form of an electronic business card.

iPAQs all have an infrared (or IrDA) port built in, allowing them to send and receive data with other infrared-equipped devices like iPAQs, most laptop PCs, certain printers, and yes, even Palm PCs. One of the coolest ways to exchange business cards with other iPAQ or Palm PC users is to *beam* your card through the IrDA port to that other iPAQ or Palm PC. In Figure 6-1, I've selected a record in the iPAQ address book and used tap-and-hold to display the context menu. (In this case, I told my iPAQ to display my contact list sorted by company name.) All I need to do now is aim my iPAQ at the other device and tap Beam Contact (and the person with the other unit must perform the necessary steps to receive it, of course). I can also send the record via Bluetooth if another Bluetooth-equipped device is within range.

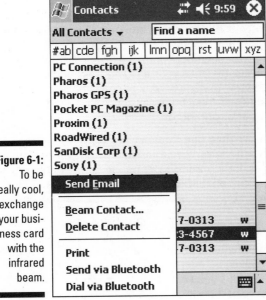

Figure 6-1:
To be really cool, exchange your business card with the infrared beam.

You may want to create more than one business card for different purposes. For example, you may not want everyone to receive all your home contact information, or you may want to create one card for business use and a different one for use in your position as a club's officer.

You can send any contact record via the infrared beam. You aren't limited to sending just your own business card. Whichever records you send, you can be certain that the other person gets a complete record without worrying that he or she wrote something down incorrectly.

To exchange data with a laptop PC, you may need to activate the IrDA port on the laptop. You may also need to install ActiveSync on the laptop if it isn't already installed. Some laptops use special applications to control infrared file transfers, so consult your laptop's user manual if you're unable to exchange information with your iPAQ. (See Chapter 5 for more information on using ActiveSync.)

Entering New Contacts

Even the New York City phone book is just a bunch of blank paper until it has all the names and phone numbers printed into its pages. Your iPAQ address book is almost as useful as that blank paper before you start adding some contact information to it — although the blank paper may be more suitable for some purposes (like making paper airplanes).

Doing it the old-fashioned way: Adding records manually

Of all the methods of adding people to your iPAQ address book, you probably spend the most time adding records manually, which isn't the easiest way to add records, nor is it the quickest. But adding records manually is the one way that's always available, and the one that gives you the most flexibility.

You need to begin by opening the Contacts application. You can open Contacts by pressing the appropriate button on the front of your iPAQ — if you remember which button does this on your unit and you haven't changed the button assignments, that is. You can also open Contacts by clicking the Start button and tapping Contacts.

Now you're ready to add a new record to the list. Begin by tapping New in the lower-left corner of the iPAQ's screen, which opens a new blank record so that you can add information. Figure 6-2 shows how a record looks after you've added information in several of the fields.

 Although the entry form shown in Figure 6-2 has so many different fields that you'd need several screens to view all of them, you don't have to use any of the fields that you don't need. In fact, when you later have a look at one of the records in your address book, you find that your iPAQ is smart enough to show a field only if it actually contains information. In most cases, this means that anyone's record can easily fit on a single screen.

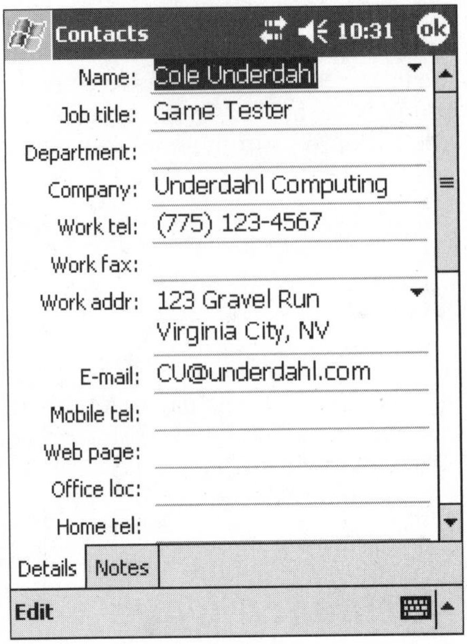

Figure 6-2:
Enter
contact
information
into any of
the fields as
necessary.

When you're done adding information, tap OK to close the new record and add it to the address book.

To confirm that the record was added correctly, you can find and view the record. Depending on just how many people you've added to your address book, finding a record can be a bit of a pain unless you understand a few of the tools that are available to help you out.

You can narrow your search in two ways so that you don't have to scroll through quite so many records in your iPAQ address book. These two ways are by using categories or by using the alphabet bar. Figure 6-3 shows both of them. In this case, I opened the menu so that I can select a category. I could also tap a section of the alphabet bar to view records in a specific part of the alphabet.

If you selected a category when you entered someone's record, you can narrow your search by clicking the category list (just below the Start button). This drops down the list so that you can choose a category to view. When you select a category, only those records that are in that category appear in your contact list.

You can easily add your own categories. To do so, tap More at the bottom of the category list, and then tap the Add/Delete tab. You can then add whatever categories you need in order to organize your list of contacts. You can add an individual to as many categories as necessary.

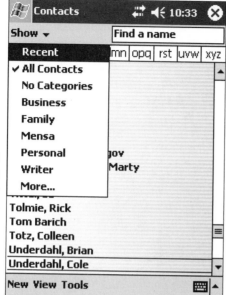

Figure 6-3:
Use
categories
to make
finding
specific
records
easier.

Remember to select All Contacts to make the full list available again when you're finished searching.

In addition to selecting a category, you can also click the alphabet bar (just above the list of records) to jump to a spot someplace in the middle of your address records, which beats using the scrollbar to move the entire distance.

When you've found the record that you want, click the record to view it. As Figure 6-4 shows, the information is condensed so that you see only those fields with information filled in.

To quickly modify the record that you're viewing, tap Edit on the menu bar. This opens the record and shows all the fields — even the ones that don't have any information yet.

Bringing records over from your desktop

As powerful as your iPAQ may be, it was never really intended to be your only computer. Your iPAQ makes far more sense as a partner to your desktop PC. One area where this partnership really shines is in sharing information — such as your address book — between your iPAQ and your desktop PC. This sharing makes it possible for you to enter the information once and then use it anywhere.

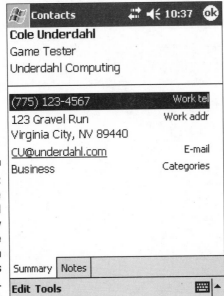

Figure 6-4:
Open the record to verify that the information you added is really there.

To share information between your desktop PC and your iPAQ, you need to use ActiveSync — a program that comes with your iPAQ. Chapter 5 covers the use of ActiveSync in detail, but you should know some important things about sharing your address book information between the two types of PCs.

You need to install Outlook

You need to install Outlook 2002 (or later) on your desktop PC in order to share contact information with your iPAQ. Outlook 2002 is included on the iPAQ Companion CD-ROM if you don't already have it installed on your desktop system.

No rule says that you have to actually *use* Outlook on your desktop, but Microsoft certainly has made it clear that they would like you to do so. Outlook is the only program that can share contact information with an iPAQ, so keeping your address book in any application other than Outlook is going to involve a lot of extra steps whenever you want to update the information in your iPAQ or your desktop PC.

You need the information in Outlook

If your contact information is currently in some program other than Outlook, you need to import that information into Outlook before you can add the information to your iPAQ. In Outlook, you can import information by using the File⇨Import and Export command. This starts the Import and Export Wizard, which helps you import your data.

You can import information from many different applications, but Outlook can sometimes be a little picky about which file formats it accepts. I've noticed, for example, that sometimes I have to try three or four different formats before I find one that works. Unfortunately, the Import and Export Wizard allows you to go through almost the entire process before it tells you that it cannot import a particular file. If this happens, going back to the original application and trying to export the data in a different format is usually the best route.

 If all else fails, see if you can export the data in *delimited* text format. Delimited text format simply writes out the data as a text file with each field separated by commas and the values enclosed in quotes. Most programs offer this as an export option, and Outlook can easily import a delimited text file.

You need to set the Contacts option in ActiveSync

After you have the address book information in Outlook, you need to enable sharing of contact information in ActiveSync. Choose Tools➪Options in ActiveSync, and then select the Contacts check box. Chapter 5 covers all the ActiveSync options so that you can see what else you may need to do.

Beam It Over, Scotty!

By far, the coolest way to add address book information to your iPAQ is to beam it over from another iPAQ, Pocket PC, or a Palm PC. After you see how fun this beaming is, you'll probably start looking for other PDA owners just so you can have beaming sessions.

Exchanging information with the infrared beams is pretty easy once you get the hang of it. To make it a bit easier, here's a step-by-step approach that works well:

1. **Select the contacts that you want to beam over to the other iPAQ by dragging the stylus across the records to highlight them.**

   You can select more than one contact to send.

2. **Tap Tools on the menu bar.**

   This displays the pop-up menu shown in Figure 6-5.

3. **Choose Beam Contacts to begin the transfer.**

   Aim the infrared ports of the two iPAQs at each other, keeping the ports within a few inches of each other. While your iPAQ is looking for the other iPAQ, you see the Align ports and Searching messages shown in Figure 6-6.

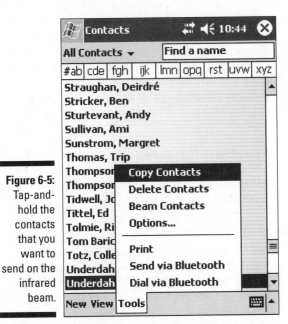

Figure 6-5:
Tap-and-hold the contacts that you want to send on the infrared beam.

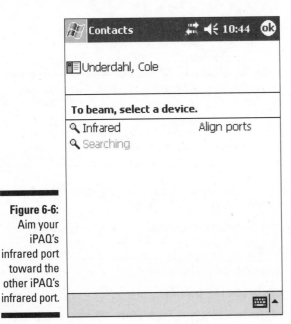

Figure 6-6:
Aim your iPAQ's infrared port toward the other iPAQ's infrared port.

4. **Tell the other iPAQ to save the records: Click Yes or Save All, depending on the number of records that you sent.**

When the receiving iPAQ has received the transmission, you see a `Receiving Data` message on the receiving iPAQ.

If the transfer didn't work, here are some tricks to try:

✔ First, try starting the transfer again. This usually resolves the problem.

✔ If you can't get the transfer working after a couple of tries, make sure that the two infrared ports really are pointing at each other. Different brands of iPAQs hide their infrared ports in different locations.

✔ Make certain there's nothing between the two iPAQs that could be blocking the infrared light beam. Really bright sunlight can be a problem. You may also be holding your iPAQ with your hand over the infrared port — but if you realize this is the problem before anyone else does, blame it on something else.

✔ Blame it on some secret encryption software that prevents anyone from stealing your data. It's not true, but how is anyone else going to know?

Using Voice Recognition to Manage Your Contacts

Your iPAQ is pretty cool all by itself, but this next program that I show you could be called the iceberg of cool! In fact, this is the program that I use when I want to impress someone by showing them how useful and advanced the iPAQ has become.

The software I'm talking about (and talking to) is *Voice LookUp* from HandHeld Speech (`www.handheldspeech.com`). This amazing application enables your iPAQ to recognize your voice so that you can look up contact records by speaking the name that you want into the microphone. After you have someone's record on-screen, placing a call to them, sending an e-mail message, or scheduling a meeting is just another simple voice command away. You can even use voice commands to switch to different applications on your iPAQ. You can download a trial copy of the program from the HandHeld Speech Web site, and register it (for just $20!) after you see how well it works. If you're going to add any programs to your iPAQ, this one should be at the top of your list!

Voice LookUp is very easy to use. After you've downloaded and installed it, you probably want to set up your iPAQ so that pressing one of the buttons on your iPAQ starts the program. (The readme file that accompanies Voice LookUp tells you exactly how to do this.) This makes it even easier for you to use Voice LookUp because you can do so just by pressing that button.

Before you can use Voice LookUp for the first time, you need to spend a few minutes training it to recognize your voice. To do so, tap the Enroll icon in the Programs folder, and then spend about five minutes reading some text. At the end of the enrollment, you can begin using the program. (However, you should continue training it as you use the program in order to improve the accuracy — see the user documentation included with the program for more details.)

After the enrollment is completed and you start the program, you see the LookUp screen. This is your starting point for using Voice LookUp.

When the LookUp screen is displayed, you see a message in the lower-left of the screen telling you that the microphone is off. Now it's time to have some fun. Press the button on your iPAQ that you assigned to LookUp (or the Record button if you didn't assign a button) so that the microphone turns on, hold the microphone on your iPAQ close to your mouth, and say "lookup" and the name of someone in your contact list. (See Chapter 3 if you need a refresher on assigning buttons.) Figure 6-7 shows the result.

Figure 6-7:
Voice
LookUp
finds and
displays
your
contacts by
listening to
your voice.

After a contact record is displayed, you can easily send an e-mail or place a phone call to that person. In Figure 6-8, I pressed the button on my iPAQ and said "send mail" to tell Voice LookUp to start an e-mail message.

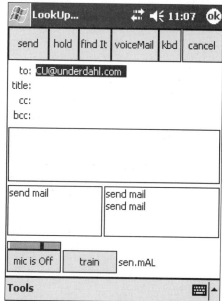

Figure 6-8:
Voice LookUp can even send e-mail messages.

As I mention earlier, you do need to train Voice LookUp in order to improve the accuracy. If you find that the program has displayed the wrong record, choose the correct record from the list above the Train button and then tap the Train button. As you continue to do this, Voice LookUp will find the correct record far more often. Tap the saveUser button to save all your training. You should do a bit of training before you start bragging to other people about how smart your iPAQ is, but it's time well spent — especially after you see the reactions on peoples' faces when they watch your iPAQ respond to voice commands!

Chapter 7

Taking Some Notes

. . . .

In This Chapter

▶ Discovering some great uses for notes

▶ Creating notes

▶ Recording notes by speaking

. . . .

As I show you in Chapter 6, your iPAQ makes old-fashioned paper address books seem pretty lame. Well, get ready to throw out your paper notepads, too. Your iPAQ makes writing notes on a pad of paper seem like the equivalent of scratching a letter out on a piece of tree bark.

If you aren't in the habit of writing yourself notes, you may wonder why anyone would need to use an iPAQ for note taking. If so, go ahead and skip this chapter — but write yourself a note to remind you to come back later when you discover that you've forgotten something important.

Finding Uses for Your iPAQ Notes

Notes are probably the most free-form type of document that exists. There's really nothing formal about all those sticky notes that people paste all over the sides of their monitors, and no rules exist to tell you what you can or can't do with a note. Notes simply are the Swiss Army knife style of documents. (Why, even using the word *document* to describe a note seems kind of pretentious, doesn't it?)

Still, you can do lots of things with notes on your iPAQ:

✔ Quickly write down a Web address that you see on a TV commercial.

✔ Create your weekly grocery list — although you may get some funny looks in the frozen food aisle.

✔ Remind yourself of the punch line to that great joke you just heard. (Just don't try to tell people the joke by reading it off your iPAQ's screen — they may laugh, but it won't be at the joke!)

✔ When you wake up in the middle of the night with that idea for a new product that's going to make you rich, write it down in an iPAQ note. You don't even have to turn on a light to see the iPAQ's screen. (However, if you want to delete that idea about the pink elephants the next morning, go right ahead.)

✔ When writing down a note just isn't possible, you can use your iPAQ's recording capabilities to record a voice note, something that can be very handy when you're in a hurry and need to capture a thought that can't wait for you to write it down.

✔ If you use the Transcriber, your iPAQ may be able to read your handwriting better than almost anyone else. So even if your handwriting is pretty sloppy, you can still create notes that someone can actually read. Don't forget to proofread it, though — the Transcriber can't produce miracles! (See Chapter 4 for information on how to use the Transcriber.)

Of course, you shouldn't try to do certain things with notes on your iPAQ:

✔ Leaving your iPAQ taped to a friend's door with a note telling him that you dropped by when he wasn't home.

✔ Writing ransom notes on your iPAQ.

✔ Using an iPAQ note to tell a bank teller that "this is a stickup." This situation could be bad if you run out with the money but forget your iPAQ — especially if you entered your real name and address in the owner information screen.

Writing Yourself a Note

The iPAQ Notes application seems like a very simple program, but you may be a little surprised to find out just how much it can really do. In addition to being a quick way to jot down a thought, this program offers some really cool options, such as voice notes as well as an electronic drawing pad that lets you draw a picture right on your screen. I want to make sure that you don't miss many of the neatest options, so here's a quick overview.

Choosing your note options

You can just go ahead and begin using the Notes program, but why not start with a little detour to see whether some of the available options suit your needs? Open the Notes program by clicking the Start button and choosing Notes from the Start menu (or from the Programs folder if you have modified the Start menu and removed Notes). When you see the list of existing notes (or a blank list if you haven't used Notes before), choose Tools➪Options to display the Notes Options, shown in Figure 7-1. Then follow along through the following four sections to see what these options do and which settings will work best for you.

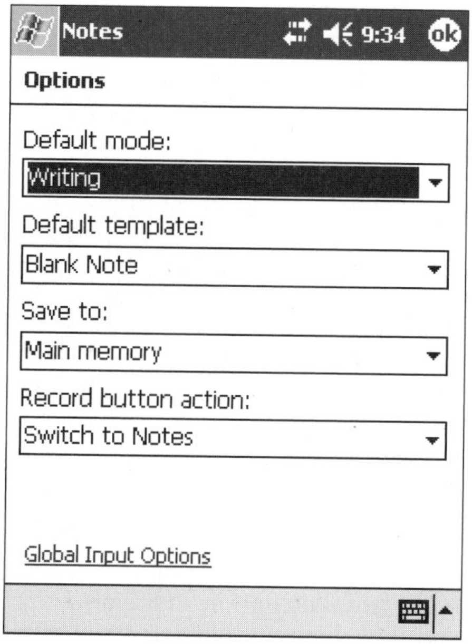

Figure 7-1:
Open the
Notes
Options
screen to
choose
how you
want Notes
to work
for you.

Notes	⇄ ◀€ 9:34	ok
Options		
Default mode:		
Writing	▼	
Default template:		
Blank Note	▼	
Save to:		
Main memory	▼	
Record button action:		
Switch to Notes	▼	
Global Input Options		
	⌨ ▲	

Selecting your entry mode

The first optional setting is the Default Mode setting. You can choose to start new notes in Writing mode or Typing mode. As you can easily guess, these modes refer to using handwriting or the on-screen keyboard to enter text into your notes.

Selecting a default input mode for notes may seem odd when you can easily select your input method using the Secondary Input Panel (SIP) selector in the lower-right corner of your screen. In reality, though, this Notes option is pretty cool because it enables you to select a different input mode for notes than the one that you typically use in other types of applications.

You could, for example, choose Writing as your Notes default and leave the on-screen keyboard selected for all other input. When you want to write out a quick note, you don't have to remember to first switch the input method (or worry about losing your train of thought when you have to attend to such details).

Using the Writing mode in Notes is not quite the same thing as using the Transcriber. When you use the Transcriber, your notes are automatically converted into text a short time after you finish writing. When you use the Writing mode in Notes, you need to choose Tools⇨Recognize to convert your handwriting into text.

Picking a template

You'll probably be pleasantly surprised by the next optional setting — the Default Template option. You may not even realize that the Notes application uses templates.

In addition to the Blank Note template, you can select from Meeting Notes, Memos, Phone Memos, and To Do templates. Each template is set up specifically to make taking certain types of notes easier, so selecting the correct template can help you produce better notes with less work. Indeed, the right template can save you a lot of trouble by making certain that you don't forget to write down an important piece of information — such as a phone number so that you can return a call.

In addition to adding fields for important information that you don't want to forget, the templates also use quite large text in the field names so that you can more easily see where and what you need to enter.

After you select a default template, any new notes you create use that template until you choose a different template option. Remember to use the Tools⇨Options command to select a different template when you want to create a different type of note.

Deciding where to save it

When you close a note that you've created, your iPAQ saves the note into the storage memory area. If you have a storage card installed in your iPAQ, you can use the Save To option to choose to save the note on the memory card rather than in the main storage memory.

Your iPAQ uses a very efficient file storage system, which minimizes the amount of memory that's used to store your files. Even so, the built-in storage memory is limited, and using an extra memory card can greatly enhance your ability to save files.

Saving your notes to a storage card rather than to main memory can be especially important if you create lots of voice notes. These types of notes can really eat up memory, especially if you select one of the higher-quality recording settings. Saving your notes to the iPAQ File Store saves notes in *flash memory* — a fairly limited space that is not available on all iPAQ models.

Setting the Save To location to a Secure Digital (SD) or CompactFlash (CF) card won't have any effect if you don't have a storage card inserted into your iPAQ. If you select the storage card option rather than main memory and then swap out your storage card for a different type of device that fits into the expansion slot, any new notes that you create are stored in main memory. If you reinsert the storage card, it's used again to store new notes, but existing notes in main memory won't automatically be moved.

Programming the Record button

Your iPAQ has a button that you can press to begin recording a voice note. (See "Recording a Note" later in this chapter for more information.) Use the Record Button Action setting to choose what you want to happen when you press the button.

Some iPAQ models have a dedicated Record button. If your iPAQ lacks the dedicated Record button, you can easily reassign one of the other buttons to the recording function. To do so, tap the Start button, choose Settings, tap the Personal tab, and then tap Buttons icon. Choose the button that you want to use and then select Record as the action that you want to assign to that button.

The Record Button Action setting controls whether your iPAQ automatically opens the Notes application when you press the Record button. Either way, your iPAQ records your voice note, but because other applications may not know how to deal with the voice note, keeping the default action set to Switch to Notes is usually best.

Starting a new note

After you know what the Notes application can do and have selected the settings that you prefer, you can begin using the program with a new note. If you haven't started the Notes program yet, click the Start button and choose Notes from the Start menu.

If you've used Notes to create other notes, you see a list of the existing notes. Tap one of them to open it so that you can read it, edit it, or simply add more to it. To begin a new note, choose New.

What you do next depends on the input method that you select. In most cases, using handwriting is probably the easiest, but you have to decide what works best for you.

Figure 7-2 shows a note that I began writing. Although it isn't necessary, I chose Tools➪Recognize after entering the first four words so that you can see how good the iPAQ is at recognizing handwriting.

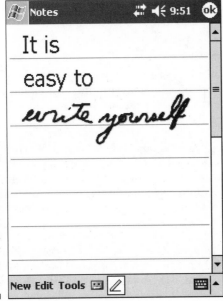

Figure 7-2:
Write your note on the screen, and your iPAQ turns your writing into text.

Editing your note

As good as the handwriting recognition may be, you may encounter errors from time to time. That's when you need to get out the red pen and begin some serious editing. (I'm not *really* advocating using a red pen — it's just that human editors traditionally used red pens to mark their corrections in a manuscript.)

Editing a note on your iPAQ will seem very familiar because you use the same commands that you've used on your desktop PC. Figure 7-3 shows the Edit menu in the iPAQ Notes program.

Editing a note by using the on-screen keyboard is often easier than doing so by handwriting recognition. If, however, you're using the Transcriber, you can teach your iPAQ to do a better job of recognizing your handwriting by training it when it makes an error. *Training* consists of selecting the letter that was incorrectly recognized and then rewriting the letter. How successful this training is depends heavily on how patient you are; you may need to repeat the process a number of times before the recognition improves.

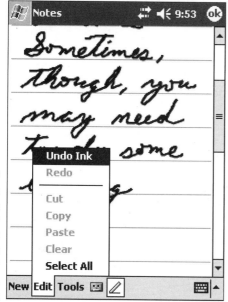

Figure 7-3:
Use the
familiar
Edit menu
commands
to edit your
notes.

To edit your note, tap where you want to make the correction. If you want to replace a word, drag the stylus across the word to select the word. Then type in your correction or use the Edit menu commands as necessary. If you want to delete the last handwriting, choose Edit⇨Undo Ink.

If you're using handwriting recognition and discover that some words are incorrect after you choose Tools⇨Recognize, select the misspelled word and then try the Tools⇨Alternates command. As Figure 7-4 shows, using the Alternates command often saves you the trouble of manual editing. If the correct word is one of the alternates, select the correction from the list. If the correct word isn't shown, edit the word manually. Just make sure that you don't select one of the non-words that often appear in the list — they're just your iPAQ's attempts at being helpful.

A picture is worth a thousand words

Sometimes showing something in a quick drawing is far easier than writing out a long description. Even a crude map can be more understandable than someone's list of directions. And you don't have to give up the ability to make a quick drawing just because you're taking notes on an iPAQ rather than on a pad of paper.

Figure 7-4:
Use Tools⇨
Alternates
as a quick
method
to correct
incorrectly
recognized
words.

Figure 7-5 shows an example of a quick map that I drew on a friend's iPAQ to show him how to find a campground where a bunch of friends were gathering. I could have added a lot more detail and even included some written directions, but even this crude map got him to the campground.

Figure 7-5:
Draw right
on your
screen to
include a
drawing in
your note.

You may be wondering how your iPAQ knows when you've made a drawing rather than some really odd handwriting. The answer is simple: When you cross three of the horizontal gridlines in a single motion, your iPAQ knows that you are using *digital ink* to make a drawing. When you complete your drawing it becomes a *bitmap* image within your note. (A bitmap is simply a graphic image where each dot in the image can be modified on its own without affecting the rest of the image.) You can tell this because tapping within the drawing displays a dotted line that indicates the borders of the drawing. Don't tap within the drawing if it's already selected, though. That will add a dot to the drawing. You can tell that the drawing is selected because the dotted line appears around a drawing when it's selected. (To find more information about the Transcriber and the horizontal guidelines that it uses, see Chapter 4.)

You can expand a drawing by starting a new line within the current boundaries of the drawing and simply continuing the line outside those boundaries. You can change the size of the drawing by tapping it to select it, and then using the handles that appear along the borders to stretch or contract it.

To edit your drawing, use the Edit⇨Undo Ink command, which removes elements from the drawing in the reverse of the order that they were added. But you aren't limited to this sequential editing mode. You can also tap an element within the drawing to select it, and then use the Edit menu commands or drag and drop to modify it. You can even use the tap-and-hold technique to display a context menu for the selected element.

Recording a Note

In addition to typing, handwriting, and drawing, you've got another interesting option for creating a note. You can record a note in your own voice — or someone else's if you can get a friend to talk into your iPAQ.

Voice notes are often the most convenient way to create a note because you can record a note while you're doing something else. You can create a voice note even when writing is pretty much impossible, such as while riding in a crowded bus on a very bumpy road.

Although recording voice notes on your iPAQ while you're driving seems mighty tempting, I don't recommend it. Even talking into your iPAQ takes too much concentration for this to be safe. If you absolutely have to record a voice note while driving, try to find a safe place to pull over so that you don't endanger everyone else (and yourself) on the road. This warning is especially important if you're using one of the iPAQ models that lacks a dedicated Record button on the side of the case.

How good do you want it to sound?

Remember those commercials for audio recording tape that asked, "Is it live, or is it Memorex?" Well, no one is going to mistake a recording you make on your iPAQ with a live voice. Quite honestly, if you really want high-fidelity recordings, you need to look somewhere else.

The voice-recording feature on your iPAQ is somewhat lacking in audio quality for one very good reason: Storing high-quality digital sound recordings takes up a lot of space. By choosing a lower-quality level, you greatly reduce the amount of memory needed for your recording.

Choosing the best recording format can be a bit of a pain. Your iPAQ offers quite a few storage settings that range all the way from about 2K for each second of recording to about 172 kilobytes per second — a ratio of 86 to 1!

Unfortunately, the choices aren't quite as simple as they may seem. The smallest-sized voice setting certainly gives you the longest recording time on a given amount of memory, but you may not be able to understand your own voice recordings if you select that option. The largest-sized files certainly sound better, but they waste half the space they use because they're in stereo format — even though you're recording from a monaural (single channel) microphone on your iPAQ. (Both channels of the stereo recording have exactly the same signal.)

To make matters worse, if you want to share your recording with your desktop system or perhaps to e-mail a voice note to someone, only some of the recording formats are likely to be usable, depending on exactly where the recording is played back. For example, the GSM 6.10 format — the one that happens to produce the smallest files — isn't playable on most desktop PCs. And it figures that the format that produces the largest files is the one that pretty much anyone is able to play. You'll probably find that it takes some trial and error to determine which recording formats are usable for other people because their particular desktop PC may not have the ability to use the format that you select. (For details on selecting the recording format, see the following section, "Choosing your recording format.")

Experiment a little before you decide on the recording format. Create a few sample files with different formats, and then try listening to those recordings on the different PCs and in the different applications that you're using. That way, you won't have any unpleasant surprises when you actually need to make an important recording.

Choosing your recording format

In order to find the best format for you, you may want to try out several different ones. To select the recording format, follow these steps:

1. **Click the Start button and choose Notes from the Start menu.**

   Make certain that you're viewing the list of notes rather than creating a new note. If you're in a note, you have to close the note in order to access the recording settings.

2. **Choose Tools⇨Options and then tap the Global Input Options link to display the Settings screen. If it isn't already displayed, tap the Options tab.**

3. **Click the down arrow on the Voice Recording Format drop-down list box, as shown in Figure 7-6, and select the option that you prefer from the list.**

4. **Click OK when you have made your selection.**

Don't waste memory selecting a stereo recording format. The equivalent mono format works just as well and takes half as much space. Besides, your iPAQ has only a single microphone, so a stereo recording would simply have two identical channels.

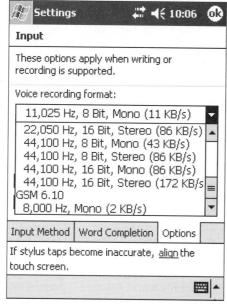

Figure 7-6: Select the recording format that suits your needs.

When you select a recording format, the frequency that's listed is the number of *samples* — little bits of data that define the sound you're recording — per second that are used to record the sound. But this number generally represents a figure that's about double the highest audio frequency that's included in the recording. As a result, selecting a format that's listed as 8,000 Hz effectively limits the recording to sounds below 4,000 Hz. This isn't as bad as it sounds. Sure, a musical recording that cuts off everything above 4,000 Hz would sound terrible, but the human voice typically doesn't use many sounds above about 3,000 Hz. So for a voice-only recording, you don't gain much by including higher frequencies.

Recording your note

The easiest way to record a note is to hold down the Record button and begin speaking into the microphone. Continue holding down the button until you're done. You can also click the Record button on the recording controls toolbar to begin a recording and click the Stop button to end the recording. (To display this toolbar, click the icon that looks like a miniature cassette tape on the Notes menu bar.) This second option is probably best if your iPAQ model lacks a dedicated Record button because it does not require you to reassign one of the other buttons.

If possible, try to make your recording in one pass. Each time you press and release the Record button on the side of your iPAQ, you create a new recording. So if you want all your thoughts to be included in a single recording, be sure to hold the button down continuously while speaking.

Using your recording

After you make a recording, you'll want to play it back, especially if you selected a new recording format — you want to make sure that you can actually understand what you recorded.

To play back your recording, tap the recording in the list of notes on the Notes screen. If you can't hear the recording, click the speaker icon on the right side of the recording toolbar to display the volume control (see Figure 7-7). Drag the slider up or down as necessary.

Understanding a recording is much easier if you listen to it with headphones rather than trying to use the built-in speaker (especially if you've selected one of the more highly compressed recording formats). Any standard stereo headphones should work, although the small ear bud type may be the most convenient to carry along with your iPAQ.

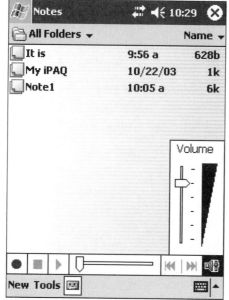

Figure 7-7:
Use the
recording
toolbar
to control
playback
and volume.

After you check your recording and find that it's okay, you can use that recording many different ways. Here are just a few ideas:

✔ **Directions:** If someone is giving you directions to someplace, ask him to record the directions on your iPAQ so that you can play them back if you get confused or turned around. You may want to have them record each leg as a separate voice note so that you can repeat a single note without listening to directions you have already completed.

✔ **E-mail attachment:** You can send a recording to someone as an e-mail attachment, which is a great way to send someone birthday greetings — especially if you sing "Happy Birthday" in the recording. What better way to get someone to stop complaining that you always forget his or her birthday?

✔ **Document insertion:** A voice note can be included in a spreadsheet or other document. When someone is viewing the document, she can click the recording icon in the document to hear your explanation justifying the cost of your latest business dinner.

✔ **Friendly blackmail:** Finally, if you have a recording of your buddy telling you he'll eat his hat if you get that promotion, you'll probably work extra hard to make certain that you actually do get the new job. And won't it be fun passing the salt and pepper?

Chapter 8

Keeping Your Mobile Calendar

In This Chapter

▶ Setting up your calendar options

▶ Creating your pocket calendar

▶ Putting your to-do list in your pocket

I bet that you're just too busy and that managing your time seems harder than it should be. Even if weeks were eight days long, you still wouldn't have enough time for everything you want to do, would you?

Your iPAQ can't create more time, but it can help you make better use of the time you have. Not only does the iPAQ help you organize your schedule, but it keeps track of your to-do list — all those things that need to get done sometime, but don't fit neatly into a schedule. And, as an added bonus, your iPAQ can keep you out of the doghouse by making sure that you never forget an important personal event like a birthday or an anniversary. (That alone could be worth whatever you have to pay for an iPAQ!)

Setting Up Your Options

When you're dealing with something as personal as your calendar, you certainly want it to reflect your way of looking at things. Luckily, you can customize the calendar by using the Calendar options, so you're sure to enjoy using it.

To begin setting the calendar options the way you want them, first open the Calendar by clicking the Start button and choosing Calendar from the Start menu. Alternatively, you can press the appropriate button on the front of your iPAQ (whichever button is set up to open the calendar on your iPAQ). Next, choose Tools⇨Options, which displays the Calendar Options screen, shown in Figure 8-1. Read on for details on each option.

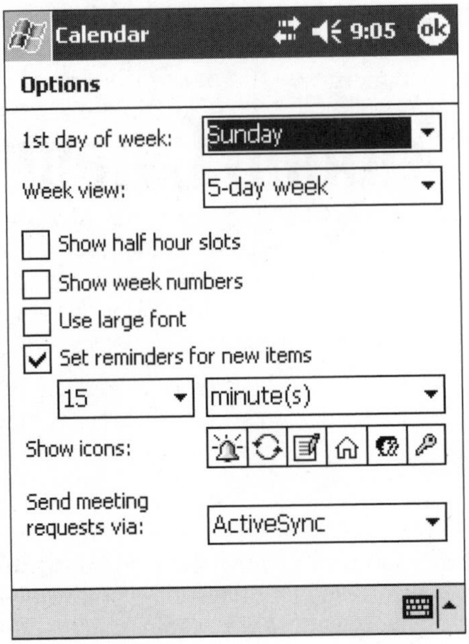

Figure 8-1:
Open the
Calendar
Options
screen to
choose your
personalized
calendar
settings.

Defining your week

Your first choice in the Calendar Options is defining your week — at least in terms of how you want to use the calendar.

Depending on your needs, you can have the calendar begin each week by showing either Sunday or Monday as the first day of the week. And you're stuck with choosing either Sunday or Monday, so if you've got one of those strange work schedules that rotate starting days or if you always begin work on a day other than Sunday or Monday, you're out of luck.

Next, you can choose the number of days in your week. Okay, so we all know that there are seven days in a week, but you can set your calendar to five, six, or seven days. The reason for this is to allow your iPAQ to display only work-days if you want. Setting the number of days is really a matter of personal choice; you're on your own in deciding what to use.

Controlling the clutter

Now get ready to decide just how cluttered you'd like your calendar to appear. Select from the following options:

✔ **Show Half Hour Slots:** Select this option if you want to be able to easily tap the exact time slot for appointments that begin at half past the hour in addition to those beginning right on the hour. Choosing to show half hour slots makes the daily schedule take up a lot more room on the iPAQ's screen, so I prefer to skip this option. You can easily set the correct time for an appointment no matter how this option is set.

✔ **Show Week Numbers:** Select this to include the *week number* — the number of weeks since the first of the year — in the calendar header when you choose the week view. Unless you really need to know the week number for some odd reason, this option seems to serve no important purpose other than adding more clutter to the screen.

✔ **Use Large Font:** Choose this option if your calendar display is just too hard to read. Of course, pulling out your reading glasses is another viable option. The larger the font, the less information the small iPAQ screen can show and the more you need to scroll.

✔ **Set Reminders for New Items:** This option automatically creates a reminder that pops up (and even turns your iPAQ on if necessary) to make certain that you don't forget your appointments. You can always set reminders for individual calendar items, but this option makes certain that you don't forget to do so.

   If you select the Set Reminders for New Items option, you can use the two boxes immediately below the option to determine how far in advance you want to be notified. I prefer more notice than the default setting of 15 minutes, but you can choose whatever works best for you.

✔ **Show Icons:** Tap any of the icons to choose the ones you want to see on your calendar. The icons (left to right) represent the following:

   • Reminders

   • Recurring appointments

   • Notes

   • Location

   • Attendees

   • Private

Select only those icons that really mean something important to you. Doing this keeps your calendar listings from being crowded out by all sorts of unnecessary icons.

Sending meeting requests

The final calendar option is the choice of how to send meeting requests. (See "Creating a meeting" later in this chapter for more information on using this feature.) Your choices here would generally be to use ActiveSync or to send the requests via e-mail (this option is listed as POP3 — a type of mail server). If you access your e-mail directly from your iPAQ by dialing in to your mail server, you may want to select the e-mail option so that the requests go out sooner. If you regularly synchronize your iPAQ with your desktop PC, and you handle most of your e-mail messages through your desktop system, select ActiveSync.

Click OK when you have finished setting your calendar options.

Setting Up Your Schedule

The iPAQ calendar is more than a pretty display of dates. By adding the items that are on your schedule, the calendar becomes especially useful: It allows you to plan ahead. After you've added your schedule, you can easily see when you're busy, when you have some free time, and when you can arrange for new appointments.

Because you probably use your iPAQ as a partner to your desktop PC, you almost certainly want to have the same list of events and appointments on both systems. Fortunately, the software that comes with your iPAQ — specifically ActiveSync — makes keeping your two calendars up-to-date a simple automated process. When you've set up the items you want to share between your iPAQ and your desktop PC, you can synchronize your calendars by simply popping your iPAQ into the cradle on your desk. Chapter 5 shows you how to set up ActiveSync so that you don't even have to think about it.

In the following sections, I cover how to set up and manage your appointments on your iPAQ. If you sometimes manage your schedule with your desktop PC, you'll find that the process is very similar no matter which PC you use.

Adding an appointment

Adding a new appointment to your schedule is very easy. At least it's easy in terms of what you need to do on your iPAQ. Finding the time to accommodate the items you've added is your problem.

Just because your iPAQ's calendar uses the fancy term *appointment* for things that you add to your schedule doesn't mean that you can add only business-related items to the list. Birthdays, anniversaries, dates, or anything else that happens on a specific date or time are also fair game. Someone had to pick a name for the items you add to your calendar, and it just so happens that the person chose *appointment.* If you'd prefer to think of these things as *rendezvous, prior engagements,* or something else, feel free.

To add a new appointment, do one of two things:

✔ Open your calendar and then choose New.

✔ Tap-and-hold a specific date and time for the appointment, and choose New Appointment from the pop-up menu that appears.

Either method works, but the second method offers a couple advantages and some disadvantages:

✔ **Advantage:** Starting by selecting the date and time enables you to quickly see if the new item is in conflict with existing items.

✔ **Advantage:** If you select a specific date and time, the New Appointment form automatically uses that date and time as the starting point for the item. Of course, you can easily change the date and time, but you don't have to if the date and time are already correct when you begin creating the schedule item.

✔ **Disadvantage:** If you're setting up an event that's far off in the future, navigating to the correct date may be a bit of a pain.

✔ **Disadvantage:** If the new item conflicts with an existing item, tapping the time of the new item opens the existing item rather than opening a new appointment form. Events conflict with each other if they share some of the same date and time on your calendar. For example, an all-day event like a birthday would conflict with a dental appointment at 10 a.m. on the same day.

Choosing a subject

Okay, you've elected to create a new appointment by one of the methods described in the preceding section. Now what? Begin by entering a subject for the item. You can select a subject from the drop-down list, as shown in Figure 8-2, or you can enter a new subject. In the figure, I clicked the keyboard icon near the lower-right corner to remove the on-screen keyboard so you would have a better view of the form.

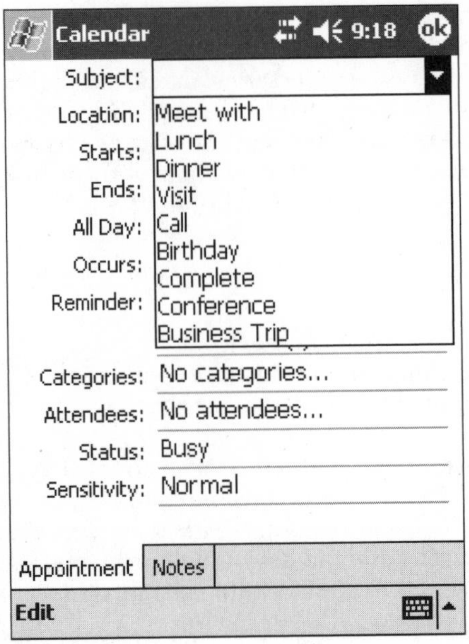

Calendar ⇄ ◀€ 9:18 ◯ḵ

Subject:	▼
Location:	Meet with
Starts:	Lunch
	Dinner
Ends:	Visit
All Day:	Call
	Birthday
Occurs:	Complete
Reminder:	Conference
	Business Trip
Categories:	No categories...
Attendees:	No attendees...
Status:	Busy
Sensitivity:	Normal

Appointment | Notes

Edit 🖮 ▲

Figure 8-2:
Make sure
that you pick
a subject
that's easy
to under-
stand.

Generally, the calendar shows only the event's subject, so picking a clear subject enables you to understand your schedule with a quick glance, even after
you've added a bunch of things to your calendar. If you can't figure out an
event from looking at the calendar, you have to open the individual items
to see what they contain. So make the subject as clear as possible for your
own sake.

Even if you pick one of the subjects from the drop-down list, you can person-
alize it by adding your own text. For example, if you select the Meet With
subject, add the name of the person that you're meeting to the subject line.

Setting the location

After you've specified the subject, you can add a location for the event.
Including a location isn't always necessary because some events simply don't
require you to be in some particular place. A good example is if the event
that you're adding is someone's birthday. In that case, the location doesn't
matter (unless you happen to be going to the birthday party, of course). You
also don't need a location if you're listing something like a phone call that
you need to make. The point is, you can leave this field (or any unneeded
field) blank.

For an event like a scheduled phone call, you may want to use the location field for the phone number that you need to call (especially if you're calling someone who isn't included in your list of contacts).

The drop-down location list starts out empty. As you set up appointments, the locations that you've used in the past are added to the list. Eventually you can select locations from the drop-down list rather than always entering them manually.

Setting the times

Now it's time to set the times for the event. Again, as with locations, not all appointments require a time. You don't have to worry about times for some all-day events like birthdays, but in most cases, you want both a starting and an ending time.

Each item that you add to your calendar is considered to run continuously from the specified starting time to the specified ending time. If you need to add an event that runs during the same hours — but not all day — on several consecutive days, you can use the Occurs field to specify a recurrence pattern. See the "Setting the pattern" section later in this chapter for details on how to do this.

To set the dates and times, tap the date or time that you want to change and either type in the correct information or select what you want from the item that drops down. As Figure 8-3 shows, if you tap one of the date fields, a calendar drops down. If you tap a time field, a list of times appears.

When you're viewing the drop-down calendar, shown in Figure 8-3, you can click a date in the calendar to place that date in the field. If the date that you want isn't visible, use the arrows at the top of the drop-down calendar to navigate to the correct month so that you can select the date you want.

You aren't limited to the times shown in the time drop-down lists. If you need to set an event for 4:11 a.m., go ahead and type in the correct time. Remember, though, that your iPAQ automatically assumes that all events run for exactly an hour, so you may need to specify both the starting and ending times.

Picking an event type

The iPAQ calendar recognizes two types of events: Normal and All Day. Choose No in the All Day field for events that have a beginning and ending time; choose Yes in the All Day field for events like birthdays that don't have specified beginning and ending times.

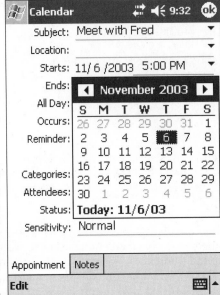

Figure 8-3:
Choose
the correct
beginning
and ending
dates and
times.

Your definition of an all-day event may differ from your iPAQ's definition. In the iPAQ's definition, an event that is all day begins at midnight and ends at the next midnight. Don't try to use Yes in the All Day field as the event type for things that really do have a beginning and ending time — such as a training class that lasts your entire workday. If you do use Yes, your iPAQ doesn't warn you if the scheduled event conflicts with other items on your schedule.

Setting the pattern

The next appointment option is the Occurs drop-down list box. Use this option to specify events that happen more than once. For example, if you have a regular staff meeting every Monday morning at 9 a.m., you need to set up only one occurrence of the meeting and then specify when it repeats.

Figure 8-4 shows an example of how the Occurs drop-down list may appear when you tap the box. Your iPAQ offers several common types of patterns to make it easy to set up recurring events.

In addition to the options presented in the drop-down list, you can set your own unique schedule. Just tap <Edit Pattern> and use the screens that follow to set up the recurrence schedule. You can, for example, schedule a meeting to run at the same time for three consecutive days or schedule a club meeting on the second Saturday of each month.

Use the fourth recurrence option — the one that specifies the same date each year — as a reminder for annual events like birthdays and anniversaries.

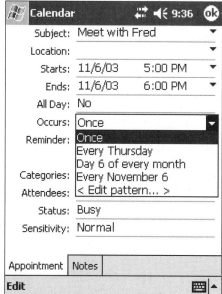

Figure 8-4:
Use the
Occurs
drop-down
list to set up
events that
happen on
a regular
schedule.

Choosing a category

If you keep different types of events in your iPAQ calendar, you may want to select categories for those events. Just tap the Categories field and select the appropriate categories for the event. These are the same categories (Business, Family, Holiday, and so on) that you use to organize your list of contacts. (In case you decided to skip around, I cover categories in Chapter 6.) I also show you more about using them with your calendar entries later in this chapter in the section "Using categories to simplify your life."

Creating a meeting

Your iPAQ helps you set up a meeting that you're scheduling by sending a message inviting each of the proposed attendees. However, you're still responsible for keeping everyone awake during the meeting — your iPAQ can't handle *all* the details!

To select attendees, tap the Attendees field and then select each of the people you want to notify. Your iPAQ sends an e-mail message to each person with all the details that you've included while setting up the event in your calendar.

You may be a little surprised when you try to select the potential attendees: Only those people in your list of contacts who have an e-mail address can be selected (which actually makes total sense because your iPAQ can't send an e-mail message unless it knows the correct e-mail address).

Specifying the status

Not all appointments are set in stone. Sometimes, you may want to set aside a period of time without making an absolute commitment. This situation certainly applies in the case where someone else is trying to set up a meeting and has asked you to set aside a couple different blocks of time while she tries to see what works best for everyone else.

The Status drop-down box offers four different choices to handle a range of possibilities: Free, Tentative, Busy, and Out of Office. You can probably figure out quite easily which one fits any event you're scheduling.

Marking it sensitive

You can specify that an appointment is a private event by selecting Private rather than Normal in the Sensitivity drop-down list box. The only real effect of this change is that if you choose to, you can flag private events with a little key icon.

If you share your iPAQ calendar with Outlook on your desktop PC, you can choose to prevent private events from appearing in a printed schedule. Use the printing options in Outlook to control just what appears in printed versions of your calendar.

Adding some notes

Preparation is one of the keys to success. When you're scheduling events in your calendar, why not take an extra step to make certain that you're prepared for your appointments?

You may notice that in addition to the Appointment tab, the form you use to create a new calendar item also has a Notes tab. You can use this tab to create a note that's tied to the appointment.

You can use handwriting or voice recording to create notes attached to events exactly the same way that you use these features to create standalone notes. If you want more help with these options, see Chapter 7.

Rescheduling an appointment

Appointments get rescheduled; it's an irrefutable fact of life. Another meeting may cause a conflict, someone may get sick, or you may just decide that the day is too nice to spend stuck inside with a bunch of boring executives. Whatever the reason, events do get moved from one time or date to another.

You can move an event from one place to another on your iPAQ's calendar in one of two basic ways:

- ✔ When viewing your calendar, tap-and-hold the event that you wish to move. Choose Cut from the pop-up menu to move the item to the Clipboard. Then, tap-and-hold the new date and time, and choose Paste from the pop-up menu. This method is simple and straightforward, but you do have to be careful to make certain you tap-and-hold the correct time slot when you paste the event. But if you have to move the event very far off in the future — say a month or so — this isn't your best choice because you have to navigate to the correct date and hope that you don't get distracted before you're done moving the event. If you do have to move an event quite a distance, try the next method.

- ✔ Open an appointment by tapping it, and then open the item for editing by choosing Edit. Use the drop-down boxes to specify new starting and ending dates and times. This method ensures that you can specify the precise times you want without error.

Changing your view

Designing a single way of looking at a calendar that fits every need is a nearly impossible task — especially on the small screen of an iPAQ. A view that makes it easy to select a date six months in the future isn't much help if you're also trying to juggle six different appointments for next Monday. So rather than trying to make you use one method of looking at your calendar, your iPAQ offers five different views. Figure 8-5 shows the Year view — you can select any of these views for use by clicking the icons on the menu bar.

Here's a quick look at the view options (as they appear left to right on the menu bar):

- ✔ **Agenda:** Shows your upcoming appointments in a condensed list. In this view, your appointments are shown in chronological order, two lines per appointment.

- ✔ **Day:** Shows your schedule for one complete day, with time slots for each hour of the day (or each half hour if you enabled that option). This view is generally the most useful — especially when you need to add new items to your schedule.

✔ **Week:** Similar to the Day view, but includes a column for each day of the week in addition to a row for each hour. This view makes it easy to see events that are scheduled for an entire week, but no details show. Still, this view is useful if you need to move an appointment because you can see an entire week's worth of time slots.

✔ **Month:** Shows the entire month and uses a small triangle in the lower-right corner to indicate which days have items scheduled. Use this view when planning your schedule a couple weeks in advance.

✔ **Year:** Shows the whole year. Use this view if you're a real long-range planner!

Tap a date in the Month or Year view to open a Day view of the selected date.

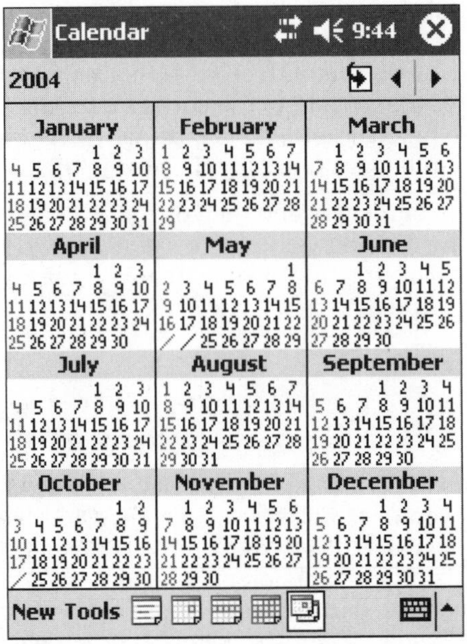

Figure 8-5:
Use the
view icons
to decide
how your
calendar
appears.

Using categories to simplify your life

If you assigned categories to the events on your calendar, you can choose to view only those items that fit into specified categories, letting you place business, personal, family, organization, or any other category of events on your calendar and still keep them separate. For example:

✔ Mark birthdays as personal or family so that you don't forget them, but reduce the clutter by excluding this category when you're setting up business appointments.

✔ Mark your club events in their own special category. Then switch to the agenda view and select just this one category. In this mode, you see only the club's activities, and you can beam them to another club member without including the rest of your schedule. (For information on beaming, see Chapter 6.)

✔ Choose to show only the business category when participating in a meeting in the office. (Certainly exclude your private meetings with the headhunter from displaying — especially when your boss wants to play around with "that neat little gadget you've got there.")

Setting reminders

Adding things to your busy schedule is only half the battle. You've also got to remember to send that anniversary card, make that important phone call, or meet that potential backer for lunch. And, to make matters worse, you've got to do those things on time!

One way to make certain that you don't forget the important details is to have your iPAQ give you a reminder of an upcoming event. Your iPAQ does this by default, but only 15 minutes ahead of the actual appointment.

When setting up reminders, you have three options to select:

✔ In the Reminder drop-down list box, select Remind Me or None. If you choose to be reminded of an event, your iPAQ sounds an audible alarm and pops up a message box at the specified time. If your iPAQ is off when the reminder is due, it automatically wakes up and gives you the reminder anyway.

✔ Use the Number drop-down list box in the next row down to set the number of minutes (or other time increment) in advance of the event to set off the reminder.

✔ Use the Interval drop-down list box to specify whether the reminder should come minutes, hours, days, or weeks in advance. One really neat aspect of your iPAQ's reminder feature is that you don't even have to remember to turn on your iPAQ to get the reminder. When the reminder time comes along, your iPAQ wakes up and chirps at you. After you get over your annoyance at this rude interruption and take a look at the iPAQ's screen, you see a reminder similar to the one in Figure 8-6.

Reminder   9:56

Reminder

Figure 8-6:
I may be
running
late, but my
iPAQ makes
certain
that I know
where I'm
supposed
to be.

Meet with Fred

10:00 AM-11:00 AM 11/6/03

Dismiss   Snooze

Snooze: 5 minutes ▼

When you're creating an appointment or other event on your schedule, be sure that you set the reminder far enough in advance to be useful. The default 15-minute reminder probably won't help for most items on your calendar. For those annual events, especially ones for which you may need to send a gift or a card, give yourself at least a week of advance notice. When the reminder does go off, you can always reset it for a later time by using the Snooze button on the Reminder pop-up.

Tracking Your Tasks List

Scheduling a specific time for tasks can be a real chore. How do you schedule something that doesn't really have a date associated with it? Still, a few tasks have at least some relationship to your calendar.

Buying Christmas presents is a good example of how tasks can relate to your schedule. You could start your shopping any time during the year, but you would certainly want to complete it before December 25. That is, this is a task that isn't something you would necessarily schedule for a specific date, but you would have a date by which it had better be finished.

Setting Tasks options

In the spirit of keeping things as simple as they deserve to be, your iPAQ keeps the Tasks options to a minimum. To set the few Tasks options that do exist, first open the Tasks application by clicking the Start button and choosing Tasks from the Start menu (or from the Programs folder if Tasks does not appear on your Start menu). Then choose Tools⇨Options to display the list of options that I describe next.

It's pretty easy to guess what the three task options do:

- ✔ **Set Reminders for New Items:** Selecting this makes certain that your iPAQ will nag you about any new tasks you add to your list until you mark them as completed. These reminders appear on the Today screen.

- ✔ **Show Start and Due Dates:** This option ties tasks more closely to your schedule by adding in a date when you should start the task and a date when the task must be completed.

- ✔ **Use Large Font:** Select this option to display your tasks in large characters so that they're harder to ignore.

Pick the blend of options that works the best for you, and then click OK to return to the Tasks list.

If you don't need to know the starting and due dates for your tasks, leave the Show Start and Due Date option unchecked. When this option is selected, each task requires an extra row on your screen — even if these dates aren't filled in.

Adding tasks

To add yet another job to your electronic job jar, choose New on the Tasks menu. You can also display the Entry Bar above your list of tasks by choosing Tools⇨Entry Bar.

Figure 8-7 shows a new task being created in my Tasks list. If you compare the new Tasks form to the New Appointment form that you use to add items to your calendar (see the section "Adding an appointment" earlier in the chapter), you notice that the two forms are similar. In fact, the differences are quite minor:

- ✔ You cannot set specific times (although you can set dates) for tasks.

- ✔ Tasks can be set to different priority levels, and your Tasks list can be sorted to show which tasks are most important.

- ✔ You don't have to set any dates for tasks if you don't want to. Giving the dog a bath can wait until you're darn good and ready!

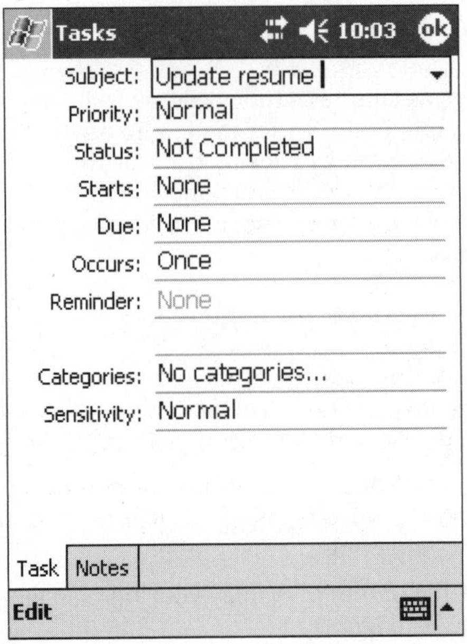

Tasks	⇄ ◀€ 10:03	ok
Subject:	Update resume	▼
Priority:	Normal	
Status:	Not Completed	
Starts:	None	
Due:	None	
Occurs:	Once	
Reminder:	None	
Categories:	No categories...	
Sensitivity:	Normal	

Task | Notes

Edit ⌨ ▲

Figure 8-7:
When you've got things to do, put them in your Tasks list so that you know when you're ignoring them.

Sorting your to-do list

As your list of stuff that needs to be done grows, you should figure out which items you can continue to put off and which ones you're just going to have to do. One way to do this is to sort the list. You can choose to sort your task list by Status, Priority, Subject, Start Date, or Due Date — depending on which order is easier for you to ignore.

The drop-down list in the upper-right corner of the Tasks screen shows the different sorting options that you can choose. When the list is not dropped down, the sorting option that you've selected replaces the words Sort By.

You can also use categories to help organize your tasks. Some good choices may be "Yeah, right," "Forget it," and "Geez, do I really have to?" However, you have to add these categories yourself. For some reason, they aren't default categories that you can select.

Part III
Putting Your iPAQ to Work

The 5th Wave   By Rich Tennant

"Well, here's what happened—I forgot to put it on my 'To Do' list."

In this part . . .

Your iPAQ includes several powerful yet easy-to-use applications that are closely related to the Microsoft Office programs that you probably already use on your desktop PC. In this part, you see how to use Pocket Word to work with your Word documents. You find out how to use Pocket Excel to create and edit Excel spreadsheets. You see how to use Pocket Money, Pocket Quicken, or another useful application to keep track of your expenses your way.

Chapter 9

Working with Pocket Word

*I*t's pretty clear to anyone who works with words that Microsoft Word has become the dominant player in the world of word processing. Word documents are everywhere. Now they can even be in your pocket thanks to your iPAQ and Pocket Word.

But is Pocket Word for real? How much word processing can you actually do on something that fits so neatly into your pocket, anyway? Well, you can do quite a bit with Pocket Word when it comes right down to it. In this chapter, I give you a taste of just how much fun you can have with Pocket Word.

Defining Uses for Pocket Word

Okay, I'll be the first to admit that there aren't too many people who are going to write a novel on their iPAQ. Tapping out a long document character-by-character on the on-screen keyboard isn't likely to fit anyone's definition of a good time. Still, Pocket Word is a very useful addition to your iPAQ. But if you do insist on creating long documents on your iPAQ, do yourself a favor and check out the external keyboard options that I mention in Chapter 4.

Comparing Pocket Word with desktop Word

One of the most important features of Pocket Word is that it can share files directly with the desktop versions of Word. Pocket Word can open and save files as both Word documents and as Word templates, which means that you can work on a document on your desktop PC, transfer it to your iPAQ, and continue to work with that document while you're away from your desk.

Pocket Word does have its own Pocket Word file format, but ActiveSync automatically converts between Pocket Word format and desktop Word format, so you don't see any difference no matter how you save your files.

Even though Pocket Word works well with most of your documents, you need to watch out for some important changes. If a Word document contains table formatting, numbered lists, or columns, those features are lost when the document is converted to Pocket Word format. The safest way to avoid any problems is to make certain that you don't include these items in documents that you intend to share between your desktop PC and your iPAQ. If you must make documents that include these features available on your iPAQ, don't save any changes to the file on your iPAQ because you will be saving the file minus the features that aren't supported on your iPAQ, and they will be lost even when you bring the file back to your desktop PC.

So, because Pocket Word can use desktop Word documents, how can you use Pocket Word? Here are some ideas:

- If someone sends you a report in a Word document, you can transfer the file to your iPAQ and read the report while you're sitting out in the local park during your lunch break. You may still be working, but at least you can get a bit of fresh air for a few minutes.

- If you've been working on a proposal for some potential new customers, you can keep a current copy of the proposal on your iPAQ so that you can make last-minute changes when you find out something that could give you an advantage over your competitors.

- You can use Pocket Word to put the finishing touches on your novel during your daily commute to the office. Of course, this isn't a good idea if you're the driver (unless you happen to sit in stopped traffic for long periods with nothing to do).

- If necessary, you can finish working on a last-minute project at the airport or on the plane when you're going on vacation. Then when you get the chance, you can e-mail the completed document back to the office. This may be the perfect solution if you have one of those bosses who always finds a way to ruin your vacation by insisting that you delay your departure to clean up the mess that he or she created.

What you can do in Pocket Word

Pocket Word has many of the features that you've come to expect in your word processing software. While it doesn't have everything that you find in desktop Word, here are some of the important things that you can do with Pocket Word:

- Open, view, edit, and save documents in a format that retains most the formatting of a standard Word document — just be certain that you note the warning in the previous section about certain formatting features that cannot be saved on your iPAQ.
- Cut, copy, and paste just as you do on your desktop PC.
- Use any standard Windows fonts in your documents.
- Apply formatting to text.
- Use paragraph formatting to control the appearance of documents.
- Create bulleted lists.
- Search for and replace specific text in a document.
- Do an automated word count to make sure that your document is a specific length.
- Spell check your documents just as you do in Word on your desktop PC.

What you can't do in Pocket Word

As powerful as Pocket Word may be, some features were left out of the program in order to keep it small enough to fit the available memory. Some of the most important of these include:

- Pocket Word lacks a grammar checker. (Many people would argue that the grammar checker in desktop Word does such a poor job that this may actually be a blessing in disguise.)
- Pocket Word has no thesaurus. As you discover later in this chapter, though, an excellent alternative exists, which you can easily add yourself.
- Pocket Word doesn't support table formatting, numbered lists, or columns. If you save a document that contains these features into the Pocket Word format, the features will be lost.
- Finally, the one thing that you probably miss the most in Pocket Word is that you can't print documents from your iPAQ unless you install a program such as the HP Mobile Printing for Pocket PC utility (which I discuss in Chapter 4).

Writing in Pocket Word

Creating a document in Pocket Word is really very similar to creating one in desktop Word. Sure, iPAQs and a desktop PCs have obvious physical differences, and Pocket Word lacks a few features, but after you get past those differences, the process is remarkably similar.

To give you a better look at Pocket Word, I've opened a Pocket Word document in Figure 9-1. As the figure shows, the document clearly has retained the formatting that was in the original.

Figure 9-1:
Pocket
Word docu-
ments can
include
nearly all
the format-
ting options
that you
find in a
standard
Word
document.

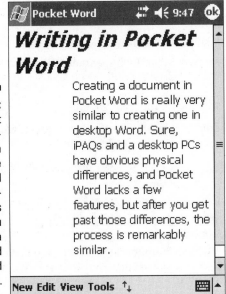

In the following sections, I show you how to use Pocket Word to create a document and to use the editing and formatting options to improve the document's appearance.

Reviewing your input options

To create a document in Pocket Word, you have many of the same options that are available in other iPAQ applications. In case you've been skipping around, here's quick look at them.

Selecting an input method

Your first and possibly most important choice in Pocket Word may be in selecting the way that you input text. You choose the input method by using the Pocket Word View menu. Your choices include the following options:

- ✔ **Writing:** Enables you to write or print directly on the iPAQ's screen. To change your writing into text, choose Tools➪Recognize. See Chapter 4 for more information on using handwriting to input information into your iPAQ.

- ✔ **Drawing:** Enables you to draw directly on the screen. Drawings are never converted into text; instead the drawing is saved as a bitmap image in your document. For more about adding a drawing to a document, refer to Chapter 7.

- ✔ **Typing:** Allows you to use the on-screen keyboard to enter text, one character at a time. If you have the Word Completion option enabled, your iPAQ can help speed your text entry by suggesting possible words that you may be entering. See Chapter 4 for more information on the text entry options.

- ✔ **Recording:** Turns your iPAQ into a voice recorder. The recording is added to your document as a sound file as opposed to text. Recording voice notes to include with your documents is covered in Chapter 7.

If you've added an alternate input device to your iPAQ (see Chapter 4), you can make your input selection by using the Secondary Input Panel (SIP) in the lower-right corner of the screen. It's the up arrow that appears there.

Choosing your document view

Almost as important as your choice of input method may be your document view option choices. These choices also appear on the View menu. Here are your options:

- ✔ **Wrap to Window:** Makes the text fit within the width of the iPAQ's screen. Selecting this option removes the horizontal scroll bar from the bottom of the screen and wraps the lines of text so that you don't have to scroll side to side to read the document. Selecting this option doesn't make any permanent changes to your document, so it still appears normally when you transfer it back to your desktop PC.

- ✔ **Zoom:** Enables you to view the text at 75, 100, 150, 200, or 300 percent of normal size. Lower zoom percentages let you see more of the document at one time, but can make the text harder to read. Larger zoom percentages can make it far easier to input text by using handwriting.

- ✔ **Toolbar:** Toggles the display of the Pocket Word formatting toolbar. You can use this toolbar to apply formatting to your text. You can also click the icon just to the right of Tools on the menu bar (the icon has an up and a down arrow) to toggle the display of the toolbar.

Editing in Pocket Word

Even though you *can* write entire documents with your iPAQ and Pocket Word, you're far more likely to use Pocket Word to do some editing of existing documents. Editing typically doesn't involve nearly as much text entry as creating a new document, so the chances are pretty good that you use your iPAQ to review and correct more often than you use it to create.

But it really doesn't matter whether you're creating new documents or editing existing ones — you still want good editing tools. The following sections offer a look at the ones available in Pocket Word.

Selecting, copying, cutting, and pasting

Figure 9-2 shows the Edit menu in Pocket Word. Here you find many of your old favorites from the Edit menu in desktop Word.

Just as on your desktop PC, commands that are gray rather than black on an iPAQ menu are currently unavailable. For example, the Cut and Copy commands can be used only after you've selected text.

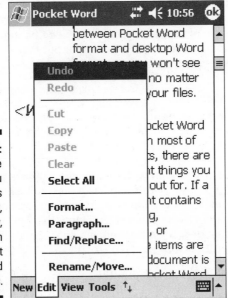

Figure 9-2:
Use the Edit menu commands to select, cut, copy, or paste in your Pocket Word documents.

Notice that the Edit menu has a Select All command but no other commands for selecting text or other objects in your document. You have to use the stylus if you want to select only part of a document. You may need to practice a little to get the hang of selecting text with the stylus. To select text, point to the beginning of the selection and then drag the stylus across the entire set of text that you want to select. If you begin your selection on one line and move to another line, all the text between the beginning of the selection and the current stylus position become part of the selection.

To make selecting text a bit faster, tap twice on a word to select the entire word. Tap three times within the paragraph to select the entire paragraph.

After you've selected some text, use the Edit menu commands to work with the selection. Unfortunately, you can't use the drag-and-drop technique that you may be used to on your desktop PC — drag-and-drop isn't supported on the iPAQ.

Finding and replacing text

If you never had to type out a letter on a typewriter in the olden days before word processors became popular, you may not realize just how lucky you really are. In those ancient times, people actually had to find their own errors by reading through their documents word by word. To correct mistakes, you had two basic options: You could retype the page (or pages, depending on how lucky you were), or you could apply correction fluid (or tape) to the error and then type over it.

Modern PCs (and this includes your iPAQ) make the whole process a lot easier by allowing you to electronically search for and replace text within your document. There's no more getting any of that white paint all over your fingers, either!

In Pocket Word, you can search for and (if necessary) replace text within your documents using the Edit➪Find/Replace command. When you select this command, Pocket Word displays the screen shown in Figure 9-3.

If you want to replace instances of a word or phrase, tap the Replace button to display a second text box labeled Replace With. Use the Match Case and Match Whole Words Only check boxes to further refine the find and replace operation.

After you've entered the search phrase (and the replacement phrase if appropriate), tap Find to locate the next instance of the phrase. Tapping Find also displays the Find/Replace toolbar, shown just above the menu bar in Figure 9-4. Use this toolbar to control the find or replace process.

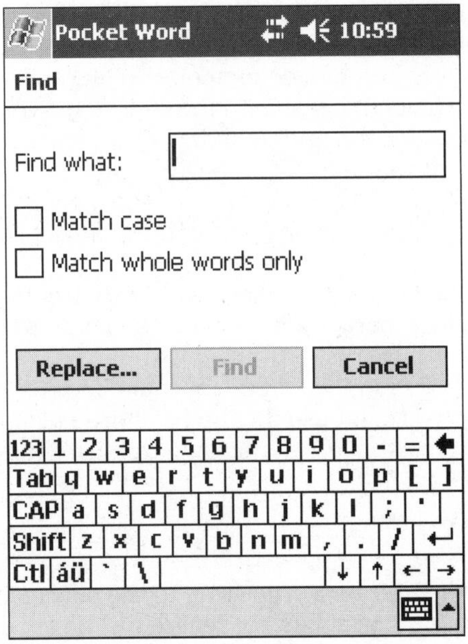

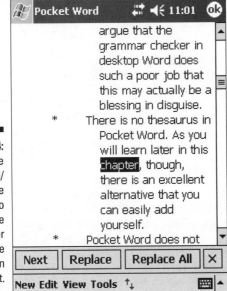

Figure 9-3:
Quickly find and correct words by using the Find and Replace commands.

Figure 9-4:
Use the Find/ Replace toolbar to continue searching or to replace items in the text.

The Find/Replace toolbar includes the following commands:

- **Next:** Moves on through the text to the next occurrence of the search phrase. The currently selected text is not changed.

- **Replace:** First replaces the highlighted text with the replacement text and then moves on to the next place where the search phrase is found in the text. Replace and Replace All are only active if you select the Replace option.

- **Replace All:** Replaces all instances of the search phrase with the replacement text and closes the Find/Replace toolbar.

- **X:** Closes the Find/Replace toolbar without making any further changes to the text.

Be careful if you use the Replace All option. It's very easy to make a mistake that could be very embarrassing. For example, if you were to decide that you had misspelled "meat" as "meet" throughout your document and used the Replace All command to change all instances of "meet" with "meat," someone may be very surprised to find out that you would like to "meat him for lunch."

Checking your spelling

Sending out a document that's filled with spelling errors is a bad idea — especially if that document is going to an important customer, to your boss, or as a cover letter along with your résumé. That's why spell checkers were invented.

To make certain that your Pocket Word documents use the correct spellings, open the spell checker by choosing Tools⇨Spell Check. Then, choose an option from the pop-up menu, as shown in Figure 9-5. The word or words in the upper section of the menu are the spell checker's suggestions. Just choose a word from the pop-up menu to replace the highlighted word with that selection. You can also choose to ignore the word or add it to your personal dictionary. As Figure 9-5 shows, however, you want to be careful about accepting the spell checker's suggestions.

Adding the date

Your iPAQ offers lots of timesaving shortcuts. In Pocket Word, for example, you can enter the current date into a document with just a couple quick taps, which can be very useful if you want to add the date to a letter or if you're creating a log of something and need the correct date to appear in the log.

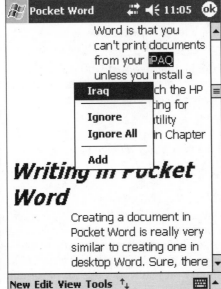

Figure 9-5:
Spell check
your Pocket
Word
documents
to make
certain that
they don't
contain
spelling
errors.

To add the date to a Pocket Word document, first make certain that the insertion point is in the correct location. The best way to do this is to tap where you want the date to appear. Next, tap-and-hold and choose Insert Date from the pop-up menu. You can also use the Tools➪Insert Date command if you don't like tap-and-hold.

To change the format of the dates that Pocket Word inserts into documents, click the Start button and choose Settings to display the Settings screen. Tap the System tab and choose the Regional Settings icon. Tap the Date tab and select the format that you prefer from the Short Date drop-down list. Click OK to make the change.

Counting your words

Sometimes you need to know exactly how many words a document contains. For example, if you're entering a 50-words-or-less contest for a trip to Hawaii, you wouldn't want to lose the contest simply because your entry totaled 51 words, would you?

To determine the exact number of words in your document, use the Tools➪ Word Count command. When you do, Pocket Word pops up a message box giving you the current count. Don't forget to send a postcard from Hawaii!

Formatting your text

One thing that separates Pocket Word from a simple text-editing program like the iPAQ Notes program is the ability to apply formatting to your text. Although Pocket Word doesn't include all the formatting options that you find in desktop Word, it does provide the options that you're most likely to want.

Take a look at the following sections for the scoop on formatting in Pocket Word.

Using the menus for formatting

To access the fullest set of Pocket Word text-formatting options, first select the text that you want to format, and then choose Edit⇨Format, which displays the options shown in Figure 9-6.

If the font that you want to use doesn't appear in the Font list, copy the font from your desktop PC to the \Windows\Fonts folder on your iPAQ by using the ActiveSync Explore function. See Chapter 5 for more information on viewing your iPAQ's files from your desktop PC.

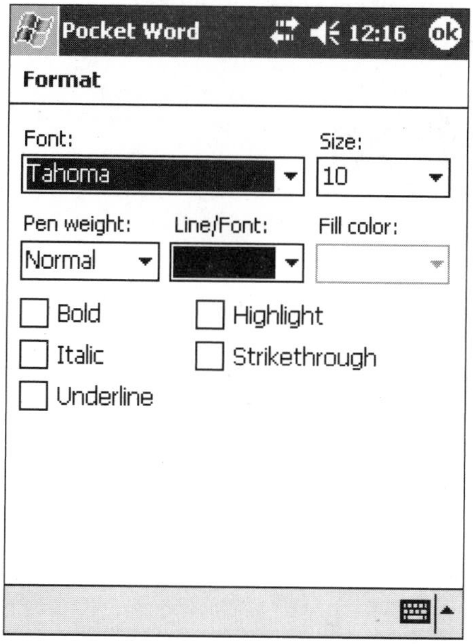

Figure 9-6:
Choose your text-formatting options on this screen.

Select the formatting options that you prefer. Any text formatting that you apply in Pocket Word remains in the document when you transfer it to your desktop PC.

The Pen Weight option isn't really a text-formatting selection. You use this option to select how thick lines are that you draw with the stylus. This option is most useful for drawings that you may want to add to a Pocket Word document, but it may also help some when you're using handwriting recognition to enter text. Your iPAQ doesn't care about the pen weight, but you may have an easier time writing if you choose a pen weight that's closer to the type of pen that you normally use for writing on paper.

Using the formatting toolbar

Some of Pocket Word's formatting options are also available on a handy formatting toolbar. As Figure 9-7 shows, the formatting toolbar sits just above the Pocket Word menu bar.

The left side of the formatting toolbar contains a button to display the Format screen as well as three of the text-formatting options. You can apply bold, italics, or underline by using these buttons. The middle section of the toolbar has buttons that you can tap to select left-aligned, centered, or right-aligned paragraph format. The right side of the toolbar has a button for creating bulleted text.

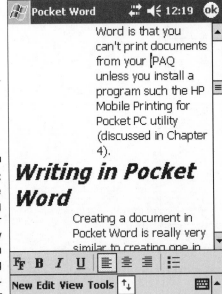

Figure 9-7:
Use the formatting toolbar to apply common formatting options.

To display the formatting toolbar, tap the button with the up and down arrows (just to the right of Tools on the Pocket Word menu) or choose View➪Toolbar. The display of the toolbar setting is a toggle — each time you select it, the toolbar appears or disappears depending on its current state.

Setting paragraph options

You can also select several paragraph format options (see Figure 9-8). To display this screen, choose Edit➪Paragraph.

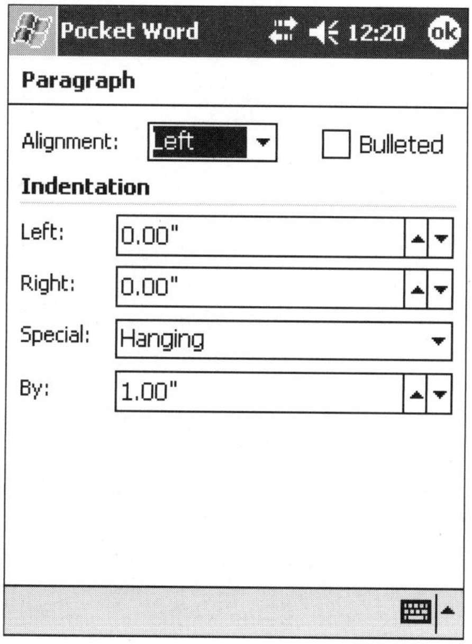

Figure 9-8:
Set paragraph alignment and margins with these options.

> ⊞ **Pocket Word**   ⇄ ◀€ 12:20 ⓞⓚ
>
> **Paragraph**
>
> Alignment: [Left ▼]   ☐ Bulleted
>
> **Indentation**
>
> Left: [0.00"]   [▲▼]
>
> Right: [0.00"]   [▲▼]
>
> Special: [Hanging ▼]
>
> By: [1.00"]   [▲▼]

You can quickly set paragraph alignment and bullets by using the formatting toolbar.

The paragraph format options include the following options:

- ✔ **Alignment:** Aligns the text in the paragraph to the left, right, or center.
- ✔ **Bulleted:** Creates paragraphs with leading *bullets* — symbols like those that appear in front of the items in this list.
- ✔ **Left:** Controls the distance the text is offset from the left margin.
- ✔ **Right:** Controls the distance the text is offset from the right margin.

✔ **Special:** Controls the first line of the paragraph separately from the rest of the paragraph. Select the First Line option to indent the first line, or select the Hanging option to outdent (move to the left) the first line of the paragraph.

✔ **By:** Controls the distance of the first line's indent or outdent.

When you set the various paragraph options, remember the limitations of the iPAQ's screen. You may not be able to see exactly how your document will appear when you go to print simply because the iPAQ's screen is too small. Even so, the options that you set are saved with the document, and they transfer with the document to your desktop PC for printing.

Saving your work

One very handy difference between an iPAQ and a desktop PC may save you from a world of trouble: The iPAQ doesn't have a hard drive, so everything is always in memory. As a result, you don't really have to save your Pocket Word documents — they're saved automatically when you click the OK button to close the document. So no more worries about saying no to a Save when you really meant yes.

However, a couple of options exist to help you control how your document is saved.

Selecting the document format

If you want to give your document a specific name, select the location where it is saved, or select the document type. Choose Tools➪Save Document As, which displays the Save As screen shown in Figure 9-9.

By default, Pocket Word uses the first few words in your document as the name of the document, something that can be really convenient or a big pain depending on the document. If every document starts out differently, using the first few words makes it really easy to remember which document you're dealing with. But if you start several documents the same way — with your address, for example — you probably want to provide a name for each new file by entering that name in the Name field.

Pocket Word saves all documents in the My Documents folder unless you specify a different destination. On your desktop PC, you probably use folders to organize your files into related projects, but this may not be necessary on your iPAQ because you aren't likely to keep hundreds of files on your iPAQ. It's your call whether you want to get fancy on this. Use the Folder drop-down list box if you want to select a different folder.

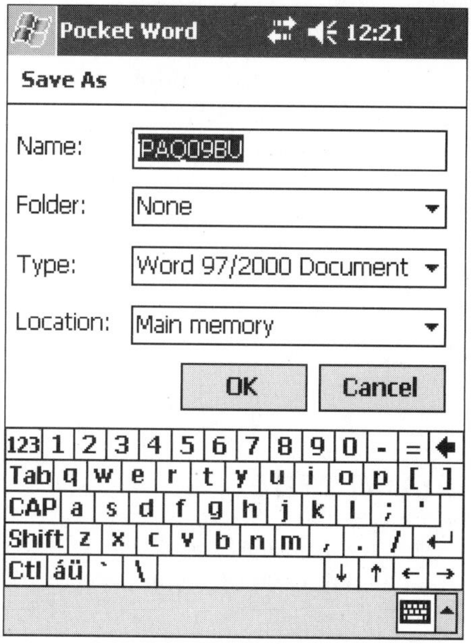

Figure 9-9:
Use this
screen to
control how
your Pocket
Word
document
is saved.

Use the Type drop-down list box to select a different format for your file. In most cases, just leaving the type set to Pocket Word Document is best — allow ActiveSync to handle any necessary conversions. However, you may want to select a different format if you intend to send the document file to someone via e-mail. (See the section "E-mailing your document" later in this chapter.)

If you have a storage card inserted into your iPAQ, you can use the Location drop-down list box to choose to store the document file on the storage card rather than in main memory. If you do choose this, remember that you won't be able to access the file if you remove the storage card for any reason — until you reinsert the storage card, of course. This is especially important to remember if you want to e-mail the file to someone and need to replace the storage card with a modem or a digital phone card to send e-mail.

Renaming or moving your document

You can rename or move a Pocket Word file after it has been saved by choosing Edit➪Rename/Move. Why the program's developers thought people would think to look on two different menus to save a file and to rename it is hard to say, but they did.

The Rename/Move screen offers the same options as the Save As screen with the exception of the Type option. The same choices apply when you're renaming or moving a file as when you're saving it in the first place.

Sending Your File

In most cases, you'll probably transfer Pocket Word documents to your desktop PC so that you can print out whatever copies you need. But because Pocket Word runs on your iPAQ, you also have additional options for sharing your document.

E-mailing your document

If you have an Internet connection for your iPAQ, you can send your Pocket Word document via e-mail, which is really handy if you need to get the file to someone quickly.

If you're going to e-mail your Pocket Word document to someone who is not using an iPAQ, save the file in a format that he can open in his desktop PC's word processor. Usually this means saving it in one of the versions of Microsoft Word, but you may have to choose Rich Text Document or even Plain Text Document depending on the type of computer and word-processing software that he's using.

To send a Pocket Word document via e-mail, choose Tools⇨Send via E-mail. If you don't already have your e-mail access configured, refer to Chapter 14 before trying this.

Sending your document on a light beam

For even more fun, you can send a Pocket Word document to another iPAQ user over a light beam. Just choose Tools⇨Beam Document and aim your iPAQ's IrDA port at the IrDA port on the other iPAQ. The iPAQ receiving the file displays a message asking if you want to accept the file. If you haven't beamed documents before, you may want to have a look back at Chapter 6, in which I show you some tips on successfully sending information via the IrDA port.

Checking Your Words

The most useful tools in any writer's toolkit are the dictionary and thesaurus. This is especially true when you find yourself looking for just the right word, and you can't quite seem to find it. Or perhaps you think that you know the word you want to use, but are you really confident that it means exactly what you think it does?

Figure 9-10 shows an example of the Oxford American Desk Dictionary and Thesaurus from Handmark (www.handmark.com). Unlike the simple spell checker in Pocket Word, the Oxford American Desk Dictionary and Thesaurus provides the full range of entries that you would find in a printed dictionary and thesaurus, including pronunciation, meaning, and synonyms. This is one tool that any word lover absolutely needs.

After you have found the correct word, you can use the Edit⇨Copy command to copy that word to the Clipboard. You can then paste the word into your document. There's no longer any reason to massacre the language just because you're working on your iPAQ!

Figure 9-10:
The Oxford American Desk Dictionary and Thesaurus is an excellent addition to your writer's toolkit.

Chapter 10

Managing Your Calculations

. . . .

. . . .

*I*t's interesting to think back to the origins of the computer and realize that its original purpose was as a giant numerical calculator. No one had any idea that computers would one day be small enough to fit in your pocket, nor powerful enough to display life-like multimedia productions. But with programs like Excel and Calculator, your iPAQ does hark back to that original purpose.

You don't have to be a mathematical whiz to find uses for Pocket Excel. In fact, that's one of the best things about being able to take Excel along in your pocket — if you can fill in the blanks, Pocket Excel can crank out the numbers you need. (Even with a powerful spreadsheet program like Pocket Excel, the iPAQ is more often thought of for its other capabilities rather than its numerical calculating ones, but this is one feature that you don't want to overlook.)

You've probably got at least one calculator buried somewhere under the papers on your desk. Simple calculators are so common and cheap that people give them away when you renew a magazine or walk into your bank on free calculator day. Why would you possibly need to use your iPAQ as a calculator?

Actually, having a calculator built into your iPAQ makes a lot of sense, if for no better reason than your iPAQ is so useful that you probably have it with you most of the time. As the old saying goes, "a program in the hand is worth two on the desktop."

Uses for Pocket Excel

To get a feel for what you can do with Pocket Excel, you first need to have an idea of just what a spreadsheet really is. Thinking of a spreadsheet as a grid loaded with formulas doesn't really do it justice. I prefer to think of a spreadsheet as a really fancy calculator that already knows how to perform hundreds of super complex calculations on data and then present it so that we simple humans can understand what's going on. Or maybe it's just all magic — you throw in a bunch of numbers at one end, and a bunch of supposedly meaningful numbers fall out of the other end.

So what can you do with Pocket Excel? Here are just a few ideas to get you thinking:

- ✔ If you work in real estate, you can create a Pocket Excel spreadsheet that takes into account the tax implications of mortgage payments, real estate taxes, and so on to convince your customers they can afford a higher-priced home to help you earn larger commissions.

- ✔ If you're an amateur astronomer, you can use a Pocket Excel spreadsheet to calculate the altitude of satellites that pass overhead. And because your iPAQ's screen has a backlight that you can easily adjust, you can use the spreadsheet when you're out looking at the sky on a dark night, too.

- ✔ A contractor can use a Pocket Excel spreadsheet to give a customer a preliminary idea of the cost of a project on the spot. Many people have no idea what it costs to build things, so being able to name your price may help you weed out the lookers from the doers without going through the entire bidding process.

- ✔ A Pocket Excel spreadsheet can help you work on your company's budget while you're commuting between home and the office. You can actually get a chance to play around with some of the numbers without being interrupted by telephones or that lousy background music that your employees insist on playing.

- ✔ If you bet on the horses, a Pocket Excel spreadsheet can help you figure out which ones you want to put your money on based on the statistics and records you've entered. Of course, there's no guarantee that you've got the right formula to produce winners, but that's part of the fun of going to the races, isn't it? Remember; just keep telling yourself, "It's only money."

- ✔ Of course, anyone who keeps a household budget knows how handy a calculator is. Think of how much handier it would be to use a Pocket Excel spreadsheet so that you can always look back at your numbers to make certain that you didn't mess things up by accidentally entering the wrong number for something.

Transferring Your Desktop Spreadsheet

Your iPAQ may be a great tool for *using* a Pocket Excel spreadsheet, but no one is going to suggest that it's a great tool for *creating* one. Sure, you can do it, but do you want to? Transferring an Excel spreadsheet from your desktop PC is much easier than creating some complex monster from scratch right on your iPAQ. Entering complex formulas by using the iPAQ's on-screen keyboard just isn't going to rank very high up on your list of fun things to do!

Transferring an Excel spreadsheet to your iPAQ takes just a few moments. As I discuss in Chapter 5, when you copy your Excel spreadsheet file into the Pocket_PC My Documents folder on your desktop PC, ActiveSync takes care of the transfer the next time you pop the iPAQ into the synchronization cradle.

Figure 10-1 shows an Excel spreadsheet that I copied from my desktop PC to my iPAQ. In this case, the spreadsheet is one that I created to quickly figure out the day of the week for any date.

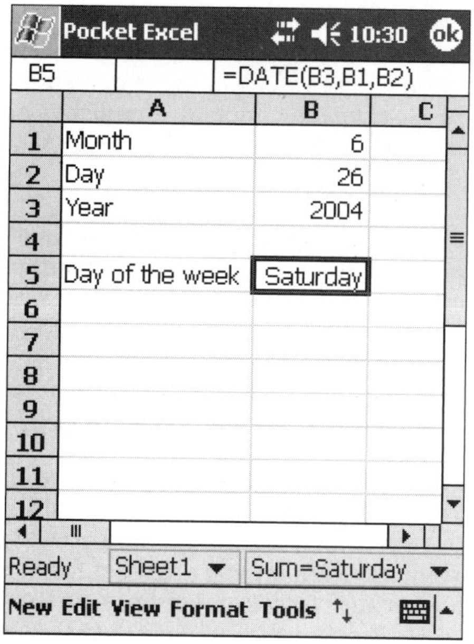

Figure 10-1:
Spread-
sheets
in Pocket
Excel look
just like
their coun-
terparts on a
desktop PC.

Excel Features Not Included in Pocket Excel

Of course, *some* differences do exist between Excel on your desktop PC and Pocket Excel on your iPAQ. Read on for a look at a few important differences.

Macros need not apply

Many years ago, the user manual for Lotus 1-2-3, the first spreadsheet program that became popular on the PC, asked the readers if they really wanted to become a programmer. This question lead in to a short description of the *macro* commands that one could use to automate certain operations in the spreadsheet. (Macros are really just a simple programming language built into many different types of application programs.) Over the years, macros became almost an institution with some users, and spreadsheet automation was the sign of a true spreadsheet guru.

As popular as macros and other programming languages were, however, they were also complex and allowed users to create spreadsheets that no one could really understand. You still see some of those monsters on occasion, but macros aren't nearly the rage they once were, which is a good thing if you want to use your spreadsheet in Pocket Excel on your iPAQ — macros simply don't work in Pocket Excel.

You don't have to worry about macro viruses in your Pocket Excel spreadsheets, either. Because macros can't run on Pocket Excel, macro viruses can't run either.

Forget the graphs, just give me the facts

Graphs are another of those spreadsheet features that don't make it across the line from desktop Excel to Pocket Excel. But how many really useful graphs have you ever seen in a spreadsheet anyway? Sure, a graph may seem to be saying something impressive, but don't you often get the impression that people use graphs simply because they can, not because they really mean anything to anyone?

Functioning in a Pocket Excel world

Functions are the meat and potatoes of spreadsheets. *Functions* are the built-in formulas that enable you to perform all sorts of fancy calculations that would take a year or three to do on your own.

Pocket Excel has over 100 built-in functions. If you need to calculate "the depreciation of an asset for a specified period using the double-declining balance method," Pocket Excel has a built-in function to do it. Just don't ask me to explain what the double-declining balance method is — I haven't got a clue. But if you need it, it's there waiting for you to insert some numbers and act like you really do know what it means. (For more on actually using functions, see the "Entering formulas" section later in this chapter.)

As bizarre as it may sound, the 100-plus built-in functions in Pocket Excel don't come close to the mind-boggling 400-plus functions in some desktop spreadsheets. For example, unlike desktop Excel, Pocket Excel can't calculate the "cumulative beta probability density function" — whatever that is.

In reality, unless you're really doing strange things with spreadsheets, Pocket Excel probably has all the functions you'll ever need. If it doesn't, maybe you need to get out into the fresh air a bit more often.

Creating a Pocket Spreadsheet

Okay, I admit that earlier in this Chapter I say that the iPAQ isn't the greatest tool for creating a spreadsheet. Your desktop PC's larger screen and more convenient means of input certainly make creating spreadsheets far less of an ordeal than it can be on an iPAQ. Still, knowing how to create or modify a Pocket Excel spreadsheet on your iPAQ does provide you with the ability to create a spreadsheet when no desktop PC is available. Besides, anyone who watches you create a spreadsheet with a stylus is going to know that you're not someone to mess with!

So, just what does it take to create or modify a spreadsheet on your iPAQ? Besides lots of patience, it takes using the tools in Pocket Excel. The following sections show the tools that you most likely need.

Entering formulas

Pocket Excel uses the same format for formulas that you're familiar with from Excel on your desktop PC. You begin a formula by entering an equal sign (=). (If you forget to lead off with the equal sign, Pocket Excel doesn't realize that you are attempting to enter a formula.) Then, reference the spreadsheet cells that you want to include in the formula. For example, if you want to sum the values from cells A1 through A4, and you want that sum to appear in cell A5, you enter the formula as =**A1+A2+A3+A4** in cell A5. Figure 10-2 shows how this formula appears in the spreadsheet. When you enter a formula in a Pocket Excel spreadsheet, the value appears in the spreadsheet, and the formula appears just above the columns when the cell is selected.

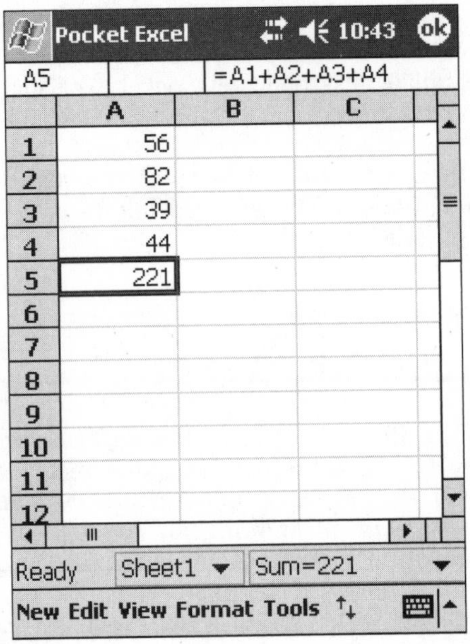

Figure 10-2:
Here's how a formula appears in a Pocket Excel spreadsheet.

		=A1+A2+A3+A4
	A	B	C
1	56		
2	82		
3	39		
4	44		
5	221		

Pocket Excel ⇄ ◀€ 10:43 **ok**

A5

Ready   Sheet1 ▼   Sum=221 ▼

New Edit View Format Tools ↑↓

You can enter a formula that references the values in specific cells by tapping those cells just the way you click cells when you use Excel on your desktop PC.

Entering formulas by using arithmetic operators like the plus sign (+) and minus sign (–) is fine for very simple calculations, but to get real power in your formulas, use some of those built-in functions that I mention earlier, in the section "Functioning in a Pocket Excel world." For example, use the SUM function rather than a series of plus signs to sum up a column of 100 different numbers. To insert a function, select it from the scrolling list of functions and click OK. You can select from the list by tapping the *fx* button to the left of the formula bar after you enter an equal sign to begin the formula.

Click the 123 button on the on-screen keyboard. This changes the keyboard to the numeric keypad and makes numerical entries somewhat easier.

I don't have the space here to describe all of Pocket Excel's built-in functions. For that detailed information, refer to a book such as my *Excel 2002 Bible* or one of the other fine titles from Wiley Publishing, Inc., that cover Excel in more depth. However, I can at least show you how to add those functions to your Pocket Excel spreadsheet. To do so, choose Tools⇨Insert Function from the Pocket Excel menu bar, which displays the Insert Function screen shown in Figure 10-3.

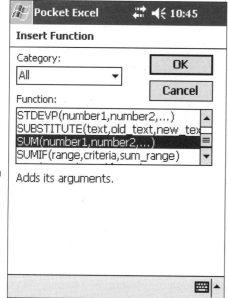

Figure 10-3:
Use this
screen
to choose
from Pocket
Excel's built-
in functions.

If you're not sure which Pocket Excel function you need, use the Category list to cut down the number of functions that are displayed by showing only functions that apply to a specific category. Then, watch the description area below the list of functions. As you highlight a function, the description area provides you with some idea of what the function does.

One problem with using functions is that nearly all of them require *arguments* — extra information (such as cell references or values) that you must enter in order to complete the calculation. This doesn't mean that the functions are angry, but even so, you may become frustrated trying to figure out what information is required for each argument — especially when you try to use some of the stranger functions that are available in Pocket Excel.

When you select a function to add to your spreadsheet, Pocket Excel includes *placeholders* (names that describe what is needed) for each argument. You have to determine the correct information to replace each of the placeholders. Some of the argument placeholders are easy to understand, such as the year, month, and day values that are required for the DATE function. Other argument placeholders — such as "number," which appears in many functions — are far less clear.

The copy of Excel on your desktop PC includes far more help than simple argument placeholders for entering functions into spreadsheets. I recommend checking the desktop version of Excel if you need more help figuring out what information to enter for each of the arguments in complex functions. Or you could turn to the *Excel 2002 Bible* that I mention earlier.

Editing your spreadsheet

We've all heard people blame their mistakes on so-called computer errors, although in reality computers seldom make errors. Sure, the results may not always be what we expect, but that doesn't mean the computer was wrong. More often, the problem is simple human error caused when someone asked the wrong question.

Spreadsheets can easily produce results that aren't what you expect. Until someone invents a computer that does what you mean rather than what you say, this will continue to be a problem. In a Pocket Excel spreadsheet, if you don't get the results that you want, it's usually because you either entered the wrong information or you have an error in a formula. Either way, you need to edit your spreadsheet to correct the problem.

For some editing chores, you can use the Edit menu commands (see Figure 10-4). For example, if you want to fill a group of cells with a sequence of values, use the Edit➪Fill command. The other Edit menu commands include:

- **Edit➪Undo:** Returns the spreadsheet to where it was before your last entry

- **Edit➪Redo:** Undoes the change made by the Edit➪Undo command

- **Edit➪Cut:** Removes a selection and places it on the Clipboard

- **Edit➪Copy:** Places a copy of the selection on the Clipboard without removing it from the spreadsheet

- **Edit➪Paste:** Adds the Clipboard contents to the spreadsheet

- **Edit➪Paste Special:** Controls how the Clipboard contents are pasted — such as just the current values of formulas rather than the formulas themselves

✔ **Edit⇨Clear:** Removes cell contents or formatting

✔ **Edit⇨Select All:** Selects everything in the spreadsheet so that the next command you issue applies to all of the selection

✔ **Edit⇨Fill:** Automatically fills a selected range of cells with a series of values

✔ **Edit⇨Find/Replace:** Locates all instances of a specific value

✔ **Edit⇨Password:** Sets or changes the password that's needed to open the spreadsheet

✔ **Edit⇨Rename/Move:** Changes the name or storage location for the spreadsheet

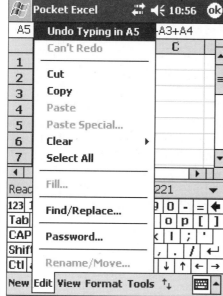

Figure 10-4:
Use the
Edit menu
commands
to modify
your spread-
sheet.

The Edit menu commands aren't very useful when you want to modify a formula. For that, you need to attack the problem directly by selecting the cell that you want to modify, and then tapping in the *formula bar* (the area just below the time display in the upper-right of the Pocket Excel screen). Figure 10-5 shows how the screen appears when you're editing a formula.

When you're editing or creating a formula, you can open the Insert Function screen by tapping the Insert Function button just to the left of the formula bar. The Insert Function button is the one labeled *fx*. Tap the other two buttons to the left of the formula bar to enter your changes (with the check mark button) or to discard any changes (with the X button).

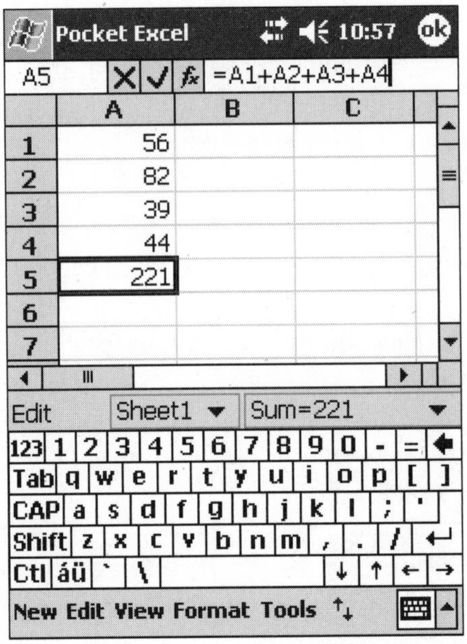

Figure 10-5:
Edit
formulas
directly in
the formula
bar.

WARNING! If you forget to tap the formula bar before you begin entering something in a cell, you replace the entire contents of the cell rather than editing it. If this happens, immediately select Edit➪Undo before you do anything else.

Controlling the view

One of the biggest problems with using a Pocket Excel spreadsheet is that you can't see very much of the spreadsheet at one time. There's just so much going on to clutter the screen that you don't have much room for useful information.

As Figure 10-6 shows, you can control just how much of that junk appears on the screen by using the View menu options. The five items at the top of this menu are all toggles, so each time you select them they either appear or disappear depending on whether they're currently visible.

TIP If possible, place all the cells into which you need to enter information near the upper-left corner of your Pocket Excel spreadsheet. That way you may be able to hide the scroll bars and still easily input data.

If your spreadsheet has more than one worksheet, choose View⇨Sheet to select a different worksheet. You can also use the worksheet selector button that appears in the center of the toolbar (just above the menu bar) if the Toolbar is visible. To make the toolbar visible, choose View⇨Toolbar.

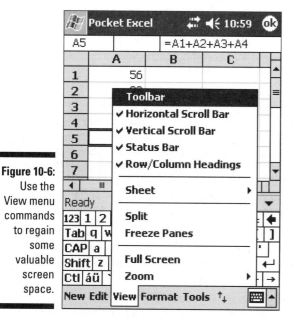

Figure 10-6:
Use the
View menu
commands
to regain
some
valuable
screen
space.

The View⇨Split and View⇨Freeze Panes commands enable you to see different areas of your spreadsheet at the same time. Although you may find View⇨Freeze Panes useful in making certain that you're working in the correct row or column, the iPAQ's screen is really too small for View⇨Split to be of much use.

View⇨Full Screen devotes the maximum possible screen area to displaying your spreadsheet. When you select this command, every Pocket Excel element that can be hidden disappears from view.

Finally, View⇨Zoom lets you zoom in or out on your spreadsheet while leaving all other screen elements normal size. This command is most effective if you combine it with View⇨Full Screen.

Formatting cells

Formatting changes the appearance but not the contents of cells in your spreadsheet. You have an extensive set of formatting options in Pocket Excel. To select the cell-formatting options, first select the cells that you want to format. Then, choose Format⇨Cells to display the Format Cells screen. This screen has several tabs that you can use to make the following changes:

- **Size:** Control the row height and column width. Normally, Pocket Excel adjusts these dimensions automatically, but you can change them for more precise control. You can also drag a row or column border to resize them just as you do in Excel on your desktop PC.

- **Number:** Select the numeric format used to display numerical values. Selecting the correct numeric format can make the difference between numbers that are impossible to decipher and ones that are instantly recognizable. For example, if a cell is supposed to indicate an important date, 6/26/2000 is probably easier to understand than 36703, the *date serial number* that corresponds to June 26, 2000. (Date serial numbers are the number of days since December 30, 1899.)

- **Align:** Control the positioning of text and numbers within cells. By default, numbers line up along the right side of the cell and text lines up to the left. The alignment options even allow you to wrap text to fit within the width of the column.

- **Font:** Use a different typeface or other font characteristics such as bold or colored text. You can use any font that is installed on your iPAQ.

- **Borders:** Add lines around cells or a background color. (This tab has nothing to do with a bookstore or emigrating to another country.)

The Format menu has several other commands that you can use to modify your spreadsheet:

- **Format⇨Row** and **Format⇨Column:** These commands enable you to hide or display entire rows or columns and to remove any changes that you may have made on the Size tab of the Format Cells screen. Note, though, that removing changes to cell height or row width by using the Autofit option only works if you actually have some entries in the same row (or column) when you select the Autofit command.

- **Format⇨Modify Sheets:** This command provides you with a tool for adding or deleting worksheets, renaming worksheets, or moving worksheets so that they appear in a different order.

- **Format⇨Insert Cells** and **Format⇨Delete Cells:** These are pretty easy to figure out. It's probably no surprise that you use these commands to add or remove cells from your spreadsheet.

Navigating in Pocket Excel

Because so little of a typical Pocket Excel spreadsheet fits on the screen at the same time, you need efficient ways to move around. You can move to a different location in your spreadsheet in several ways:

✔ Use the scroll bars to change the visible area of the spreadsheet. Remember, though, that until you tap a new cell, the cell that was selected remains selected. It doesn't matter that you're viewing a different set of cells — viewing is not the same as selecting!

✔ Use the arrow keys on the on-screen keyboard to move around. Because this method does move the cell selector, it also selects a new cell, and that cell is the one that receives any input when you start typing.

✔ Use the navigation button just below the center of your iPAQ's screen. This button moves the cell selector as you rock the navigation button left, right, up, or down.

✔ To move a long distance, choose Tools⇨Go To to display the Go To screen, shown in Figure 10-7. You can enter either a cell address or a name if your spreadsheet has names assigned to cells.

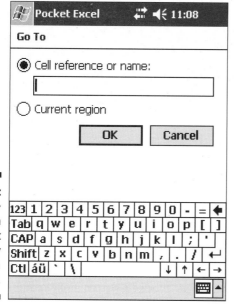

Figure 10-7:
Use Tools⇨ Go To when you want to quickly jump to a distant cell.

The easiest way to move to a different worksheet is to use the worksheet selector button in the status bar.

Exchanging Spreadsheet Data

Pocket Excel uses the same three-ring circus for exchanging data with other computers that you've grown familiar with from other iPAQ applications. But just in case you've forgotten, your choices are

- ✔ **Tools➪Beam Workbook:** Beams your spreadsheet to another iPAQ user. Doesn't this almost make you feel like you're back in grade school passing notes?

- ✔ **Tools➪Send via E-mail:** Sends your spreadsheet file as an e-mail attachment. May as well spread the work around, right?

- ✔ **ActiveSync:** If you have ActiveSync set up to synchronize your files, your spreadsheet is copied to your desktop PC when you pop your iPAQ into the cradle.

Pocket Excel spreadsheets may not be the most exciting way to use your iPAQ, but they sure can put a lot of power in your pocket. Almost any Excel spreadsheet from your desktop PC will run on your iPAQ, so maybe one day you can convince your boss that you were late because you had to stop and run some budget numbers on your way to work.

Calculating the Uses of the Pocket Calculator

You already know a dozen different uses for your desktop calculator, but the calculator in your iPAQ has some unique uses, too. Here are a few of the ways that you can use your iPAQ calculator:

- ✔ If you're writing a note on your iPAQ and need to do some quick calculations to figure out how much more business you need to do to increase revenues by 7.8 percent next year, you can pop open the calculator and get some good numbers. And because you can copy and paste from the calculator, you don't need to retype those numbers.

- ✔ When you're out for lunch with those stingy people who never seem to remember to add in their part of the tax and tip, you can use the calculator to let them know what their share of the bill really is. (Or you can simply use the Address Book to choose a better dining companion in the future.)

- ✔ If you're using Pocket Money or Pocket Quicken to manage your finances, you can use the calculator to add up your bank deposits and then copy the results directly into your transactions (see Chapter 11).

✔ Finally, you can gather up all those funky calculators that you got for free and clear a bunch of space on your desk. And because everybody likes to get something for nothing, you could walk around the office giving everyone the gift of a free calculator and make everyone think that you're really a nice person. Just watch out when the office gardener comes by trying to give away zucchini — you'll probably be on the top of his list!

Doing Some Calculations

To open the iPAQ's calculator, click the Start button and choose Programs from the Start menu. Then, tap Calculator in the Programs folder. Figure 10-8 shows the calculator.

The calculator includes a currency conversion feature for those of you who travel in countries where you may need to know how the local prices compare to Euros. To use this feature, tap the third icon in the Toolbar (the icon with three different money symbols).

When the calculator is open, tap the buttons to enter numbers and perform calculations. As you enter numbers, they appear in the box just above the keys. This box also shows the results of your calculations.

If the on-screen keyboard pops up when you open the calculator, tap the keyboard icon next to the lower-right side of the menu bar to hide the keyboard. Although you may think the on-screen keyboard could be useful when entering symbols like parentheses in a calculation, the iPAQ's calculator ignores any such attempts to get fancy. What you see on the face of the calculator really is all you get.

I'm sure that you can figure out most of the keys, but a few keys you may not recognize or realize just how powerful they are:

✔ **M+** adds the current value into memory so that you can use it later in a calculation. Because the calculator lacks *nesting* — essentially, the ability to perform sub-calculations through the use of parentheses — you have to use the calculator's memory if you need to get very fancy.

✔ **MR** recalls the value that's stored in memory. You can recall the same value as often as necessary, so you can store a value that you want to apply in a series of calculations (such as marking up prices by a set percentage).

✔ **MC** clears the current value stored in memory. Memory stores a cumulative value, so clear the memory first if you want to replace what is in memory rather than adding to it.

✔ **+/–** switches the sign of the currently displayed value so that positive numbers become negative, and negative numbers become positive. Use this key if you want to subtract the displayed value from whatever is currently stored in memory.

✔ **CE** clears the currently displayed value without messing up your existing calculation. Use this key if you make a mistake entering a value and don't want to go back to the beginning and re-enter all your numbers.

✔ **C** clears the entire calculation so that you can start fresh.

✔ **√** gives you the square root of the currently displayed value. Even though most roots are actually a lot closer to round, if you really need a square one for something, this is the place to find it.

✔ **1/x** inverts a number. Essentially, inverting a number means that the calculator divides 1 by the number that is currently displayed. My favorite number to invert is 0.

The rest of the calculator keys are for entering numbers or performing simple calculations.

Even though the iPAQ's calculator has only a single memory, you can store two values if you're tricky enough. Use the memory keys to store one value and use Edit➪Copy to store the other. Choose Edit➪Paste when you want to reinsert the value that you stored by using Edit➪Copy.

You can also use Edit➪Copy and Edit➪Paste to share values with other iPAQ applications.

Figure 10-8:
The iPAQ's calculator is always handy whenever you're using your iPAQ.

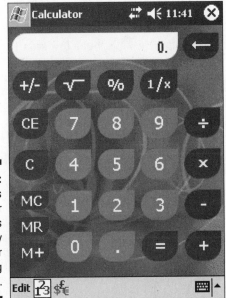

Chapter 11

Tracking Your Money

*Y*ou've probably noticed that keeping track of your money is awfully important. This is especially true if you have business expenses that you need to manage or an expense account to prepare. Your iPAQ is the perfect tool for helping you with this sometimes-tedious task.

In this chapter, I show you several options for tracking your money on your iPAQ. You can probably determine the best choice for you based on how you currently manage your expenses. If you happen to use Microsoft Money on your desktop system, Microsoft Money for Pocket PC is likely your best option. If you are a Quicken fan, Pocket Quicken is right up your alley. If you don't use either Money or Quicken, you may want to try out one of the other options that I mention. Regardless of your choice, your iPAQ makes it far easier to remember where all the money went.

Handy Uses for iPAQ Expense Managers

Your iPAQ is very adept at helping you manage your money. But maybe you're having a hard time figuring out how you can use this capability in your daily grind. Well, never fear; I'm going to give you some ideas that will have you reaching for that stylus in no time. Here are just a few of the ways that you can use an expense manager on your iPAQ:

➤ If you have an expense account, you probably end up paying lots of business-related expenses (like bridge tolls, parking meters, umbrellas, and so on) out of your own pocket simply because it's too much trouble to keep track of those miscellaneous expenses. With an expense manager, you can easily keep track of those costs along with a complete record of the date and time of the expense. And after you've entered an expense one time, these programs typically remember most of the details so that you can enter it far more quickly the next time around. You'll probably end up getting far more than the cost of your iPAQ back in extra expense money for all those little items that used to be too much trouble to track!

✔ Even if you aren't on an expense account, you can keep better track of your business-related expenses so that you don't forget to claim them at tax time. Guess what? These programs are as handy at making sure that you get all the business deductions you deserve as it is at making certain that the other lucky guy gets his expenses reimbursed.

✔ If you handle petty cash for your organization, you can use your iPAQ expense manager to track where all the money goes. There's no sense letting anyone have any questions about whether you're being honest, is there?

✔ If you're the person who's always getting stuck making the lunch run for the office, why not use your expense manager to keep track of everyone's running bill? That way, you're more likely to get paid back on payday — especially if you've got some people with poor memories who always seem to forget at least some of what they owe you.

✔ Some of these programs can also keep track of the stocks in your portfolio. Whenever you go online to check your e-mail, they can let you know if now is the right time to announce your retirement party or if you need to ask for a bit more overtime.

Managing Your Money with Microsoft Money for Pocket PC

Microsoft Money for Pocket PC is a little money manager program that's available for your iPAQ. This handy program helps you keep track of where all your money went. It works seamlessly in conjunction with Microsoft Money on your desktop PC.

You must have the 2004 (or later) version of both Microsoft Money and Microsoft Money for Pocket PC if your iPAQ uses Windows Mobile 2003. If you have an earlier version of Windows Money, you must upgrade to the current version before you can install the program on your iPAQ.

If you already use Microsoft Money on your desktop PC, Microsoft Money for Pocket PC should be quite familiar and easy to use. Microsoft Money for Pocket PC concentrates on a few basic money management functions rather than trying to cover all the bases. Getting to know Microsoft Money for Pocket PC takes only a few minutes, and it's time well spent.

Setting Microsoft Money for Pocket PC's options

Microsoft Money for Pocket PC has very few options, but take a quick look at them to help you understand how the program works. To begin, open Microsoft Money for Pocket PC by clicking the Start button and choosing Programs from the Start menu to display the Programs folder. Then, tap the Microsoft Money icon. When Microsoft Money for Pocket PC opens, choose Tools⇨Options to display the Options screen.

You probably want to leave all three of the following options selected:

- ✔ **AutoComplete+:** This option makes Microsoft Money for Pocket PC far easier to use because you don't have to do nearly as much typing. When this option is selected, Microsoft Money for Pocket PC fills in most entries for you by using its best guess based on previous entries. If you eat the same lunch at Joe's Diner a couple times each week, Microsoft Money for Pocket PC can fill out the whole transaction as soon as it recognizes that you're starting off with "Joe's" as the payee.

- ✔ **AutoFill:** This option helps you by entering the same amount and category for a payee. You can easily overwrite these entries, but if they are correct, you don't have to.

- ✔ **Use Large Font:** This option simply makes it easier to read the iPAQ's screen when you're using Microsoft Money for Pocket PC. There's really no reason not to choose this option.

Almost no one needs the options on the Proxy Server tab. (Those of you who do already know who you are, don't you?) *Proxy servers* are special computers that provide access to the Internet while preventing unauthorized traffic. In the case of Microsoft Money for Pocket PC, the proxy server settings are used only if you set up Microsoft Money for Pocket PC to track your investments and you need to use a proxy server to access the Internet. Confused yet? Don't worry about it — if none of this sounds familiar, it's a good indicator that it doesn't apply to you. Your online broker is the most likely source of information on this subject.

If you find yourself using Microsoft Money for Pocket PC often, click the Program Button link near the bottom of the Options screen to assign one of the buttons on the front of your iPAQ to opening Microsoft Money for Pocket PC. You have to decide which of the currently assigned buttons to reassign to Microsoft Money for Pocket PC. To reassign the front panel buttons on your iPAQ to any other application, tap the Start button, select Settings, and then tap the Buttons icon.

After you select the three options, tap OK to close the options screen.

Using a password

For many applications, passwords can be more trouble than they're worth. After all, if someone else uses your Internet account for a few minutes, who cares? (As long as they stay away from your e-mail account, that is.) Most likely, your Internet account is set up for unlimited access, so if a friend needs to get on the Internet, you're probably quite willing to let her use your PC and your account.

For Microsoft Money for Pocket PC, though, a password can be really important because you enter your account numbers and other confidential information that you probably don't want to broadcast to the world. And you certainly want to make getting into your account harder in case a thief tries to steal your iPAQ.

To add a password that's needed to even open Microsoft Money for Pocket PC, choose Tools⇨Password to display the screen shown in Figure 11-1.

Enter your password in both boxes and tap OK. You need to enter the same password twice to make certain that you've actually typed in what you thought you did. If the two entries don't match, Microsoft Money for Pocket PC rejects them.

Figure 11-1:
Create
a password
to prevent
unauthor-
ized access
to your
Microsoft
Money
for Pocket
PC files.

Be awfully careful when you're creating a password for Microsoft Money for Pocket PC. If you forget what you entered, you won't be able to open Microsoft Money for Pocket PC or access the data in it. It's a really good idea to close Microsoft Money for Pocket PC as soon as you've added a password and then re-open the program. That way you can check that your password is correct before you spend a lot of time setting up accounts or entering information. If you can't remember your password, you have to use ActiveSync to remove Microsoft Money for Pocket PC from your iPAQ and then re-install it. Any data that you've entered in Microsoft Money for Pocket PC will be lost if you do this.

Setting up a new account

You have to set up an account in Microsoft Money for Pocket PC before you can use the program. An *account* is simply your checking account, a petty cash account, a credit card, or something similar. You can set up as many different accounts as you need. Each account is separate from all the others, so it's fine to set up special accounts for specific purposes.

To create a new account, choose New on the Microsoft Money for Pocket PC menu bar. This displays the account setup screen, shown in Figure 11-2.

Figure 11-2:
Create
all the
Microsoft
Money for
Pocket PC
accounts
that you
need to
manage
your
finances.

Fill in the blanks on this screen as follows:

✔ **Account Name:** In this field, enter a descriptive name for the account. If you're going to be sharing information with Money on your desktop PC, use the same account name as the one on your desktop PC. Enter a name that makes it easy for you to select the correct account so that you don't accidentally enter transactions into the wrong account.

✔ **Account Type:** Select the type of account from this drop-down list box. Microsoft Money for Pocket PC uses the account type to control how it handles transactions, so be sure that you choose the correct type. For example, if the account type is a checking account, Microsoft Money for Pocket PC automatically enters sequential check numbers to record transactions.

✔ **Opening Balance:** Use this field to indicate how much money is currently in the account. Here you need to remember that Microsoft Money for Pocket PC is going to start off with the amount that you enter here, so enter the amount in the account as it exists just before you enter your first transaction. For example, if you're going to track your checking account, enter the amount of money shown in your check register just before the first check you're going to record in Microsoft Money for Pocket PC.

✔ **Credit Limit:** For a credit card or credit line account, use this field to indicate your total credit limit for this account.

✔ **Interest Rate:** If the account is an interest-bearing account, enter the appropriate rate in this field.

Next, click the Optional tab. Here you enter information that you may need to access your account (like your account number).

The information on the Optional tab is optional for a good reason. You don't want to make it easy for someone else to access your accounts without your authorization. If you fill out this tab, make certain that you have password protected Microsoft Money for Pocket PC, as I discuss in the preceding section.

Click OK when you have finished setting up the account.

Organizing your money by using categories

One of the best ways to keep track of where you've spent your money is to organize things into categories. You can have categories like office expenses, business travel, groceries, entertaining, and that all-important one — chocolate! If you want to use categories in Microsoft Money for Pocket PC, you have to set them up yourself. To make certain that you actually use the categories when you finally do enter transactions, set up at least some basic categories before you start entering transactions.

To create your categories, follow these steps:

1. **Click the View list (the list just below the Start button that indicates what is currently being displayed).**

   If you've just added a new account, the View list is probably showing "Account Manager."

2. **Select Categories from the View list.**

3. **When the View list indicates Categories, choose New to create a new category.**

4. **Use the boxes on this new category screen to enter the information about your categories.**

   Each category must have a unique name — you can't have the same category listed as both an income and an expense category. Slight variations can be used if you can't think of a creative way to name a category.

5. **If you want to break down a category further, use the Subcategory Of drop-down list box for the new categories that are a part of the category.**

   For example, you might want subcategories of your Medical category for dental, doctor, and drug-related expenses.

6. **To make a note reminding yourself of something special about a category, enter your note in the Memo text box.**

7. **Click OK when you finish setting up each category.**

Entering your transactions

After you create accounts and set up categories, you can start throwing in some transactions. Now you get to see where the money is really going.

Start by selecting Account Register from the View list. If you've set up more than one account, select the account that you want to use from the Account list to the right of the View list. Figure 11-3 shows how your account register appears after you've entered several transactions.

To add a new transaction, choose New to display the new transaction screen. As you begin filling in the Payee text box, Microsoft Money for Pocket PC tries to help out by entering the matching information for the last transaction with this same payee.

After you complete the fields on the Required tab, you can use the fields on the Optional tab to add more information about the transaction. (The Optional tab is where you select a category to help organize your accounts.)

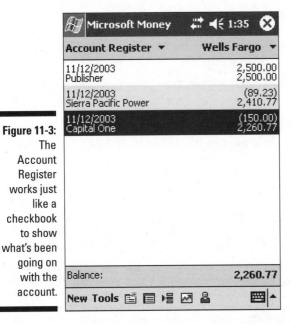

Use the Void option in the Status drop-down list box to record checks that you voided so you don't forget and get in a panic trying to remember what happened to the missing check.

When you're finished entering information, tap OK to complete the transaction.

If you enter a transaction in error, tap-and-hold the transaction in the transactions list, and then tap the Delete Transaction button. Microsoft Money for Pocket PC asks to confirm that you really do want to send the transaction to the dump.

You can edit an existing transaction by tapping it to open the transaction screen. Make your changes and then click OK.

The bottom of the transaction screen has a menu item called Split. Use Split to create transactions that are a bit more complicated, such as bank deposits that include funds from more than one payee. When you create a split, you need to allocate the money between different sources. You enter each individual part of the transaction in the Split screen, specifying the amount of the individual part. For example, if you make a bank deposit that includes $500 from your paycheck and $20 that you won in the office football pool, you create one entry for $500 and one for $20. When you are finished entering the individual entries in the split transaction, tap OK to enter the total transaction into the transaction record.

Tracking your investments

Microsoft Money for Pocket PC can also keep track of your stock market investments. If you have an Internet connection on your iPAQ, you can even get delayed stock quotes. But your iPAQ doesn't offer hot stock picks — you still have to rely on your brother-in-law for that type of information.

To add your favorite stocks to the Microsoft Money for Pocket PC Investments list, select Investments from the View list. Then, choose New and enter the name of the investment and the other details in the appropriate fields (the stock ticker symbol, the price per share, and the number of shares you own) about the investment. Click OK when you're finished.

Be sure that you enter the correct stock market symbol for each of your investments. Microsoft Money for Pocket PC uses the symbol to locate the current market value.

After you enter your stocks, choose Tools➪Update Investments (or click the Update Investments button just to the right of the Tools menu) to get a delayed market price for those stocks. You need an Internet connection through your iPAQ (see Chapter 12) to get this update.

Sharing the numbers with Money

If you have Microsoft Money loaded on your desktop PC, you can share the Microsoft Money for Pocket PC information from your iPAQ with Money. By sharing this information, you can keep track of expenses on your iPAQ and then update the files on your desktop PC.

To share information between Microsoft Money and Microsoft Money for Pocket PC, you must select Money as one of the synchronization options in ActiveSync (see Chapter 5). Unfortunately, if you use a different money management program (such as Quicken), you can't share information between Microsoft Money for Pocket PC and the other program on an ongoing basis. In fact, you can share your Quicken data only if you first load Money on your desktop PC and then import your Quicken data into Money. That's why Quicken users should read the following section on Pocket Quicken, of course.

If you intend to share information between Microsoft Money for Pocket PC on your iPAQ and Money on your desktop PC, make certain that you have set up Money on your desktop PC and have established the synchronization before you add information to Microsoft Money for Pocket PC. Otherwise, you have to remove Microsoft Money for Pocket PC from your iPAQ and then reinstall it to add the synchronization option to your iPAQ.

Data sharing between Money and Microsoft Money for Pocket PC is strictly a one-to-one relationship. You can't share the same information between an iPAQ and two desktop PCs, nor can you share information between two iPAQs and one desktop PC.

Managing Your Money with Pocket Quicken

If you're already a Quicken user, you probably put the idea of switching to Microsoft Money right up there with slamming a car door on your hand — or maybe worse. Unfortunately, if you want to use Quicken on your desktop, you won't find Microsoft Money for Pocket PC to be very friendly because the two programs simply don't work well together.

Actually, you can share your desktop Quicken data with your iPAQ and Microsoft Money for Pocket PC, but only one time, and then only to send data to your iPAQ. But this arrangement requires you to manually update Quicken on your desktop after you've added information into Microsoft Money for Pocket PC if you want the two to agree.

A far better option for Quicken users is Pocket Quicken from LandWare (www.landware.com). Pocket Quicken works directly with the version of Quicken on your desktop (Quicken 99 or later) and automatically synchronizes your accounts between your desktop and your iPAQ.

Setting up Pocket Quicken

Pocket Quicken automatically sets up the accounts on your iPAQ to match those on your desktop version of Quicken. As a result, you probably don't have to spend much time setting up Pocket Quicken on your own. Figure 11-4 shows an example of how Pocket Quicken might look when you first open the program on your iPAQ.

Entering your transactions

Entering transactions in Pocket Quicken is also extremely easy because the program fills in a lot of information for you (just the way desktop Quicken does). To enter a transaction, choose New and choose the type of transaction you wish to record from the drop-down Ref field. Figure 11-5 shows how the screen appears when entering a payment.

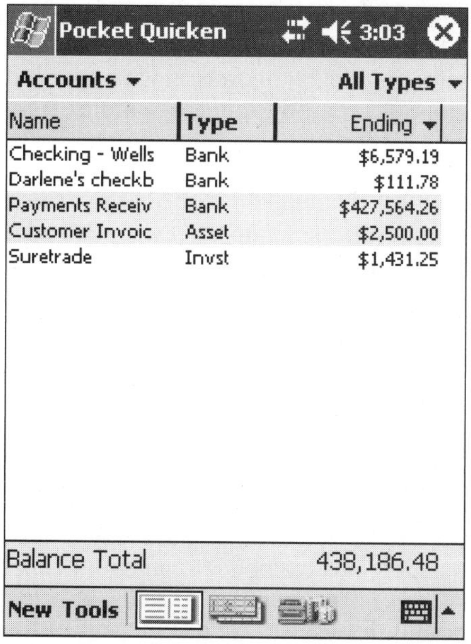

Figure 11-4:
Pocket
Quicken
automatically sets
up your
accounts
with data
from your
desktop PC.

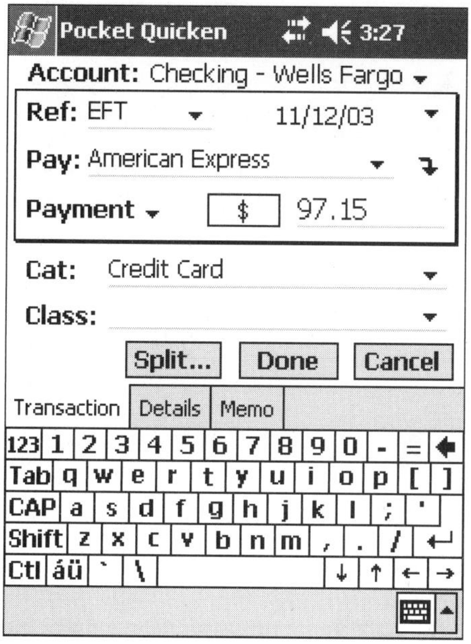

Name	Type	Ending ▼
Checking - Wells	Bank	$6,579.19
Darlene's checkb	Bank	$111.78
Payments Receiv	Bank	$427,564.26
Customer Invoic	Asset	$2,500.00
Suretrade	Invst	$1,431.25

Pocket Quicken — Accounts ▼ — All Types ▼ — 3:03

Balance Total — 438,186.48

New Tools

Figure 11-5:
Enter your
transactions
in Pocket
Quicken.

Pocket Quicken — 3:27

Account: Checking - Wells Fargo ▼

Ref: EFT ▼ 11/12/03 ▼

Pay: American Express ▼

Payment ▼ $ 97.15

Cat: Credit Card ▼

Class: ▼

Split... | Done | Cancel

Transaction | Details | Memo

Tap the Details tab to set or find out the status of a transaction. Use the Memo tab to create a free-form note to yourself to remind you of important details that you might otherwise forget — such as the reason why your lunch was so expensive. You can also use the Split button for more complex transactions, such as bank deposits from several sources.

When you tap the Done button, Pocket Quicken records the transaction on your iPAQ. The next time you synchronize your iPAQ with your desktop, the transaction will automatically be added to your desktop Quicken files. You don't have to worry about remembering to enter the transaction on your desktop.

Organizing your budget

Pocket Quicken does have one feature that it doesn't share with desktop Quicken. As Figure 11-6 shows, Pocket Quicken enables you to create budgets on your iPAQ. You can set specific goals for both income and expenses and let your iPAQ keep track of your success. To use this feature, select Budgets from the drop-down view list, and then select New and choose the type of budget that you wish to create.

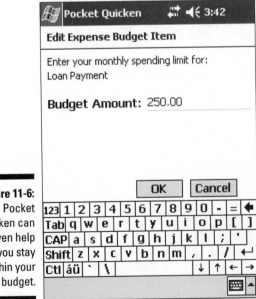

Figure 11-6:
Pocket Quicken can even help you stay within your budget.

Exploring Other Options

Okay, so maybe you're just not a Microsoft Money or Quicken type. You don't want to be told how to manage your money, do you? Well, if that's the case, perhaps you should check out a couple other money management options for your iPAQ.

Cash Organizer

Cash Organizer from Inesoft (www.inesoft.com) is designed as a complete iPAQ-based financial planning and management program. It does not rely upon a desktop PC-based money management program, but rather it offers some pretty powerful features all by itself. Figure 11-7 shows a typical transaction entry in Cash Organizer.

Even though Cash Organizer is designed to be an independent solution, it can both import and export data in a number of formats. You could, for example, import information from Microsoft Money or Quicken, or you could export information to Excel. In addition, Cash Organizer automatically uses your iPAQ contact list so that you don't have to retype existing contact information.

Figure 11-7: Cash Organizer enables you to do all your financial work right on your iPAQ.

EZ-Expense

EZ-Expense from Soft Pocket Solutions (www.softpocketsolutions.com) is by far the simplest, most focused program covered in this chapter. EZ-Expense does one very important job — it manages your expenses. As such, it is especially useful for any iPAQ user who must turn in expense account reports in order to get reimbursed for all the costs of doing business.

As Figure 11-8 shows, EZ-Expense concentrates on making life easy — at least when it comes to filing expense reports, that is. When you incur an expense, you just pull out your iPAQ, start EZ-Expense, tap an icon, and enter the expense. With specific icons corresponding to different expense categories, it's pretty clear where to place the various little charges.

Although EZ-Expense is not intended for full financial management duties, it does offer the option of exporting your expense reports in an Excel spreadsheet. This makes it a very simple task to create your expense report in whatever format your company requires.

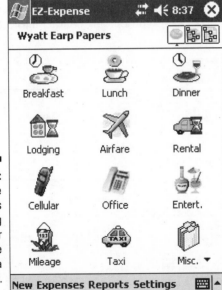

Figure 11-8:
EZ-Expense
makes
tracking
your
expense
report a
breeze.

Part IV
The iPAQ and the Internet

"Most of our product line is doing well, but the expanding
touch pad on our iPAQ keeps opening unexpectedly."

In this part . . .

You discover how you can use your iPAQ to access the Internet as well as your local network. Here you find out just how you can surf the Internet and handle your e-mail virtually anywhere. You may even be able to make use of some wireless Internet options as well as the more familiar wired connections. I also show you why the new Wi-Fi option is so popular as a means of being connected with your iPAQ.

Chapter 12

Connecting Your iPAQ

These days, whether you'll want to connect your iPAQ to the Internet is no longer a question; the only real question is *how* you'll connect it. And with all the options now available, you may even choose more than one way to connect so that you can always send that e-mail or check on the latest news on the Web.

Nowadays, it's easier than ever to go online with your iPAQ. In this chapter, I cover the options so that you can decide which ones are best for your needs. Along the way, you also see how many of these same options can enable you to access your own network for faster synchronization or even to use your iPAQ to control and run applications on your desktop PC.

What You Need to Connect

You can connect your iPAQ to the Internet or your local network in many different ways. In some cases, the necessary hardware is built into your iPAQ, but that isn't always true. In the following sections, I go over a number of things that you need to consider to determine just what you need to get connected.

I'm sorry to be the one to tell you this, but your iPAQ needs help when it comes to the Internet. iPAQs don't come with the hardware necessary to connect directly to the Internet. For that, you're going to have to get some extra pieces, which I go over in the following sections.

Understanding the iPAQ hardware realities

If being able to connect your iPAQ to the Internet is such a big deal, why doesn't every iPAQ simply include all the necessary pieces to make the connection? Unfortunately, this is one of those problems that's a lot more complex than it seems. When it comes to connecting an iPAQ to the Internet, a solution that's perfect for me may not work at all for you. Indeed, a solution that works perfectly for you in some cases may be totally useless in others.

Here are some things to consider:

- Some iPAQ models have built-in *Wi-Fi* (or 802.11b) — wireless networking. (The 802.11b is simply a standard for this type of wireless networking.) If you have access to a wireless network, this may be an ideal way to connect. But Wi-Fi isn't built into every iPAQ, so you may need to buy a Wi-Fi adapter card if you want to use this option.

- The most common type of expansion slot on iPAQs is the *Secure Digital* (SD) slot. The SD slots on most iPAQ models are actually SDIO slots, which are slots that can be used for more than just memory cards — they can also be used for input or output (the IO part of SDIO). But if you want to use the SD slot for a memory card — as is so often the case — then you'll have no place to add a Wi-Fi adapter card.

- A few iPAQ models also offer a *CompactFlash* (CF) expansion slot. This gives you two slots instead of just one. With two slots you can add both a memory card and a Wi-Fi (or other type) adapter.

- Most iPAQ models also include built-in Bluetooth capabilities. Bluetooth is another type of wireless connection, but it's typically not very useful for connecting to the Internet unless you happen to have one of those very rare Bluetooth-enabled cell phones. Bluetooth is awfully handy for some other uses, though. See Chapter 19 for one great example.

- If you don't mind being connected via the sync cable to your desktop PC, you can connect your iPAQ to the Internet via the *pass through* feature of ActiveSync. Of course, if you're close enough to your desktop system to be connected with the sync cable, you'll probably prefer surfing the Net with the larger screen on your desktop PC.

- Certain wired modems enable you to connect your iPAQ to the Internet via an ordinary phone line, but so far none of these fit an SD slot — you need a CF slot for this.

- *Wireless modems* are currently available as CF devices. These essentially connect via the cell phone network and are typically quite expensive to buy and use. Also, they tend to be quite slow and are really only suitable if you absolutely must always be connected, and no better option exists.

✔ Another slow wireless connection option is the *digital phone card* that connects via your cell phone. Digital phone cards are specific to certain brands and models of cell phones. You must get the correct one for your phone, and you must have a CF slot in your iPAQ to use one.

Understanding the service availability realities

Before you get your hopes set on one type of Internet connection option for your iPAQ, you've also got to consider another very important factor: Can you even use the hardware in the area where you are? Here are some very important considerations:

✔ You probably take it for granted that you can plug a regular wired modem into most regular phone jacks and make a connection. While this is mostly true, you do have to be aware that some phone jacks can kill your modem. Digital phone lines — such as the ones in many businesses — produce voltages that will fry your modem. So if you want to use your wired modem, you may not be able to do so from your office or hotel room unless you can plug into an analog phone line. You definitely want to check this by asking the hotel before plugging in.

✔ Wi-Fi connections are becoming more common, but you may not always be able to find a service that you can log onto. A lot of companies are setting up *hotspots* in places like coffee shops and airports, so those can be good places to look for a signal. In most cases, you need to use a credit card to sign up for access, but you can usually do so online. (I offer more information about hotspots later in this chapter in the section "Connecting to public hotspots.")

✔ Wireless modems typically require *Cellular Digital Packet Data* (CDPD) service. Unfortunately, CDPD coverage is not available in all areas. You can most likely find good coverage in large metropolitan areas, but it's not widespread enough yet that you can take it for granted.

✔ Digital phone cards require a digital phone and digital service. If your cell phone is analog, you can't use a digital phone card. If your cell phone is digital, but the signal in your area is only analog, you can't connect with a digital phone card.

✔ Wireless modems typically require a separate service contract from your cell phone contract, which can get quite expensive — especially when you consider that a digital phone card generally allows you to connect with little or no extra charge other than your airtime. If you have a cell phone contract that leaves you with lots of unused airtime each month, the difference could be considerable.

Online versus offline viewing

Just how important is the difference between *live* (online) and *static* (offline) viewing? There's an easy answer for that question: It depends.

Obviously, a lot of Web pages don't change very often. You probably don't expect a Web page that contains the text of an old Norwegian folktale to be much different today than it was yesterday. That folktale — and that Web page — probably will remain pretty much the same for quite some time. If you download a copy of the page today, it will still be just the same as the copy that you downloaded last month.

On the other hand, a Web site that brings you the latest news changes constantly. The copy that you downloaded some time ago may not tell you what you really want to know. For example,

if a severe storm is threatening your area, last hour's weather status probably doesn't do you much good. You may not know that a tornado is about to strike if you depend on the one-hour-old weather report showing that the storm is still 50 miles away.

And, of course, there's e-mail to throw into the picture, too. If you're trying to negotiate a big deal with someone and you're using e-mail messages every few minutes to clinch the deal, it would certainly help to be able to keep things moving while you're commuting. (You don't want your competitor to step in and make a better offer to steal away the business.) But being unconnected when you're on the go may prevent you from responding until it's too late.

Check with wireless service providers to see what service is offered in your area before you get too hung up on selecting one type of Internet connection for you iPAQ. There's no sense in wasting time researching options that simply aren't available to you.

Choosing Your Hardware Options

After you've decided on the type of service that you want to use to connect your iPAQ to the Internet, you need to pick out the hardware — assuming that your iPAQ doesn't already include the proper connection option, of course. By picking the type of service first, you don't waste any time buying the wrong equipment.

Here I take a quick look at the hardware options that you may want to consider.

Wi-Fi

Wi-Fi is the nickname given to 802.11*x* wireless networking. For iPAQs, this usually means 802.11b, but it can also mean 802.11g (a faster version, but generally compatible with 802.11b). Another standard, known as 802.11a, is incompatible with the iPAQ version of Wi-Fi.

If your iPAQ has Wi-Fi built in, Wi-Fi is almost certainly your first choice for connecting. Later in this chapter, in the section "Understanding your network connection options," I show you some ways that you can easily add Wi-Fi if your iPAQ doesn't have this capability built in.

In addition to your own wireless network, you can use a Wi-Fi connection to connect to public hotspots.

Bluetooth

Bluetooth is another wireless networking standard and is built into many current iPAQ models. It's hard to recommend attempting to make your Internet connection via Bluetooth, however, because Bluetooth is really only intended for very short-range operations (typically a maximum of about 30 feet). Still, Bluetooth may be viable if you happen to have a Bluetooth-enabled cell phone.

Wired modems

Wired modems may not be the coolest way to connect your iPAQ to the Internet, but they offer some real advantages over some other options. Not only are wired modems inexpensive and fast, but you can connect through the regular Internet account that you use on your desktop PC. But even if you were to set up a separate Internet account just for your iPAQ, unlimited access is generally quite reasonable. The one really big problem with wired modems, though, is that they typically require a CF expansion slot — something that few iPAQs offer.

Digital phone cards

If you already have a digital cell phone, a digital phone card may be available for your phone. These phone cards plug into your iPAQ and your cell phone and let you connect to the Internet wherever a digital cell phone signal is available. But like the wired modems, digital phone cards require a CF expansion slot, so this may not be an option for you.

Wireless modems

Wireless modems function something like a cell phone for data. To use a wireless modem, you must subscribe to a *wireless IP service plan* from a carrier such as AT&T Wireless, GoAmerica, or Verizon Wireless. These plans can be very expensive, so it pays to shop around for the best deal.

Most wireless modems were actually designed to fit the PC Card slot on a laptop, and simply won't work with your iPAQ. You might be able to find a CF wireless modem, but this will only be useful if your iPAQ has a CF expansion slot.

Setting Up a Wired Modem Connection

Before I show you how to set up a Wi-Fi connection, I take a quick look at how to set up a wired modem connection. Setting up your wired modem to work with your iPAQ probably seems fairly familiar — especially if you've ever added a modem to your desktop PC. Your iPAQ automatically recognizes your new modem, so all you have to do is set up the connection.

Be sure that you've pushed the modem fully into the expansion slot before you begin.

Here's the step-by-step procedure:

1. **Click the Start button and choose Settings to open the Settings screen. Then, tap the Connections tab (see Figure 12-1).**

2. **Tap the Connections icon to open the Connections screen.**

3. **Tap the Add a New Modem Connection link.**

4. **Enter a descriptive name for this connection in the first text box near the top of the screen.**

   Make this name distinctive enough that you can tell your different connections apart when you're ready to connect.

5. **Choose which modem you want to use from the Select a Modem list box. If you have more than one type of modem, you see several options in this list box.**

6. **Tap Next to continue.**

7. **Enter the correct dial-up number for your Internet service provider (ISP).**

   If you're setting up a connection to use while you're traveling, be sure to enter the correct area code (and country code if you'll be in another country).

8. Add your user name and password to the top two text boxes.

You probably don't need to fill in the Domain text box unless your ISP has specifically told you to do so.

9. Tap Finish.

In most cases, you don't need to change any of the advanced settings.

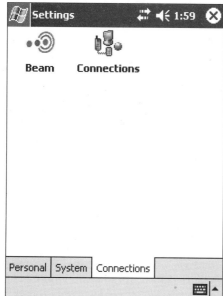

Figure 12-1:
Every new connection begins on the Connec-tions tab.

Be sure to take your iPAQ out of the cradle (or disconnect the sync cable) before you attempt to use your modem. Your iPAQ can have only one active connection at a time, and a connection to your desktop PC will prevent your iPAQ from opening the modem connection.

When you're finished using the connection, disconnect to free up the phone line. (Your iPAQ eventually disconnects after a period of inactivity, but this can take a half an hour or more.) To break the connection, tap the connection button on the title bar and then tap End.

Even though modems use very little power when they aren't in use, you can extend your battery life a bit by removing the modem when you aren't using it.

Using Wi-Fi with Your iPAQ

By now, it should be pretty clear that a Wi-Fi connection really is the best option for connecting your iPAQ to your own network and to the Internet. A Wi-Fi connection offers faster data transfers than virtually any other method that you might use, and because Wi-Fi is wireless, it's certainly the most convenient to use.

Understanding Wi-Fi

Wi-Fi connections use very small, low-powered two-way radios to exchange data. These connections operate by using a number of different frequencies in the 2.4 GHz radio band. These frequencies are in a range of *unlicensed* frequencies. This means that many different devices and users all share the same set of frequencies — which can lead to interference, but this usually doesn't have much affect on Wi-Fi networks. In addition to Wi-Fi networks, here are some other gadgets that use this same frequency band:

- Microwave ovens
- 2.4 GHz cordless telephones
- Bluetooth devices

Did the last item surprise you? Yes, it's true that Bluetooth and Wi-Fi share many of the same frequencies. Fortunately, they seldom interfere (at least not enough to cause major problems). That's why some iPAQ models can include (and use) both Wi-Fi and Bluetooth capabilities.

Connecting to your network

Setting up a wireless network should be pretty easy, especially with an iPAQ running the Windows Mobile 2003 operating system (OS). After all, Microsoft touts "Zero-Configuration Wi-Fi" functionality as one of the benefits of this latest version of the OS. In reality, though, I've generally found that it helps an awful lot to know how to modify various settings if I want to avoid major frustration.

Even if you have set up your own wired network in the past, you may not be familiar with setting up a wireless network. However, the whole process is fairly simple and you can be up and running in just a few minutes. Read on for a look at a typical wireless network configuration.

In this example, I'm using D-Link DWL-2000AP 802.11g Access Point to provide access to the network (see Figure 12-2). Because this particular access point uses the 802.11g standard, I can use both 802.11b and 802.11g wireless network cards on my network. The 802.11g cards can run nearly five times as fast as the 802.11b cards. You can find out more about this access point at the D-Link Web site (www.dlink.com).

Figure 12-2:
This D-Link
Access
Point
provides
wireless
access to
my network.

Here's how to quickly connect to your wireless network (you can skip these steps if your iPAQ has Wi-Fi capabilities built in):

1. **Connect the access point to the hub, switch, or router on your network.**

   The access point connects to your desktop PC or your router with an ordinary Cat-5 network cable. To maximize the range, place the access point as high as possible. Or you may want to add a high-gain antenna as I discuss later in this chapter in the section "Extending the range of your Wi-Fi network."

2. **Place your iPAQ in the sync cradle and make certain that ActiveSync connects to your iPAQ.**

3. **Insert the CD-ROM that came with the wireless network cards and install the drivers.**

   Typically, the driver setup runs automatically when the CD-ROM is inserted into the drive. Make certain that the drivers are fully installed on your iPAQ before continuing.

4. **Remove your iPAQ from the sync cradle and turn it off.**

You may also have to do a *soft reset* by pressing the iPAQ Reset button with the stylus — check the directions that came with the wireless network card. I have found that a soft reset at this point is generally a good idea even if the instructions don't mention it.

5. **Insert the wireless network card into your iPAQ.**

Your iPAQ will automatically turn itself back on once the card is inserted. At this point, you need to wait a few moments while your iPAQ detects the network.

If your iPAQ model has built-in Wi-Fi capabilities, you must turn on the radio before you can use your wireless network. To do so, select iPAQ Wireless from the Start menu to display the iPAQ Wireless screen shown in Figure 12-3. Features that are turned off are orange, and those that are on are green. Tap the WLAN icon to turn on the Wi-Fi radio. The radio defaults to being turned off, so you should always check this setting first if you're having trouble connecting.

After your iPAQ has detected the network, two arrows (pointing left and right) appear just to the left of the speaker icon on the Today screen title bar. Tap these arrows to display the Connectivity pop-up shown in Figure 12-4. The first time your iPAQ detects a network, you may see a pop-up asking if you want to connect — if you see this message, be sure to confirm that you do indeed want to connect.

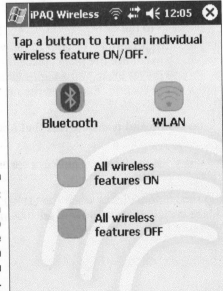

Figure 12-3: The built-in Wi-Fi radio must be turned on before you can use it.

Figure 12-4:
This
message
shows that
you have
made a
wireless
connection.

Adjusting the wireless configuration

In most cases, you should not have to do anything else except begin using your wireless connection. However, if you do have any problems connecting to either your network or the Internet, follow these steps:

1. **Tap the two arrows to display the Connectivity pop-up, and then tap the Settings link, which takes you to the Connections Settings screen.**

2. **Tap the Advanced tab, shown in Figure 12-5.**

3. **Tap the Select Networks button to display the Network Management screen shown in Figure 12-6.**

4. **Choose the network settings from the drop-down list boxes.**

   In virtually every case, you should select the My Work Network option in both list boxes. This setting enables your iPAQ to use your wireless connection to access your desktop PC via ActiveSync and also to access the Internet via your network's shared Internet connection. If you select My ISP, instead of My Network, you can only connect to the Internet and not to your own network.

5. **Tap OK to return to the Connections Settings screen.**

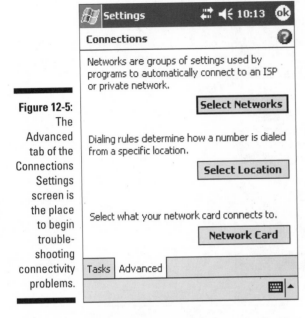

Figure 12-5:
The
Advanced
tab of the
Connections
Settings
screen is
the place
to begin
trouble-
shooting
connectivity
problems.

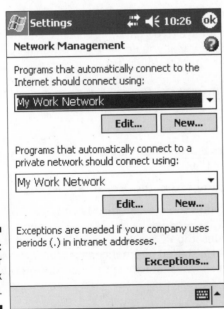

Figure 12-6:
Choose your
network
connections.

6. **Tap the Network Card button to display the Configure Wireless Networks screen shown in Figure 12-7.**

   If you want to use your iPAQ to connect to public hotspots (which I discuss later in this chapter in the section "Connecting to public hotspots") make certain that you select the Automatically Connect to Non-Preferred Networks option.

Figure 12-7: Choose your network connections.

7. **Tap your connection in the list box to display the screen shown in Figure 12-8 (this screen is also called Configure Wireless Networks).**

   Select Work from the Connect To drop-down list box so that your iPAQ can connect to your desktop PC via ActiveSync.

8. **Tap the Authentication tab, shown in Figure 12-9.**

9. **Select the proper security settings for your network.**

   You can enable the security features for your network to prevent other people from accessing your files. You need to enter that same key value here that you entered when enabling security on your wireless access point.

10. **Tap OK three times to close the Settings screens.**

Your wireless network should now be functional. Next, I look at some hardware options that you can use to make the wireless connection possible.

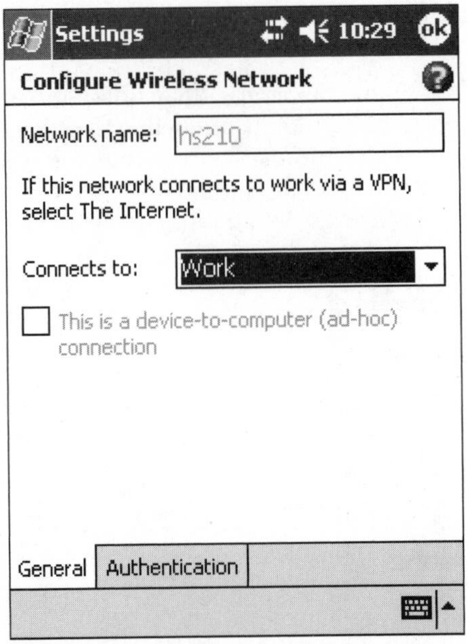

Figure 12-8:
Choose your network connections.

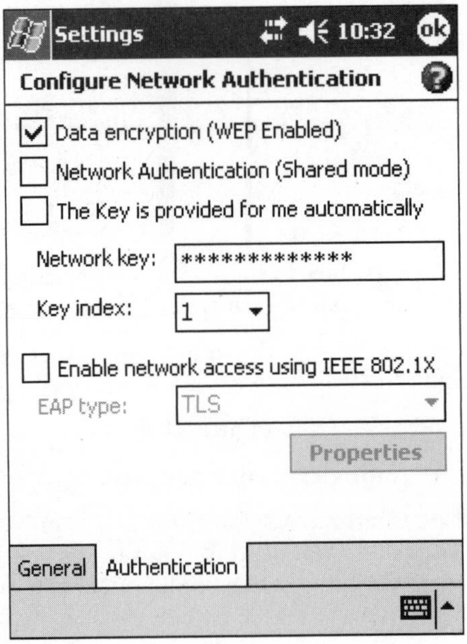

> **Settings** ⇄ ◀€ 10:29 **ok**
>
> **Configure Wireless Network** ❓
>
> Network name: hs210
>
> If this network connects to work via a VPN, select The Internet.
>
> Connects to: Work ▼
>
> ☐ This is a device-to-computer (ad-hoc) connection
>
> General | Authentication

Figure 12-9:
You need to specify the proper key to connect to networks with security enabled.

> **Settings** ⇄ ◀€ 10:32 **ok**
>
> **Configure Network Authentication** ❓
>
> ☑ Data encryption (WEP Enabled)
> ☐ Network Authentication (Shared mode)
> ☐ The Key is provided for me automatically
>
> Network key: *************
>
> Key index: 1 ▼
>
> ☐ Enable network access using IEEE 802.1X
> EAP type: TLS ▼
>
> Properties
>
> General | Authentication

Understanding your network connection options

If your iPAQ lacks built-in Wi-Fi capabilities, you still have a number of excellent options for connecting to wireless networks. These vary according to the type of expansion slots that you have available, of course.

If your iPAQ has a single SDIO expansion slot and no CF expansion slot, you may have to choose between adding Wi-Fi capabilities and expanding your iPAQ's memory. As this is being written, SanDisk has announced but not yet released another option that you may wish to consider — an SD Wi-Fi adapter card with 256MB of memory included. See the SanDisk Web site for more information (www.sandisk.com).

Figure 12-10 shows three of the Wi-Fi adapters that I tested while writing this book.

Figure 12-10: Any of these Wi-Fi adapters can enable your iPAQ to connect to your network wirelessly.

From left to right, the Wi-Fi adapters shown in Figure 12-10 are:

- ✔ SMC SMC2642W Wireless CompactFlash Card (www.smc.com)
- ✔ SanDisk SD Wi-Fi Card (www.sandisk.com)
- ✔ D-Link DCF-660W Wireless CompactFlash Card (www.dlink.com)

Each of these adapters worked quite well, but the SMC and D-Link Wi-Fi cards can only be used in iPAQ models that have a CF expansion slot.

Socket (www.socketcom.com) offers an SD Wi-Fi card that is similar to the SanDisk card. Figure 12-11 shows just how small an SD Wi-Fi card really is. The figure shows the card photographed next to a United States quarter. If you buy one of these cards, be careful not to lose it!

Figure 12-11:
SD Wi-Fi
cards really
define
the term
compact
power.

Each of the Wi-Fi adapter cards suffered from its own set of problems during testing. These problems were mostly resolved by downloading and installing updated drivers, but the SD Wi-Fi cards seemed to have a few more compatibility problems than the CF Wi-Fi cards had with different access point brands. One way to reduce compatibility issues is to buy your adapter cards and access points from a single manufacturer.

Wi-Fi security considerations

In doing research for this book, it became clear to me that quite a few people really don't understand just how vulnerable they can be when they install a wireless network. It's true that a wireless network makes it extremely easy for you to move around and still access your network without the bother of dragging a bunch of cables, but this same ease and convenience also makes it quite simple for neighbors or strangers to connect to your network, too. And this could give them easy and free access to your sensitive files, your user names and passwords, your financial data, or even to your bank and credit card accounts. Are you scared yet?

Actually, it's not difficult to keep most unauthorized people from accessing your wireless network, but it seems like most people don't realize just how simple the access process is. Rather than protecting themselves they seem to take the attitude that "no one would be interested in what's on my computer." Tell that to anyone who has been the target of identity theft and see if they agree with you.

If you want to keep the snoops out but still want the convenience of a wireless network, you're going to have to do a small amount of work. It takes only five minutes or so, but you can sleep better tonight knowing that you've made some effort to protect yourself. Your first step is to dig out the user manual for your access point — you know, it's that little book that you ignored that came with the access point. Find the section on configuring the access point (each brand is a little different). Then, be sure to change the password (and user name if you can). Next, change the SSID (the network name of the access point). Don't use a name that easily identifies whose network this is. Turn on the highest level of security that's offered and enter a key value that's so difficult that you have to write it down to remember it. You also have to modify the settings on your iPAQ and any other devices to match. These steps won't keep out crooks or governmental goons, but they at least prevent the casual passersby from getting in.

Connecting to public hotspots

One of the really cool ways to use Wi-Fi is to connect to the Internet through a public hotspot (a place where wireless Internet access is available) such as those you might encounter in a coffee shop, a restaurant, or an airport. Just whip out your iPAQ, turn it on, and you could be surfing the Web or handling your e-mail. The wow factor when people see you pulling up Web sites with no dangling wires is enough to start some awfully interesting conversations with a whole bunch of perfect strangers.

Finding hotspots

You have to find the hotspots before you can connect to them. Many businesses are installing hotspots, so this probably won't be too much of a problem — especially in large cities. Your iPAQ will even tell you when you're within range of a hotspot by popping up a message box. You do, however, have to do a couple of things to make this happen:

✔ Your Wi-Fi radio must be on. iPAQs with built-in Wi-Fi radios default to turning the radio off to save power, so you need to check this before you go hotspot hunting.

✔ The Automatically Connect to Non-Preferred Networks option must be selected (see "Adjusting the wireless configuration" earlier in this chapter). If this is not selected, your iPAQ simply ignores most public hotspots.

✔ In most cases, you need to set up an account with the hotspot provider before you can log on and use the Internet or e-mail. In some cases, this requires setting up an account *ahead* of time, but increasingly, hotspots allow you to enter your credit card information and sign up immediately.

✔ Finally, you must be within range of the hotspot. The range varies considerably, but I have found that iPAQs tend to be able to connect further from the hotspot than most Wi-Fi–equipped laptops.

Using pocketWiNc

Even though your iPAQ is pretty adept at finding and connecting to Wi-Fi hotspots, you would probably be very surprised to see just how many connection opportunities exist. Sure, your iPAQ will tell you about some of them, but I have found a tool that makes your iPAQ into a top notch Wi-Fi finder. This program, pocketWiNc, goes far beyond the ordinary and shows you every Wi-Fi signal that it can detect. It even shows you which Wi-Fi networks are open and available, and which ones require you to enter the proper security key to connect. (See the nearby sidebar titled "Wi-Fi security considerations.")

Figure 12-12 shows pocketWiNc in use. The top portion of the screen shows all Wi-Fi access points that are currently detected by your iPAQ. The lower portion of the screen shows the names of networks that you have connected to recently. You can find out more about this great tool at the Cirond Web site (www.cirond.com/site/products/wifispotter/download_software.htm).

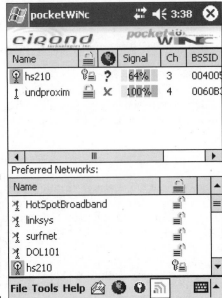

Figure 12-12:
You can use
pocketWiNc
to snoop
around and
find Wi-Fi
networks.

Extending the range of your Wi-Fi network

Have you ever tried to put a telephone or a small kitchen appliance in just the right place only to find that the cord was just two inches too short to reach the nearest outlet? If so, you can certainly understand how frustrating it can be to set up your wireless network in your home office and then discover that your iPAQ doesn't get quite the signal that it needs for a reliable Wi-Fi connection in your family room.

Wi-Fi networks operate at a very high frequency — 2.4 GHz. They also transmit signals at a very low power level. These two factors combine to limit the ability of Wi-Fi signals to penetrate the walls in your home. As a result, a Wi-Fi signal is actually usable over a much longer distance outdoors than indoors. In fact, the difference is often four to ten times as much, depending on how clear the path between the two Wi-Fi units is.

In some cases, you may be able to correct a marginal Wi-Fi signal situation by moving your access point to a different location. For example, placing the access point on top of a high cabinet rather than on your desk might do the trick.

Figure 12-13 shows another option that works far better than moving your access point. This is the 6dBi Desktop Directional Range Extender Indoor Antenna from Pacific Wireless (www.pacwireless.com/html/apxtender.html). To use this antenna, simply unscrew the little antenna from the back of your access point and connect the cable from the new antenna. Then place the new antenna as high as possible and point it in the direction where you would like to increase your Wi-Fi signal. In my testing, this compact little unit effectively doubled the distance over which my iPAQ could make a reliable connection to my network.

Figure 12-13: You can easily extend the range of your Wi-Fi network with this antenna from Pacific Wireless.

Working Remotely

If you have an iPAQ and a wireless connection, you have options that can get you out of the office. By itself, that might be worth the cost of an iPAQ!

No one would claim that an iPAQ can do everything that a desktop PC can do. However, with the options that I show you next, your iPAQ can do virtually anything that your desktop PC can do.

Figure 12-14 shows something that probably looks a little familiar, yet not something you're used to seeing on your iPAQ: an ordinary Windows-based PC and Windows Media Player. In this case, I'm controlling of one of the PCs on my network — our home media center — by using NetOp Remote Control (www.netop.com). You can download a trial version, but you'll need to buy a license if you want to continue using it after the trial period ends.

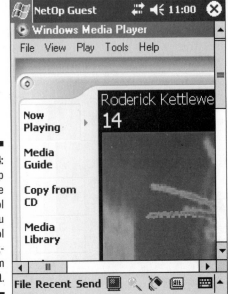

Figure 12-14:
NetOp
Remote
Control
enables you
to control
your desk-
top PC from
your iPAQ.

NetOp Remote Control can do far more than simply show your desktop's screen on your iPAQ. Indeed, when NetOp Remote Control is running, you can use anything on your desktop system with your iPAQ. You can run the programs on your desktop, change settings, and even perform file-management functions.

It helps to use your imagination when you use a program like NetOp Remote Control. Sure, the business applications for this type of program are obvious, but you can have some fun with it, too. For example, you can use your 802.11b wireless network connection to access your desktop system while you're sitting out in your backyard with your iPAQ. Then, you can play music through your home stereo system that's connected to your desktop system's audio card. Your iPAQ can control Windows Media Player and even adjust the volume.

If you use NetOp Remote Control (or any other remote control software) to allow remote access to your desktop PC, make certain that you activate the security features included in the program. Otherwise, someone else might be able to gain control of your desktop system and do all sorts of mischief.

Chapter 13

Surfing the Internet

. . . .

In This Chapter

▶ Getting to know Pocket Internet Explorer

▶ Browsing the Internet on your iPAQ

▶ Viewing Web pages offline

▶ Getting the most out of Pocket Internet Explorer

▶ Using an alternative browser

. . . .

*E*ven though surfing the Web on your iPAQ will never be quite the same as browsing with a huge desktop monitor, there's a lot to be said for both the convenience and sheer coolness of being able to whip out your iPAQ and find something on the Web. While everyone else has to wait until they can fire up their desktop PC, you're able to go online whenever you want. That alone is worth the price of admission, isn't it?

In this chapter, you see how to use Pocket Internet Explorer on your iPAQ to do some real Web browsing. In addition, I show you an alternative to Pocket Internet Explorer that makes use of the entire iPAQ screen to present Web pages in a whole new way. Whichever browser you choose, your iPAQ really does function as a powerful and convenient way to access the Internet.

Introducing Pocket Internet Explorer

Pocket Internet Explorer is a Web browser designed for the small screen of the iPAQ. A *Web browser* is a program that displays Web pages more or less as the Web page designer intended. On your desktop PC, you probably use Internet Explorer, Netscape, Mozilla, or Opera as your Web browser, but you can't run any of those on an iPAQ. Pocket Internet Explorer, of course, is similar to Internet Explorer, but these two programs have many differences.

Understanding the Pocket Internet Explorer screen

Figure 13-1 shows the Pocket Internet Explorer screen that you see the first time you open Pocket Internet Explorer. You don't need to be connected to the Internet to see this screen because it's stored right on your iPAQ. In fact, you don't need to connect at all until you actually want to visit a Web site.

Right off the bat, you probably notice that the Pocket Internet Explorer screen looks quite different from any other Web browser that you've used in the past. For one thing, it has far fewer buttons and toolbars cluttering up the screen. Because Pocket Internet Explorer has far less room to waste, Web pages tend to have a more compact appearance with less empty space between the various bits and pieces. (Later in this chapter, in the section "Making the Best Use of Your Screen Real Estate," I show you how to maximize your viewing area.)

Even with a more compact view of Web pages, you still need to be able to move around. Fortunately, if you're familiar with Internet Explorer, you don't need to know anything new to navigate Web pages with Pocket Internet Explorer. You can still click a link to load a different Web page. You can still use the address bar to enter a URL (although you may have to choose View⇨Address Bar to display the address bar first because it's often hidden to give you more browsing room). And you can still scroll to other areas on a Web page by using the scroll bars that appear when the Web page is too large for a single screen.

Figure 13-1:
Pocket
Internet
Explorer
enables you
to surf the
Web on
your iPAQ.

You can also use the navigation button below the center of the iPAQ screen to move around on a Web page.

Setting your general options

Pocket Internet Explorer has a number of options that you can set to control how the program works. You may want to have a quick look at these options before you actually begin browsing with Pocket Internet Explorer to be sure that you understand exactly which options will work the best for you.

To begin setting the options, choose Tools➪Options to display the General tab (see Figure 13-2).

Here's a brief explanation of the options on the General tab:

- **Home Page:** These buttons enable you to choose a specific Web page to view whenever you open Pocket Internet Explorer. Click Use Current if you're viewing a Web page that you want as your home page. Click Use Default to reset your home page to the Web page shown in Figure 13-1.

    Choosing a Web page that's always available is a good idea. Because your iPAQ isn't likely to be connected to the Internet all the time, this means choosing a Web page that's stored on your iPAQ. Because the default Web page is stored on your iPAQ, you don't need to connect in order to view the page. If you choose an online Web page, Pocket Internet Explorer won't be able to load the page unless your iPAQ is connected.

- **History:** These options enable you to control how long Pocket Internet Explorer maintains a record of your browsing. The longer links remain in the History list, the more likely you'll be able to find the link when you want to return to that neat page you remember visiting but can't quite remember the Uniform Resource Locator (URL). Of course, like with most everything else on your iPAQ, use some moderation in choosing how long to keep things in the history: Everything you store does eat up some memory. (For more on the History list, see the section "Browsing your History list" later in this chapter.)

- **Temporary Internet Files:** In this section, use the Delete Files button to remove any Web pages and their associated files from temporary storage. These files are stored so that you can more quickly reload a Web page that you've visited recently.

- **Delete Files** and **Clear History:** If you're really running low on memory, click these buttons. Doing this typically doesn't free up very much room, but it may be enough to temporarily solve the problem.

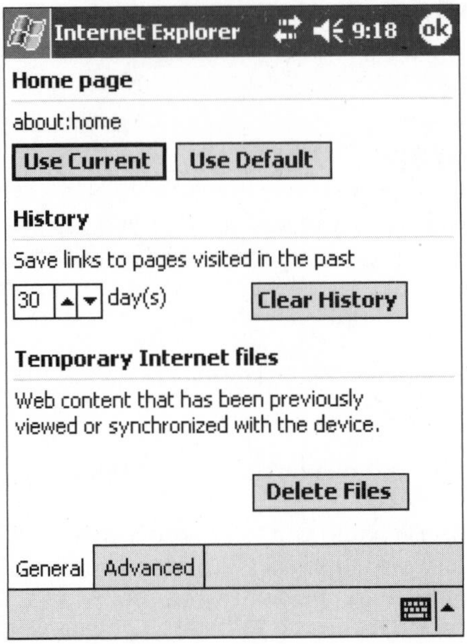

Figure 13-2:
This page
shows a
few of the
Pocket
Internet
Explorer
options that
you can
control.

Playing with the advanced options

To get to the Advanced tab, shown in Figure 13-3, choose Tools⇨Options and click the Advanced tab. Here you find some very useful options.

Here's a quick look at the advanced settings:

✔ **Cookies:** These settings let you control those files that Web sites can place onto your iPAQ when you visit a site. Some people hate the idea that Web sites can use cookies to track some of your Web browsing activity, but other people like the convenience that cookies provide — such as the ability to shop online. Choose the cookie settings that make you feel comfortable, and don't forget the milk.

✔ **Security settings:** In this section, the Warn When Changing to a Page That Is Not Secure option is very important on an iPAQ. On your desktop PC, your browser provides visible feedback to tell you whether the Web page that you're visiting is secure. This makes it far safer for you to enter sensitive information because you can easily tell if someone is asking you to enter your credit card number on a page that isn't encrypted. (If the site isn't encrypted, *don't* enter any sensitive information.) However, on an iPAQ it's harder to tell if the page you're visiting is secure — especially if you've hidden the address bar to get more browsing area. That's why it's a good idea to receive a warning when you go from a secure page to one that isn't secure.

✔ **Language:** This selection can be important if you visit a lot of foreign language Web pages. You may need to play around with this setting to see which selection does the best job of displaying the Web pages that you visit.

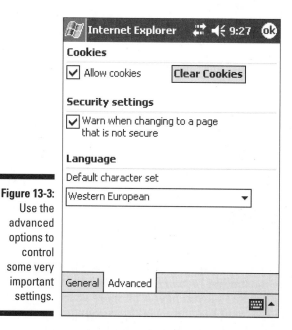

Figure 13-3: Use the advanced options to control some very important settings.

Surfing the Connected Web

Okay, I'm sure that you want to stop this fooling around and start surfing! It's time to see what Web browsing on an iPAQ is really like.

To begin having fun on the Web, first click the Start button and choose Internet Explorer. Most likely, you see the default home page shown earlier in Figure 13-1, but you may see a different page instead if you've entered a new home page. Figure 13-4 shows how Pocket Internet Explorer appears after an online Web page has been loaded.

Entering URLs

A unique address, called a URL, identifies all Web sites. If you want to view the Wiley Publishing Web site, for example, you can enter the address www. wiley.com, and your Web browser finds and loads the page you've asked for.

Internet Explorer 9:46

"Just to open a book is worthwhile" —
from a fortune cookie

Brian Underdahl-the only
"officially licensed" Writer in the
state of Nevada

View Tools

Figure 13-4:
Pocket
Internet
Explorer
displaying
my Web
site.

Like all Web browsers, Pocket Internet Explorer has an address bar that you use to enter URLs. But unlike most other browsers, Pocket Internet Explorer often has the address bar hidden so that you have a bit more space for viewing Web page content. When you want to enter an address, you first have to display the address bar so that you have a place for the address.

To display the Pocket Internet Explorer address bar, choose View⇨Address Bar. This option is a *toggle,* like a light switch, so you use the same command a second time to make the address bar go away again. Figure 13-5 shows Pocket Internet Explorer after I've displayed the address bar, entered a URL, and clicked the Go button (the curved green arrow to the right of the URL box) to load a new page.

The small down arrow at the right side of the address bar displays a list of URLs you've visited. To return to one of those Web sites, click the down arrow and tap the URL of the site you want to visit.

Following links

Almost all Web pages include links that you can follow to visit other Web pages. It is, in fact, those links that inspired the name *Web* in the first place. The Web really is an endless web of links that lead here and there. Links are also one of the most fun things about the Web. You never know where you'll eventually end up if you start following interesting-looking links. You might even end up someplace like the Beer Church Home Page (www.beerchurch.com) when you least expect it.

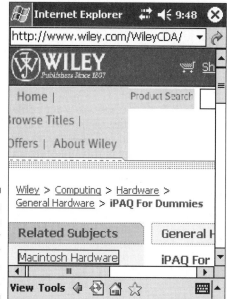

Figure 13-5:
Use the
address bar
to enter
Web page
URLs.

Links can have several different appearances. You can usually tell which words are links because they're underlined and appear in a different color from regular text. Tapping the underlined text moves you to the new page.

If you accidentally tap a link and find yourself on the wrong page, click the Back button (the left-pointing arrow on the menu bar) to return to the previous page.

Going home

After you've followed a bunch of interesting-looking links, you may find yourself wanting to return to your home page. When you get this urge, just click the little house symbol on the Pocket Internet Explorer menu bar. Pocket Internet Explorer reloads your home page. Too bad it can't also make your house payment while it's at it.

Reloading pages

You have probably encountered Web pages that just don't seem to load properly the first time. It's really hard to pin down why this happens, but when it does, your first action should probably be to tap the Reload button. Any time you need to reload a Web page, click the Reload button (the button with the two curved arrows in the middle of the Pocket Internet Explorer menu bar), and Pocket Internet Explorer sends a new request for the page to the Web server.

The Reload button helps in several different instances:

✔ If you're trying to view images, but all you see are placeholders where images belong on the Web page, hit the Reload button to ask for the page and images to be sent again. (To find out how to stop images from loading, see "Getting rid of graphics" later in this chapter.)

✔ If you're viewing a Web page with frequently updated contents — such as news headlines or stock prices — tap Reload to see an updated view.

✔ If you're trying to access a Web site that won't respond because too many people are trying to view it at the same time, clicking the Reload button may be all it takes to hit that small window of opportunity when the server will actually respond and send you the page.

Viewing the page properties

Unless you're really curious, there's probably not much reason to view the properties of the Web pages that you're visiting. Still, you can find out a few useful pieces of information by choosing View⇨Properties. The Properties screen appears, and here you can see the address (or URL) of the page that you're viewing and see whether it's secure. Secure Web pages have a URL that begins with https:// and non-secure pages begin with http://. You can also verify which type of page you are viewing by noting what the Security line just above the URL says.

Make certain that you're on a secure Web page before you enter confidential information like credit card numbers. Otherwise, you will send that information across the Internet as plain text that anyone can intercept and read along the way.

Sending a link

As you surf the Web, you're bound to come across Web pages that you'd like to share with someone else. Pocket Internet Explorer provides a very easy way to do this by allowing you to send the URL in an e-mail message. The recipient can then click the link and view the page.

To send a Web page link to someone, first make certain that you're viewing the page you want to send. Then choose Tools⇨Send Link via E-mail to open a new e-mail message. Address your message and include an explanation so the recipient knows why you're sending the link. Chapter 14 covers e-mail on your iPAQ in more detail.

Pocket Internet Explorer doesn't include an option for sending a complete Web page to someone — you can send only the link to that page. And because you can send only a link, the page may have changed or even disappeared before your e-mail message recipient tries to view the page. If it's important that the recipient sees the same information that you're seeing, you may want to open Internet Explorer on your desktop PC and send the page — not just the link — from there by choosing File⇨Send⇨Page by E-mail. Or you may want to copy the information, which I discuss in the next section.

Copying information you want to keep

One thing that's certain about the Web is that you can't trust it to remain the same. Pages are updated or can disappear without warning, and this can mean that important information may not be there when you return. If you want to preserve what you've seen on a Web page, the most reliable way to do so is to save the page on your own computer.

Pocket Internet Explorer doesn't offer you a way to save a Web page on your iPAQ, so if you want to save the information from a site, you need to use a slightly different approach. What you have to do is copy the information that you want and then paste it into your own document. Remember, though, that you may be violating someone's copyright by copying the information. You may need to ask the owner of the material for permission if you intend to use it commercially or on a Web site.

To copy information from a Web page in Pocket Internet Explorer, follow these steps:

1. **Open the Web page that contains the information that you want to preserve.**

2. **Drag your stylus across the information you want so that you select the information. Alternatively, choose Tools⇨Select All Text to select all the text on the page.**

   Unfortunately, although you can save the text from a Web page, you cannot save any images from the page.

3. **Choose Tools⇨Copy to copy the selected data to the Clipboard.**

4. **Open the document to which you want to add the information and choose the Paste command.**

   You find the Paste command on an Edit menu, a Tools menu, or on some other menu depending on the application that you're using.

If you chose the Select All Text method of coping, you probably need to do a bunch of cleanup to remove the junk that got pasted into your document along with the stuff you wanted.

Browsing your History list

Pocket Internet Explorer keeps a record of the URLs of the Web pages you visit so that it's easier for you to return to those same pages. Consider how often you've wanted to return to a site that you visited earlier, but you couldn't quite remember the correct URL. Maybe you visited the page a few days ago and just now realized that it contained some information you really need. Well, the History list can get you back there in no time.

To use the History list, choose View⇨History. As Figure 13-6 shows, this displays a list that you can scroll through. You return to a page by tapping the correct link.

You can view the URLs by tapping the down arrow to the right of Page Title and selecting Address, which may be helpful if you want to return to the main page on a Web site rather than to a page that you've already visited. This may also help you locate the information you need if the page that you visited earlier has disappeared.

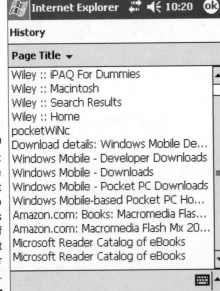

Figure 13-6:
Use the History list to return to Web pages even if you don't remember the URL.

Playing favorites

Even though you can browse through your History list to find links to Web pages that you've visited, the History list is not the most ideal way to store links to Web pages that you want to visit in the future. Not only do links disappear from the History list after a certain period of time, but all the History list links can be instantly cleared away with a tap of your stylus.

Pocket Internet Explorer provides a better way to store the Web page links that you really don't want to lose. You save them as *favorites* and they remain available until you decide to get rid of them.

Viewing your favorite Web sites

To return to your favorite Web sites, you use the Favorites list instead of the History list. Figure 13-7 shows the Favorites list. To display this list, tap the Favorites button — the button that looks like a star — at the right side of the Pocket Internet Explorer menu bar.

Saving favorite Web sites

So how do your favorite Web sites magically get placed onto your Favorites list? Simple: You put them there by using the Add/Delete tab (see Figure 13-8).

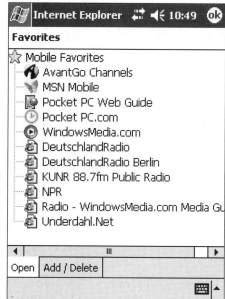

Figure 13-7:
Use the Favorites list to quickly return to your favorite Web sites.

Figure 13-8:
Add your
own favorite
Web sites
to the list.

When you arrive at the Favorites screen, it asks which items you want to delete. On the Add/Delete tab, deleting is the default activity. To add a Web site to the list, you've got to do just a bit more:

1. **Open the Web page that you want to add to your list of favorites.**

2. **Tap the Favorites button.**

3. **Tap the Add/Delete tab.**

4. **Click the Add button.**

5. **If you want, modify the page name in the Name text box to something more descriptive.**

6. **Click Add and then tap OK to close the Favorites screen.**

If you're having a hard time figuring out which Web sites to add to your list of Favorites, here are some ideas:

✔ Include the logon page for your online stockbroker. That way, you're can quickly access your account and make those trades as soon as you hear some interesting news.

✔ If you travel often, add the online ticket reservation sites for your favorite airlines. If you have a wireless connection, you can quickly book a flight if you find that you need to change your schedule at the last minute.

  ✔ Add a weather forecasting site if you'd like to see whether it's a better idea to fly off to the mountains for skiing or to the coast for some sunshine.

  ✔ Of course, you want to include `www.dummies.com` so that you can find out when your favorite author comes out with a new title. You wouldn't want your collection to be incomplete, would you?

Offline Pocket Browsing

Connecting to the Internet may not always be practical, but that shouldn't keep you from viewing Web pages that contain interesting or useful information. You may, for example, want to catch up on the weather forecast or some local news stories while you're riding to work in your car pool even though everyone else just wants to listen to a talk show or the sports. You could, of course, use a wireless Internet connection if you have one available, but there's no reason why you can't do a little browsing even when you can't connect.

The key to offline browsing on your iPAQ is ActiveSync. By using this tool, you can set up your desktop PC to automatically download certain Web pages to your iPAQ so that you can view them when it's convenient for you. To do so, choose Tools⇨Create Mobile Favorite on your desktop PC. Then, use the Options command in ActiveSync and select Favorites. That way, your iPAQ has your weather, news, or whatever you want all ready when you grab it on your way out the door in the morning.

Making the Best Use of Your Screen Real Estate

I doubt that anyone complains that the screen on the iPAQ is too large. When you're viewing Web pages in Pocket Internet Explorer, it's pretty clear that Web site designers aren't giving too much thought to how their pages look on the iPAQ's screen. You've got to make the most of a small area, and fortunately Pocket Internet Explorer has a few tricks up its sleeve to help you out.

Getting rid of graphics

One thing that you can do to fit more text onto your iPAQ's screen is to choose to not display the graphics that appear on most Web pages. After all, do you *really* want to view all those banner ads? You can turn off the graphics by tapping the View⇨Show Images command in Pocket Internet Explorer. Another plus: Your Web pages load faster because you aren't downloading any images. You can tap the button again to redisplay the graphics.

Expanding the usable screen area

Even if you want to see the images on Web pages, you can still make better use of the little bit of screen that you've got. Choose View and then use the following options:

- ✔ **Fit to Screen:** Choose this option to make Pocket Internet Explorer scrunch things together by reducing wasted space. When you select this option, you won't need to scroll nearly so much because Pocket Internet Explorer uses as little space as possible to display the Web page contents.

- ✔ **Address Bar:** Choose this option only when you need to enter a URL, and then deselect this option after you've loaded the Web page. The address bar is necessary only while you're entering an address, and hiding the address bar gives you a touch more room for viewing Web pages.

- ✔ **Text Size:** This option is for choosing the size of the characters used to display Web pages. Selecting a smaller size fits more onto the screen at one time, but if you go too small, you may need to get stronger reading glasses. Of course, you can choose a larger text size if you have trouble reading the text, too.

Browsing the Web on your iPAQ can be a lot of fun — whether it's online or offline browsing. Your iPAQ certainly makes it possible to surf the Web at times and places where doing so would otherwise be impossible.

Using an Alternative Browser

It isn't hard to argue that surfing the Web with Pocket Internet Explorer can be somewhat frustrating. Here are just a few reasons why this is so:

- ✔ Most Web pages are designed for viewing on a screen that is wider than it is high. The iPAQ screen, of course, is just the opposite.

- ✔ Even when you eliminate the address bar, a large portion of what little space is available is eaten up by the title bar and the menu bar — items you can't remove.

- ✔ No matter what you do, most Web pages require so much scrolling — both horizontally and vertically — that it can be a real chore to find the things you really want on the iPAQ's screen.

Figure 13-9 shows the ThunderHawk Web Browser. This browser is designed to address these issues and make your iPAQ browsing a much more enjoyable experience.

Figure 13-9:
The Thunder-Hawk browser gives your iPAQ a whole new way to display Web pages.

One of the first things you may notice about the ThunderHawk browser is that it uses a landscape layout so that it can display Web pages in a format similar to that of a desktop Web browser. When you're using ThunderHawk, you need to turn your iPAQ on its side to view the screen. In addition, except for a very small scrollbar, the entire iPAQ screen is used to display Web page content. The title bar, menu bar, and address bar aren't there to spoil the view.

You may be wondering about just how useful a Web browser without an address bar or any other visible controls really is. Well, rest assured that the ThunderHawk browser does have the missing controls, but it only displays them when necessary. Figure 13-10 shows how the controls are displayed when you press any of the program buttons on the front of your iPAQ. (The navigation button is used for navigation rather than displaying the controls.)

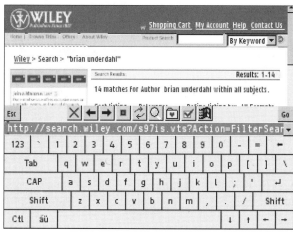

Figure 13-10:
Press a button on the front of your iPAQ to display the Thunder-Hawk browser's controls.

Another area where the ThunderHawk browser differs from Pocket Internet Explorer is that the ThunderHawk browser is sold on a subscription basis. You can, however, download a 30-day trial version so that you can see if Thunder-Hawk is really for you. You can find out everything you need to know about this browser at the Bitstream Web site (www.bitstream.com/wireless/getthnow.html).

Be sure to try out the 30-day trial version before signing up for a ThunderHawk subscription. During testing for this book, I was unable to get ThunderHawk to work on a newly released iPAQ model (although the manufacturer advised that this support would likely be available in the near future).

Chapter 14

Keeping Track of Your E-Mail

In This Chapter

▶ Setting up your e-mail account

▶ Creating and sending messages

▶ Synchronizing messages with your desktop PC

A nyone who gets too few e-mail messages just isn't trying hard enough. These days, virtually everyone wants your e-mail address, and few of us can remember what life was like back when you had to pick up a phone if you wanted to quickly communicate.

Your iPAQ is especially well-suited to helping you manage your e-mail. Its size is small enough that you can carry it with you anywhere — so you can deal with e-mail messages when you would otherwise be wasting time waiting for something else to happen. It's also convenient because you can whip out a message when a thought hits rather than waiting until you're back at your desk. And because your iPAQ can share e-mail messages with your desktop PC, you don't have to stay late at the office to handle that rush of messages that arrived just before quitting time.

Connecting to Your Mail Server

E-mail messages circulate over the Internet in much the same manner that letters travel through the postal system. E-mail moves a lot faster than ordinary mail, of course, but the two methods have certain similarities. First, like letters, all e-mail messages need to be sent to a specific, unique address. In addition, e-mail messages travel through *mail servers* — the electronic equivalent of post offices. Just as it's necessary for the post office to know that you've built a house and are now living at a particular street address, it's also necessary for you to establish your e-mail address with a mail server.

Sending and receiving e-mail messages with your iPAQ requires that you first set up your iPAQ with the proper mail server and address information. You can get started by setting up and configuring your iPAQ to use e-mail.

Setting up your e-mail account

You probably want to set up your iPAQ to use the same e-mail account as your desktop PC so that you can more easily share e-mail between the two. This isn't required, of course. If you want, you can set up an e-mail account specifically for your iPAQ — but I leave it to you to figure out how you're going to keep track of more than one e-mail account (and how to deal with twice as much spam).

You can use two basic types of e-mail with your iPAQ: online and offline. *Online* (Web-based) e-mail services typically require that you read, compose, and send messages while you're online and using a Web browser. Your Internet service provider (ISP) probably also provides you with a more traditional e-mail account that enables you to handle your e-mail offline. *Offline* (non-Web-based) e-mail servers are also known as IMAP4 or POP3 mail servers, depending on the particular mail protocol they use. You have to select the correct mail server type when you're setting up e-mail on your iPAQ, but it should be quite easy to get the server type from your ISP.

To set up your e-mail account on your iPAQ, follow these steps:

1. **Click the Start button and choose Inbox to run the program (or choose Inbox from the Programs folder if it does not appear on your Start menu).**

2. **Choose Accounts⇨New Account to display the E-mail Address screen, shown in Figure 14-1.**

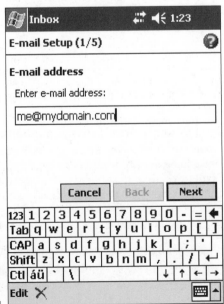

Figure 14-1: Enter your e-mail address.

3. **Enter your e-mail address in the text box.**

4. **Tap Next to display the Auto Configuration screen, shown in Figure 14-2.**

   At this point, your iPAQ attempts to connect and configure itself correctly. Wait until the Status box says Completed before continuing.

5. **Click Next to display the User Information screen, shown in Figure 14-3.**

6. **Enter your user name and your password in the text boxes if you want your iPAQ to be able to send and receive e-mail automatically.**

   If you either skip the password or don't enable the Save Password option, you have to enter the information manually each time you want to access the mail server.

7. **Click Next to display the Account Information screen, shown in Figure 14-4.**

8. **In the Account Type drop-down list box, select the type of mail server that your ISP provides.**

   In most cases, the default POP3 is the correct choice.

9. **Enter a name for this mail service in the Name text box.**

10. **Tap Next to display the Server Information screen, shown in Figure 14-5.**

11. **If the server names are not filled in, enter the correct names that were supplied by your ISP.**

In most cases, you don't need to enter anything into the Domain text box. The Domain setting primarily applies if you send and receive e-mail through a Windows NT network mail server.

Figure 14-3:
Use this screen to enter your user name and password.

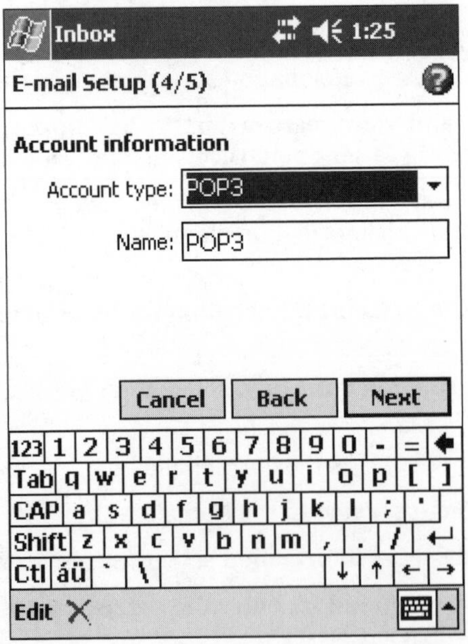

Figure 14-4:
Here you control how Pocket Inbox handles mail.

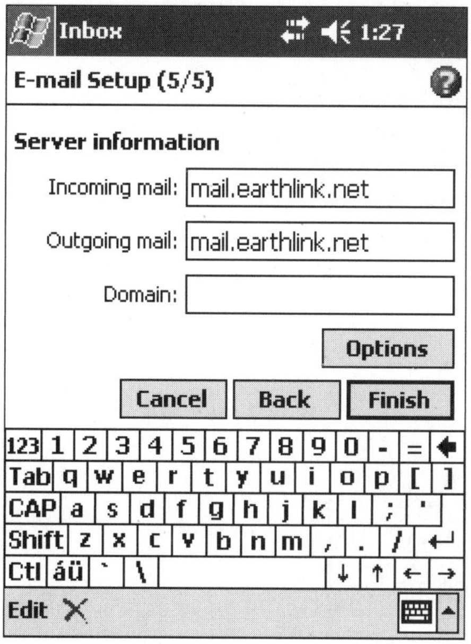

Figure 14-5:
The server
information
often fills
in auto-
matically.

12. **To adjust the settings for this mail server, tap Options to display the first Options screen, shown in Figure 14-6.**

13. **Select the mail service settings that work best for you.**

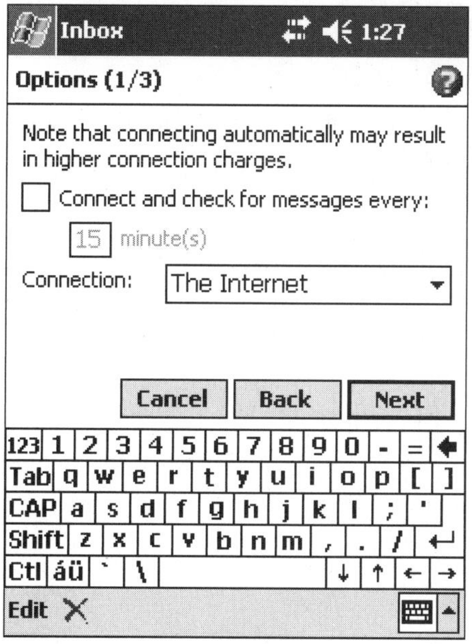

Figure 14-6:
Choose your
e-mail
options.

14. **Click Next to display the second Options screen, shown in Figure 14-7.**

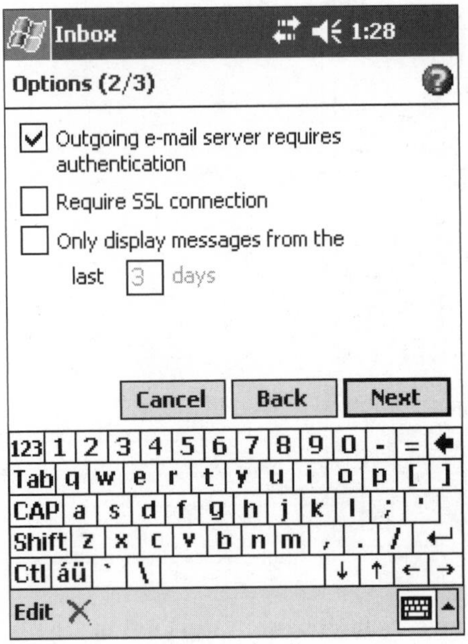

Figure 14-7:
Choose the
correct
server
settings.

15. **Choose the options that match what your server requires.**

Make sure that the Outgoing E-Mail Server Requires Authentication option is correctly enabled or disabled for your iPAQ — otherwise you will be able to receive but not send e-mail from your iPAQ. Your ISP should give you the proper information.

16. **Tap Next to display the final Options screen, shown in Figure 14-8.**

You might want to only download the message headers (which contain information such as who sent the message and the subject) or you might want to limit the download to a certain size (such as 2K). This would be especially true if you use a wireless connection where you are charged by the amount of data that's transferred or if your Inbox tends to be swamped by spam. You could later download the entire message to your desktop system.

17. **Tap Finish to complete the setup.**

Congratulations! You're now the proud parent of a brand new e-mail account.

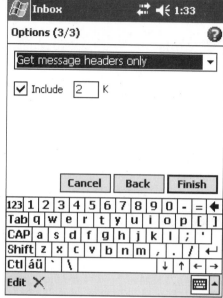

Figure 14-8:
Decide how
much of the
messages
you want
to see on
your iPAQ.

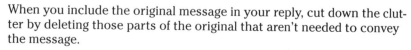

Choosing your message options

Before you begin using a new mail service, at least review the message
options that are selected for the mail service so you can be sure that Pocket
Inbox is handling mail the way you prefer.

To check the message options, open Pocket Inbox and choose Tools⇨
Options. Then, click the Message tab (see Figure 14-9).

Here's a brief description of these options:

- ✔ **When Replying, Include Body:** Use this option to include the original
  message when you send a reply to someone. If you don't select this
  option, people could have a very hard time remembering which message
  you're replying to.

  When you include the original message in your reply, cut down the clutter by deleting those parts of the original that aren't needed to convey
  the message.

- ✔ **Indent** and **Add Leading Character:** If you include the body text in
  replies, make certain that both of these boxes are selected. Using these
  options makes it easier for the recipient to recognize the text that you're
  replying to. Don't try to get fancy with the leading character, though.
  Everyone recognizes the greater than (>) symbol as signifying a reply. If
  you decide to use a different character, you'll only confuse people.

✔ **Keep Copy of Sent Mail in Sent Folder:** Enable this option if you want to keep a record of messages that you send. It's tempting to try and save storage space by not selecting this option, but then you won't have any way to determine if you've actually sent a message or simply thought you should and then forgot.

✔ **After Deleting or Moving a Message:** Select an option from this drop-down list to determine how you want Inbox to respond when you're finished with a message. You may need to experiment with the three possibilities to see which one fits your way of working.

✔ **Empty Deleted Items:** Finally, use the selections in this drop-down list to tell Inbox what to do with messages that you delete.

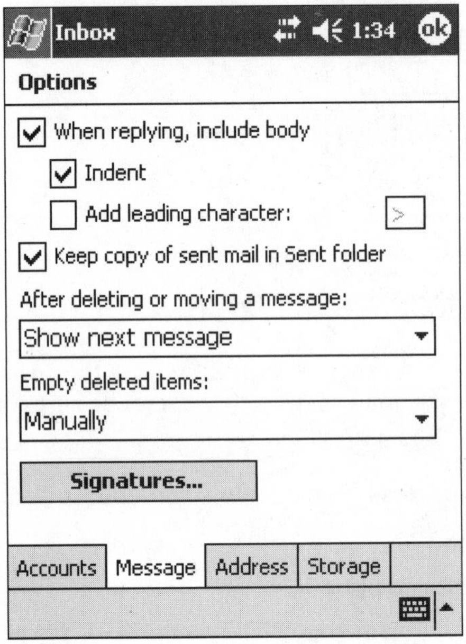

Figure 14-9:
Set the
message
options the
way you
want them.

Getting e-mail addresses

Chapter 6 helps you play around with the iPAQ address book to add contact information for the people you deal with. Now that you're about to use e-mail on your iPAQ, you begin reaping the benefits from those efforts.

Pocket Inbox can use the e-mail addresses contained in your contacts list. It can also use online address books to verify e-mail addresses. To control how these options work, open Pocket Inbox and choose Tools⇨Options to display the Options screen, and then click the Address tab, as shown in Figure 14-10.

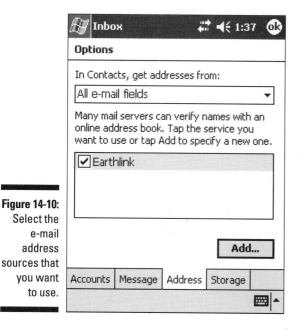

Figure 14-10:
Select the
e-mail
address
sources that
you want
to use.

Use the In Contacts, Get Address From drop-down list to determine which
fields in the contacts list to use for e-mail addresses when you enter a name
rather than an e-mail address. In most cases, this doesn't matter because
the majority of your message recipients probably each use one main e-mail
address. This can make a difference if you regularly send e-mail to a group
of people who each have separate home and work e-mail addresses. In that
case, you can use one e-mail address field for their home address and a different one for each person's work address.

If you use your iPAQ only to read and compose e-mail messages, and then use
ActiveSync to transfer those messages to Outlook on your desktop PC for
sending, make certain that you don't select a mail server for verifying e-mail
addresses on your iPAQ. (Refer to Figure 14-10.) If you do select this option,
your iPAQ may lock up when it searches for the mail server and can't find it.
For information on using ActiveSync, you may want to refer to Chapter 5.

Setting your message storage location

If you have a memory storage card for your iPAQ, you can use the storage
card to store any messages and any attachments. To select this option,
choose Tools⇨Options to display the Options screen, and then click the
Storage tab (shown in Figure 14-11). Enable the Store Attachments on Storage
Card check box.

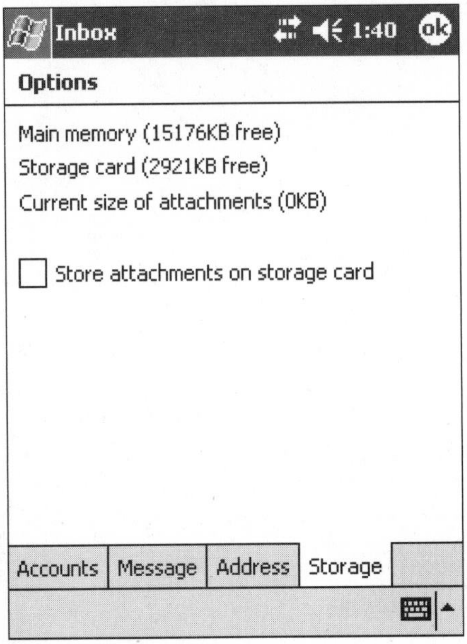

Inbox   📶 ◀€ 1:40   ok

Options

Main memory (15176KB free)
Storage card (2921KB free)
Current size of attachments (0KB)

☐ Store attachments on storage card

| Accounts | Message | Address | Storage |

Figure 14-11:
You can store messages and attachments on a storage card if you have one inserted into your iPAQ.

Sending and Receiving E-Mail

E-mail was really one of the great inventions of the computing age. E-mail made it possible to send a quick message at any time and to have that message delivered almost instantly. And unlike other forms of communication, e-mail is also cheap and has the ability to bridge time differences between people anywhere in the world. You can send a message to your friend half way around the world when it's convenient for you, and you don't have to worry about waking them with an expensive phone call. They, of course, can respond when they're available — whether that's right now or hours from now.

Your iPAQ has the ability to make e-mail even more convenient. Now you can use e-mail almost anywhere and at any time.

Creating a message

Creating an e-mail message is a very simple process. It's almost the same as writing out a quick note except that, in an e-mail message, you need to add the recipient's address and a subject line.

To create an e-mail message, choose New on the Pocket Inbox menu bar. This opens a blank message form like the one I'm using in Figure 14-12. Then, follow these steps:

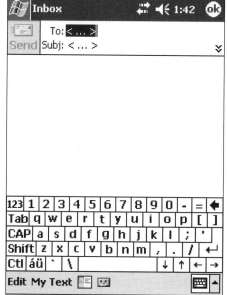

Figure 14-12:
Enter your
e-mail
message
using the
message
form shown
here.

1. **Tap the double down arrows to the right of the subject line to display the Cc, Bcc, and Account fields in addition to the To and Subj fields.**

   You can hide the extra fields by tapping the double up arrows. The Cc field enables you to send a copy of your message to an additional recipient without making them the primary recipient. Use the Account field to choose the method for sending the message.

   The Bcc (blind carbon copy) field is a really handy tool. People you list only in the Bcc field get the message, but their names and e-mail addresses don't appear on anyone's copy of the message. You can use this to great advantage if you need to send the same message separately to a whole bunch of people, because no one knows who else was listed in the Bcc field of the message, and therefore they don't know who else got the message. The Bcc field offers two other advantages, too. If you print an e-mail message, the message header normally prints at the top of the message, and the header contains a list of the recipients. By using the Bcc field for most recipients, you reduce the amount of paper needed to print the message. Also, by using the Bcc field, you eliminate the problem of someone responding by clicking the Reply All button; because no recipients are shown, you're the only person who gets the reply.

2. **Enter the name of the recipient or his e-mail address in the To field.**

   You can click To if you want to select the message recipients from your address list. If you click To, you see a screen where you can select from only those people in your address list who have e-mail addresses.

3. **Use the Subj line to briefly describe your message. When you tap the < . . . >, you can enter the subject text, which replaces the < . . . > as you type.**

   Coming up with a good subject line can be a real art because you want to distill your meaning down to just a few words. The message recipient needs to be able to grasp how important the message is just from seeing the first few words of the subject line — long subject lines probably can't display completely in his or her Inbox.

4. **After you've finished composing your message, click the Send button to place the message into your Outbox folder.**

   Items in the Outbox folder go out the next time the mail server is contacted.

Sending and receiving messages

If you configured Pocket Inbox to automatically send and receive e-mail, you don't have to do anything special to send the messages from your Outbox. Those messages go out and any new messages are received as soon as your iPAQ connects to the mail server.

You can, however, tell your iPAQ to send and receive messages immediately by clicking the Send/Receive button (the button with two envelopes at the right side of the Inbox menu bar). Depending on your settings, you may need to connect to the Internet manually, and you may need to enter your mail server's user name and password.

Organizing messages in folders

By default, Pocket Inbox creates several folders for organizing your e-mail messages. Figure 14-13 shows the typical array of folders that you see if you click the view list just below the title bar. (In the figure, the title of the list is Show because I am deciding what I want to show — normally, it shows the name of the selected folder.)

Getting the entire story

If you want to get a quick overview of the status of your messages, simply choose Tools⟳Status. As Figure 14-14 shows, you can easily see what needs to be done.

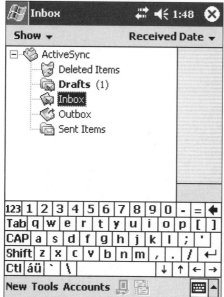

Figure 14-13:
Folders
make it
far easier
to organize
your
messages.

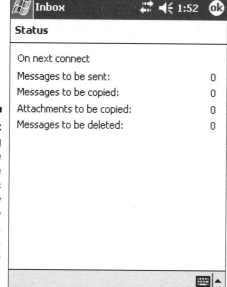

Figure 14-14:
Checking
the
message
status tells
you how
many
message
tasks are
currently
pending.

Don't depend on the Message Status screen to tell you if you have any incoming messages waiting to be retrieved. Inbox has no way to determine if you have any incoming messages until you actually connect to the mail server.

Exchanging Messages with Outlook

Just as you can use your iPAQ for offline browsing when you're not connected to the Internet, you can use your iPAQ for offline e-mail. In both cases, the key component is ActiveSync, because ActiveSync allows your iPAQ and your desktop PC to share important information in a controlled manner.

Because you need to use Outlook on your desktop PC to share e-mail with your iPAQ, the HP iPAQ Companion CD-ROM includes a full version of Outlook 2002. If you have not already installed Outlook 2002 (or later), you need to get out your HP iPAQ Companion CD-ROM and do so before you can continue.

After you install Outlook on your desktop PC, you can share e-mail messages between your iPAQ and your desktop PC by selecting the Inbox option in ActiveSync. To do so, open ActiveSync and click the Options button to open the Options screen. Then, make certain that the Inbox check box is selected. If you like, you can click the Settings button for more precise control over the way e-mail is shared.

You can share e-mail only between your iPAQ and one desktop PC. If you use two different desktop PCs, carefully choose one for sharing e-mail messages because you can use only that one desktop PC.

Part V
Multimedia Time

The 5th Wave   By Rich Tennant

"Oh, well shoot! Must be that new paint program on my iPAQ."

In this part . . .

*N*ow it's time to have some fun with your iPAQ. In this part, you see why your iPAQ can be a great musical companion, how you can read all sorts of the new electronic books on your iPAQ, how to make your iPAQ into the perfect partner for your digital camera, and why your iPAQ is the ultimate handheld game machine. You also see how to replace that heavy old laptop and use your iPAQ as the ultimate way to carry along your PowerPoint presentations.

Chapter 15

Using Your iPAQ for Music

*T*hese days, it seems like every store is trying to sell you one of those single-purpose, pocket-sized music players. Well, you can save your money because your iPAQ can easily master that little task — and even throws in a bunch of extras that those other boxes simply can't match. This chapter shows you how to do it all and make those iPod users wish they had iPAQs in their pockets!

Using Windows Media Player

Your iPAQ uses a special version of Windows Media Player to play music and other multimedia files. You can also use Windows Media Player on your desktop PC to create music files for use on your iPAQ and then to transfer them to your iPAQ.

If you haven't already, be sure to upgrade the Windows Media Player on your desktop PC to the latest version. This ensures that you have the best possible version for preparing music to share with your iPAQ. Just open Windows Media Player by clicking the Windows Media Player icon on your desktop or Quick Launch toolbar, and then choose Help⇨Check For Player Updates to see if any free updates are available.

Copying music illegally can get you into a heap of trouble. Recording companies and artists quite rightly wish to protect their property by enforcing their rights under copyright laws. These laws generally prohibit you from making copies of music and then selling, trading, or giving away those copies. Making a copy of music that you own — such as a purchased audio CD — for your own private use on a device such as your iPAQ is generally considered acceptable. Unfortunately, no one really knows what the courts may decide tomorrow, so be very careful when it comes to copying any music, no matter what the source or reason.

Transferring music to your iPAQ

Audio CDs are a great medium for distributing music. They're relatively small, fairly immune to casual damage, and they produce very high-quality sound. But unless you've got awfully big pockets, audio CDs aren't all that great as a portable music source. Not only are they too big, but they're also prone to skipping — even when played in really good portable CD players.

Audio CDs hold uncompressed sound recordings, which means that a complete recording can use up to 700MB of space. Your iPAQ, of course, probably has nowhere near that much storage room. Windows Media Player can compress audio tracks to a fraction of their original size. Some sound quality is lost when compressing an audio track, but you don't notice the difference when listening to music on your iPAQ. But even with compression, you likely don't want to copy an entire audio CD to your iPAQ unless you add a memory storage card. See "Expanding your iPAQ's Musical Capabilities" later in this chapter for more information.

You may have to connect your iPAQ to your desktop PC by using the sync cable (see Chapter 5) in order for Windows Media Player to detect your iPAQ.

To copy music from an audio CD to your iPAQ, follow these steps:

1. **Open Windows Media Player on your desktop PC.**

2. **Insert the audio CD into your CD drive.**

3. **Click the Copy from CD button on the left side of the screen to display the tracks on the audio CD.**

   If you have an Internet connection, Windows Media Player attempts to obtain the track information from a music database located on the Internet.

   Figure 15-1 shows how the Windows Media Player appears when it's ready to begin copying the tracks.

4. **Make sure that the tracks you want are checked. Then, click the Copy Music button to first copy them to your desktop's hard drive.**

5. **Click the Copy to CD or Device button on the left side of the screen.**

Windows Media Player examines your iPAQ to see how much space is available and then displays the music files in the currently open media library as well as the music files on your iPAQ. Note that Windows Media Player compresses the music files as it copies them to your iPAQ so that more music fits into the available space.

6. **Select the tracks that you want to copy to your iPAQ and then click the Copy button. Figure 15-2 shows how this process appears as files are being copied.**

Figure 15-1: Copy the music tracks to your desktop PC's hard drive first.

Figure 15-2: When the music is on your hard drive, you can copy it to your iPAQ.

Creating a play list

After you have copied the music files onto your iPAQ, you can create a play list by selecting the music that you want to hear. If you have enough storage to store several different complete audio CDs on your iPAQ, you may even want to create several different play lists.

To set up a play list, follow these steps:

1. **Click the Start button on your iPAQ and choose Windows Media from the Start menu on your iPAQ.**

2. **Choose Playlist on the menu bar, and then tap the plus sign (+) at the far lower-left side of the toolbar to display the list of songs.**

3. **Select the songs that you want to include (see Figure 15-3), and then click OK.**

    In this case, I want to include several of the songs and I tapped the information icon at the lower-left to view information about the current selection.

4. **Tap OK.**

Figure 15-3: Choose the songs that you want in your play list.

Playing your music

After you set up your play list, you can listen to the music. Figure 15-4 shows the Windows Media Player in action.

Figure 15-4:
It's time
to enjoy
the music
that you've
stored on
your iPAQ.

To hear the recording in stereo, use headphones. You can also play back the music through a set of small battery-powered amplified speakers like the ones often used with desktop PCs.

Music playback can be a major drain on your iPAQ's battery. Be sure that you're starting out with a fully charged battery and that you've turned off the backlight on your iPAQ.

If you're using headphones, look for a small *R* on one earpiece and a small *L* on the other. That way you can be certain that the right and left channels are playing in the correct ear.

Setting the Windows Media Player options

You can make your iPAQ more convenient as a music player by customizing the buttons on the front of your iPAQ so that they have special functions for playing music. You don't have to worry about screwing up the normal operation of your iPAQ — the buttons assume their special functions only when Windows Media Player is open.

To set up these special functions, open Windows Media Player and choose Tools⇨Settings⇨Buttons, which displays the Options screen shown in Figure 15-5.

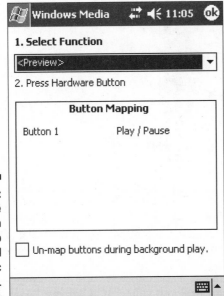

Windows Media   11:05   ok

1. Select Function

<Preview>

2. Press Hardware Button

Button Mapping	
Button 1	Play / Pause

☐ Un-map buttons during background play.

Figure 15-5: Set up the buttons on your iPAQ to control music playback.

To assign a function to one of the buttons, first choose the function from the drop-down list. Then, press the button that you want to use for the function. You can remove an assigned function from a button by selecting <Un-map> from the drop-down list and then pressing the button. Tap OK when you're finished.

Because Windows Media Player continues to play in the background when you switch to another application on your iPAQ, it's best not to select the Un-Map Buttons During Background Play check box because doing so makes it harder for you to control Windows Media Player when it plays in the background.

Expanding Your iPAQ's Musical Capabilities

The iPAQ is easily expanded to provide even more music playback capabilities. I take a quick look at a couple of options that you may find quite interesting.

Adding storage space

You may have noticed that my iPAQ had lots of room for storing music. (Refer to Figure 15-2.) One of the problems with using an iPAQ as a portable music player is that it doesn't have much room for music files in the standard storage space that comes built into an iPAQ. Fortunately, it's easy to expand your iPAQ's capacity by using a memory storage card. In my case, I added a 256MB Secure Digital (SD) memory card from SanDisk (www.sandisk.com) to allow my iPAQ to store several hours of music. You can also find excellent memory cards from SimpleTech (www.simpletech.com).

Internet radio for Wi-Fi users

If you have a Wi-Fi connection for your iPAQ, a whole new world is literally open to you — Internet radio. Stations all over the world now broadcast over the Internet, and iPAQs using the Windows Mobile 2003 operating system can let you listen to them by using Windows Media Player. If you can't find something interesting to listen to with the whole world available to you, you probably aren't trying.

To find live Internet radio stations, you use Pocket Internet Explorer (see Chapter 13). For example, Figure 15-6 shows the live stream selection available at DeutschlandRadio (www.dradio.de).

I generally find that it's easier to locate my favorite Internet radio by using the radio tuner feature in Windows Media Player on my desktop PC. The Windows Media Player on the iPAQ doesn't offer this feature, but when you've located the correct URL on your desktop, it's easy to enter that same URL on your iPAQ.

Figure 15-6:
Look for a
Windows
Media live
stream
option with
Pocket
Internet
Explorer.

Figure 15-7 shows how Windows Media Player appears when playing a live stream from an Internet radio station. Although you cannot tell from the figure, the station, Deutschlandfunk, was playing "We're Men in Tights" from the famous Mel Brooks movie, thus making it nearly impossible to complete this chapter because I was laughing so hard.

Figure 15-7:
Windows
Media
Player is
playing a
live stream
from an
Internet
radio
station.

After you find some Internet radio stations that you enjoy, choose Tools⇨Add Web Favorite in Windows Media Player to save the URLs of those stations on your iPAQ. You can then use the Playlist command to open the same station in the future without going through Pocket Internet Explorer.

Conduits Pocket Player

Windows Media Player isn't your only option for playing music on your iPAQ. Figure 15-8 shows the Conduits Pocket Player (www.conduits.com), which you may want to consider getting — especially if you want some cool features like visualizations and a graphic equalizer. Visualizations are graphics that display to visually represent the sounds that are playing, and the graphic equalizer allows you to tailor the frequency response precisely during playback.

Figure 15-8:
Conduits
Pocket
Player is an
interesting
alternative
media
player for
your iPAQ.

Conduits Pocket Player offers full support for the new Ogg Vorbis music file format — a feature that you can't find in Windows Media Player.

When you're playing MP3 or Ogg Vorbis music files, Conduits Pocket Player offers the option of displaying a graphic equalizer so that you can adjust the characteristics of the sound playback. For example, you might want to boost the mid frequencies to make vocals easier to understand or you might want to pump up the bass to compensate for the limited low frequency capabilities of most ear bud headsets.

Chapter 16

More Multimedia

. . . .

. . . .

Although playing music may seem like the most obvious way to use multimedia content on your iPAQ, that's clearly not the limit of what your iPAQ can do. In fact, as this chapter shows, your iPAQ is an excellent video content delivery machine, too. You can display and edit digital photos, watch movies and other types of video, and you can even let your iPAQ replace a bunch of heavy books.

Working with Photos

If you've got a digital camera in addition to your iPAQ, you've probably given some thought to using the two devices as partners. After all, your iPAQ is a computer, and digital images are in their natural element on a computer. Why not use your iPAQ to put those finishing touches on your digital images?

Sharing photos with your digital camera

In order to work with digital images on your iPAQ, you first have to move those images from your digital camera to your iPAQ. This can be very simple in some cases and very difficult in others — depending on a number of hardware and software factors that I show you in the following sections. For example, in some cases you may be able to simply share a memory storage card, but in others you may even need to bring your desktop PC into the act between your iPAQ and your digital camera.

What's on your iPAQ?

As you may have guessed, different iPAQ models come with different image viewing applications — or none at all. In fact, the h1900 series lacks several applications that are included with the other models, and the h2200 series and h4100 series share one application (Pictures) but have a different second one (iPAQ Image Viewer versus iPAQ Image Zone). It also appears that Hewlett-Packard may even be changing the set of standard applications depending on when a particular iPAQ was built.

This confusing situation means that it really isn't possible to provide meaningful coverage of the graphics programs that may or may not be included with each iPAQ.

To make things easier on you, I show you a couple of third-party programs that run on any iPAQ model and that offer far more capabilities than any of the built-in applications that Hewlett-Packard provides. These programs are useful no matter which iPAQ you use.

Most digital cameras store images in JPEG, BMP, or TIFF file format. Of these, JPEG is often the best to work with on an iPAQ if for no better reason than the fact that JPEG images are generally *compressed* — they take less storage space.

Sharing digital images on memory cards

The most straightforward method of sharing digital images between your digital camera and your iPAQ is to use a memory card that's compatible with both units. If this is an option, you can typically just pop the memory card out of the camera, plug it into your iPAQ, and you're ready to go — almost.

Your iPAQ generally needs a bit of help finding files that are stored on a memory card if those files aren't stored in a folder called My Documents. Digital cameras, of course, typically have little (if any) need for folders, so they often store image files on the memory card without using any directory structure. Therefore, you may need to explicitly tell whatever software you're using on your iPAQ to look on the memory card for image files because they won't be stored in the iPAQ's preferred location.

Of course, life is often more complicated than we may like. Not all digital cameras use iPAQ-compatible memory cards. Even those that do may not be able to handle a memory card that has as much capacity as the ones that you can use in your iPAQ.

If you want to share memory cards between a digital camera and an iPAQ, you may want to spend some time researching memory card compatibility *before* you buy a digital camera. Then, get a camera that uses the same memory cards as your iPAQ. Of course, if you already bought that digital camera, you may just get lucky and find out that it can use the same memory cards as your iPAQ.

Connecting to your digital camera

The one foolproof method of transferring image files from your digital camera to your iPAQ is to first transfer them from your digital camera to your desktop PC. You can use the software that came with your digital camera to do this. Then, use ActiveSync to send those files to your iPAQ.

Editing photos on your iPAQ

You aren't going to find highly sophisticated photo-editing software bundled with your iPAQ — no matter which model you have. Fortunately, though, you can easily correct this problem by adding an inexpensive piece of software to your iPAQ.

Downloading and installing new software on your iPAQ is pretty simple, but it's a subject that I in detail in this chapter. If you want to try out the software shown in this chapter, you may want to hold off until you've had a chance to read Chapter 18 (or you can skip ahead, of course).

Realize that no matter how good the software is, your iPAQ is far more suited to fairly simple image-editing tasks than it is to professional-level photo manipulation. Graphic artists have a good reason to use desktop PCs with large monitors: Editing photos is easier when you can see more detail, and the iPAQ's screen is too small to show much detail.

Of course, digital photo editing is a subject that can easily take up several complete books. Rather than try to cover the topic badly in a few pages, I'm simply going to show you one of the tools that's available for the iPAQ so that you can get an idea of the possibilities.

The tool that I've selected is Pocket Artist from Conduits Technologies. You can download a trial version from www.conduits.com. Figure 16-1 shows an example of the items that are available when you choose Pocket Artist Menu⇨Tools.

When you take photos with your digital camera, some adjustment of the brightness, contrast, or colors can often really improve the images. As Figure 16-1 shows, Pocket Artist gives you easy access to these adjustments.

If you want to go beyond basic adjustments and get creative, Pocket Artist provides tools to help there, too. For example, Figure 16-2 shows the list of tools that appear when you tap the Paintbrush icon on the toolbar.

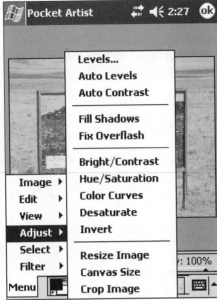

Figure 16-1:
Pocket
Artist gives
you all
the basic
image-
editing tools
that you
need to fix
up your
digital
photos.

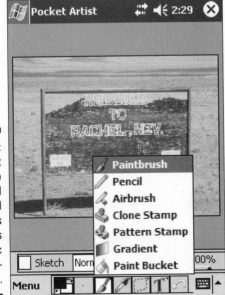

Figure 16-2:
Pocket
Artist also
goes well
beyond
the basics
with tools
for artistic
manipu-
lation.

No matter where you manipulate images — on your iPAQ or on your desktop PC — working with a copy of important files rather than with the original is always a good idea. When editing an image, you can easily go too far and then want to go back several steps. Working with a copy is the safest way to ensure that you can always go back to the original.

Displaying your photos

If you've ever tried to show people the digital photos that you've taken, and tried to use the display screen on your digital camera to do so, you know how difficult and frustrating that can be. Not only is the screen too small for good viewing, but cycling through the images usually requires pressing the right buttons.

One alternative is to use your iPAQ and create a slideshow of your images. ACDSee Mobile (www.acdsystems.com) can easily do this, and as Figure 16-3 shows, it can also display zoomed views of the images on your iPAQ.

ACDSee Mobile is one of the few iPAQ applications that can display TIFF images.

Figure 16-3: You can zoom in on the images on your iPAQ with ACDSee Mobile.

Video on Your iPAQ

You may be surprised to discover just how capable your iPAQ is at playing video content. In most cases, you don't even need anything beyond the software that's already installed, and you can watch streaming content from the Internet, videos that you've created, or even TV shows that you've recorded on your desktop PC.

Streaming video from the Internet

If you have a Wi-Fi connection, you can watch streaming video from various Web sites that offer video content. Figure 16-4 shows an example of the movie trailer for *Pirates of the Caribbean* playing in Windows Media Player on an iPAQ. This example was from the Windows Media Mobile Web site (`windowsmediamobile.theplatform.com`).

Figure 16-4: You can play streaming video on your iPAQ using Windows Media Player.

To view video full screen on your iPAQ, choose Tools➪Settings➪Audio & Video in Windows Media Player. Then, select your preferred setting from the Play Video in Full Screen drop-down list.

Creating your own movies

Finding streaming video on the Web is still a bit difficult, but you can use the free Windows Movie Maker (version 2 or later) to create video to play on your iPAQ. This might be an excellent option if you're taking a long flight on one of those budget airlines whose only customer amenities are six-month-old, dog-eared magazines. You can use Windows Movie Maker to make highly compressed copies of your favorite movies and then store them on a Secure Digital (SD) memory card. Figure 16-5 shows one of my home movies playing on my iPAQ after being converted to Pocket PC format by using Windows Movie Maker.

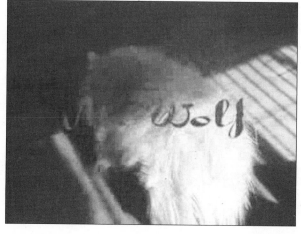

Figure 16-5:
You can use Windows Movie Maker to convert your movies for playback on your iPAQ.

Although I don't have room here to show you how to use Windows Movie Maker, I must mention one setting that's very important when producing a movie for use on your iPAQ. When you reach Step 3 in Windows Movie Maker and click the Save to My Computer to Launch the Save Movie Wizard button, select Other settings on the second wizard screen. Then, you can select one of three settings specifically designed for playback on a Pocket PC. The movie in Figure 16-5 was created with the Video for Pocket PC (Full Screen 218 Kbps) setting. This setting allows you to store over 90 minutes of video on a 256MB SD memory card.

Watching TV on your iPAQ

To watch TV shows on your iPAQ, you need a means of recording, compressing, and transferring those shows to your iPAQ. The system that I've found that best handles this whole process is SnapStream PVS (`www.snapstream.com`). SnapStream PVS uses a TV tuner card installed in your desktop PC to record TV shows from any available source so that you can watch the shows when it's convenient. This program also has a number of other really cool features, such as the capability of supplying streaming video to any PC on your network.

After you've recorded the show using SnapStream PVS, you can then compress that recording and transfer it to your iPAQ by using PocketPVS. PocketPVS uses Windows Media Player on your iPAQ to display the video.

At the default settings, you need about 1MB of storage space for every minute of video that you store on your iPAQ. This means that you can probably just fit a typical full-length movie onto a 128MB storage card. If you compare the postage stamp size of a 128MB SD memory card with the size of a standard VHS video tape, this has to be one of the more amazing feats of miniaturization around. No one could ever mistake TV viewing on the tiny iPAQ screen for a big screen, high definition TV broadcast, but the quality is certainly good enough to be enjoyable.

If you don't have a TV tuner card in your desktop PC, SnapStream offers some very good ones at quite reasonable prices on their Web site.

Displaying PowerPoint Slides on Your iPAQ

Okay, I admit that the screen on your iPAQ is too small to be very effective if you want to give a PowerPoint presentation to a crowd. Even if everyone is really friendly, that tiny screen just isn't going to do the job. If you want to make a good impression, your iPAQ is going to need a little help. Fortunately, that help is finally here.

I've found a couple very handy adapter cards that enable your iPAQ to display an image by using a large screen monitor, a digital projector, or possibly even a large TV set. With these cards, your iPAQ can show the world (or at least a large group of people) your PowerPoint presentation or pretty much anything else that appears on your iPAQ's screen.

Your iPAQ's screen has a resolution of 240 x 320 pixels — far lower than the typical computer monitor or even a TV set. Fortunately, both of the video adapter cards that I discuss have the ability to display a much higher resolution when connected to a large display. In fact, in some cases they're able to display up to 1024 x 768 pixels.

The two iPAQ video display cards that I tested are:

- ✔ Margi Presenter-to-Go (www.margi.com)
- ✔ Colorgraphic Voyager VGA CF (www.colorgraphic.net)

As I write this, these cards are both available in the CompactFlash (CF) format. In addition, Margi has a new SD card. If your iPAQ has both types of expansion slots, I recommend the CF card — it's both a bit tougher and more convenient (because using a CF card leaves the SD slot open for a memory card).

Depending on the expansion slots that are available on your iPAQ, either of the video adapter cards may work well for you, but the two units do have some differences. Here's a list of the most important differences that I found:

- ✔ The Margi Presenter-to-Go includes a remote control that works through your iPAQ's infrared port. This makes it possible to control a PowerPoint presentation from some distance away.

- ✔ The Colorgraphic Voyager VGA CF has the ability to display your presentation on a TV set that has a standard composite video input (an RCA jack). This means that you can give a presentation even if a large screen monitor or a digital projector isn't available.

- ✔ The Margi Presenter-to-Go includes a basic application for displaying PowerPoint slides. The Colorgraphic Voyager VGA CF includes a shareware version of Conduits Pocket Slides for this purpose. Because the iPAQ has no native version of PowerPoint, you need special applications like these in order to show PowerPoint slides with your iPAQ.

Regardless of the video adapter card that you choose, using your iPAQ for presentations certainly makes it easier for you to bring your show along in your pocket.

Reading eBooks

It's pretty clear to anyone who uses an iPAQ that having a computer that fits easily into your shirt pocket opens a whole new range of possibilities. The *eBook* represents a great example of just how much these new ideas can change the way we do ordinary things. In this case, that ordinary thing is something you're doing right now in the old traditional way — reading a book. If this were an eBook, you wouldn't be looking at ink printed on paper, but rather words on your iPAQ screen.

What are eBooks?

People have been reading text on computer screens for as long as there have been computer screens. It's reasonable to ask, therefore, just how eBooks are different from the plain old on-screen text that you've been seeing since you started using computers. Actually, plain document text and eBooks have several differences:

- ✔ Because your iPAQ is about the size of a paperback book, it's easy to hold your iPAQ in your hand while you read an eBook. This makes reading eBooks far more like reading "real" books than like reading text on a computer screen.

- ✔ The Microsoft Reader program that you use to read eBooks allows you to search, bookmark, and annotate eBooks. You can even ask for the definition of unfamiliar words as you're reading.

- ✔ Many popular books — including current best-sellers — are available as eBooks but not as plain text files because the eBook format allows publishers to control the distribution of titles. This way, both the authors and publishers can earn the money that they deserve from their efforts.

- ✔ With your backlit iPAQ screen, you can read an eBook in the dark without trying to find a flashlight with working batteries.

eBooks are stored in a highly compressed format that greatly reduces the amount of storage space that's needed. This format also allows publishers to control who can read an eBook. Because of their special format, you need a special program to read eBooks. On your iPAQ, that program is Microsoft Reader.

Downloading eBooks

In order to read an eBook on your iPAQ, you've got to first get those eBooks into your iPAQ. The process is similar to copying other files to your iPAQ, but with a few differences.

Building your eBook library

The first thing that you need to do is find some eBooks that are worth reading. For this, you may want to visit the Microsoft Reader Web site (www. microsoft.com/reader/us/shop/default.asp) where you can find links to several different eBook sellers. Some sites offer a selection of free eBooks in addition to titles that you can purchase.

Unfortunately, many things fit loosely into the definition of eBooks. A lot of what are called eBooks aren't designed to be read on your iPAQ. When you download eBooks, make certain that you're downloading files that are specified as being Microsoft Reader–compatible files. Otherwise, you're wasting your time (and maybe money) by downloading files that you can't use on your iPAQ.

Understanding digital rights management

When you buy a printed book, the mere fact that it's printed on paper and bound together means that it's really convenient for only one person to read that copy at a time. If you think that the printed book is really good, you may tell a friend about it so that she can buy her own copy. Or you may loan her your copy when you're finished reading the book. But it's unlikely that you can both share one copy at the same time — that would be pretty inconvenient, wouldn't it?

In the past, the ease with which eBooks could be copied and shared has made it difficult to find a lot of really good books in the eBook format. Unfortunately, this ease of copying means that some people feel that it's okay to give other people free copies of any eBooks they may buy. Needless to say, authors and publishers get discouraged when people give away hundreds of copies for each copy that's sold!

In an attempt at making publishing books in eBook format more popular, Microsoft has made the Microsoft Reader Activation Pack available on your iPAQ. This software adds something known as *digital rights management* (DRM) to your iPAQ's Microsoft Reader program. Why should you care about this? It's simple, really. After you run the Microsoft Reader Activation Pack, your copy of the Microsoft Reader can then use eBooks that are copy protected. That is, you can buy premium quality books to read on your iPAQ because those books cannot be copied and shared with other people. In effect, this makes the premium eBooks that you buy act more like printed books, and this gives publishers and authors an incentive to publish more premium eBook titles, so everyone wins.

Managing your eBook library

Managing your eBook collection is easy. The main tasks are to control where your eBooks reside on your iPAQ and to delete eBooks that you no longer need, which frees up space for other uses. Here are some points to consider:

- **Storing:** A memory card is an excellent place to store your eBooks. You don't need any other accessories like modems to read eBooks, so you could keep your entire eBook collection on a memory storage card that you pop in whenever you want to view your library. Remember to place the eBook files in the My Documents folder on the memory storage card.

- **Encountering an error message:** You may encounter a cryptic error message if you try to delete an eBook by using tap-and-hold and selecting Delete from within Reader. If you do, this probably means that the file is set to read-only mode and you can't delete it from within Reader. If this happens, you need to use the next method to delete the file.

✔ **Managing files:** You can use the File Explorer on your iPAQ to delete or move files. Even so, you may find that it's easier to click the Explore button in ActiveSync on your desktop PC and then manage those files from your desktop PC.

✔ **Backing up:** Backing up your eBooks on your desktop PC (see Chapter 5) is an excellent idea — especially if you have purchased some premium titles. That way, you're protected in case anything happens to the file on your iPAQ.

Reading an eBook

Some people build up big collections of fancy-looking books but never read a single one of them. Your eBook collection is probably far more practical — especially because eBooks just don't have the same panache as a library full of leather-bound law books.

To open an eBook, follow these steps:

1. **Click the Start button and choose Programs⇨Microsoft Reader to open the library (see Figure 16-6).**

2. **Tap a book title to open that book.**

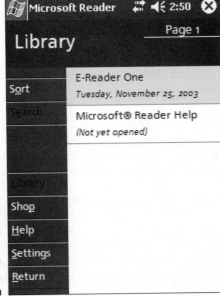

Figure 16-6:
The library shows all the eBooks that are currently on your iPAQ.

Navigating an eBook

Reading an eBook is most definitely different from reading a bound paper book or even from reading a text document on your desktop PC. For one thing, how do you flip the pages?

The title page of each eBook contains several options that you can tap to navigate your way through the book. To begin at the beginning, tap the Go To button and then choose Begin Reading from the menu that pops up. The Microsoft Reader program also keeps track of how far you've read and the last page that you were viewing — so you don't need to try to dog-ear any of the pages!

When you begin reading, the Microsoft Reader program shows several things on each page (see Figure 16-7), and you can use these to navigate your way through the book:

Figure 16-7:
You can navigate by using the arrows on the page.

✔ **Down arrow:** This arrow, located just to the right of the book title, pops up a menu that you can use to return to the beginning, open your list of annotations, view the guidebook, open the library, change the view settings, or return to the last page that you were viewing.

✔ **Left arrow:** Located by the page number, this arrow returns you to the next lower-numbered page. This may not necessarily be the last page that you were reading if you jumped to a page from an annotation or from the index.

✔ **Right arrow:** Displays the next higher-numbered page. The current page number appears between the two page navigation arrows.

✔ **Riffle control:** If you tap-and-hold the page number, you display the *riffle* control along the bottom of the screen, as shown in Figure 16-7. (The riffle control shows the page number and the total number of pages.) Drag the stylus along this control to quickly move through the manuscript pages.

You can also use the Navigator button on the front of the iPAQ to move through the book. Pressing the right side or the lower side of the button moves you forward, and pressing the left side or the upper side of the button moves you back.

One thing that's very different about reading eBooks on your iPAQ compared to reading a text document on your desktop PC is that eBooks always jump an entire page at a time. You don't see the line-by-line scrolling that's common when you're viewing text documents.

Adding notes and such

Have you ever found yourself writing notes on one of those sticky notepads and then placing the note into a book that you were reading? Eventually, it becomes almost impossible to read the book without knocking the notes out of place. And even if they stay where they belong, it can be really hard to remember where you made a note about this and where you made one about that.

When you're reading an eBook, it's really easy to add your own notes to the text and to later go back and refer to those notes. To do so, tap the word or phrase that you wish to annotate, and then choose Add Text Note from the pop-up menu that appears, as shown in Figure 16-8.

Type in your note in the notepad that appears after you choose Add Text Note, and then tap outside the notepad area to complete your note.

After you add notes to the text, you can review your notes with the annotation index. When you open the index, tap the note that you'd like to see, and the Reader opens the note as well as the page where you've added the note. You also see a small note icon next to any line that contains a note.

Tap the keyboard icon to hide the on-screen keyboard when you're viewing existing notes. This enables you to view the eBook page in addition to simply seeing the note itself. You can also tap the *i* in the upper part of the notepad to see the note in context.

You can also add highlighting, a bookmark, or a drawing to the text by choosing the proper option from the pop-up menu that appears when you select text. If you want to quote the text exactly, you can copy the selected text.

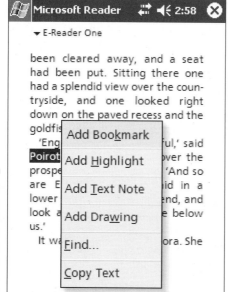

Figure 16-8:
Use this
menu to add
bookmarks
and notes
to your
eBooks.

Reading Laridian PocketBible

The Bible is probably the most popular book of all time for both scholarly and religious reasons, so it's only natural that it's also a popular thing to read on an iPAQ. Laridian (www.laridian.com) makes it easy for people to read and study the Bible through their PocketBible for the iPAQ.

You may well wonder what advantages there might be to reading the Bible on an iPAQ as opposed to simply picking up a printed version. Actually, several come to mind:

- ✔ **Reading translations:** You can read and study from multiple translations of the Bible on your iPAQ. This makes it easy to compare the different versions so that you can more easily understand passages that may seem a little confusing.

- ✔ **Searching quickly:** You can find what you want by using the find features in PocketBible. This makes it much easier to find references to specific topics.

- ✔ **Making notes:** You can add your own notes, with hyperlinks to Bible verses so that it's easy to keep track of your references.

- ✔ **Using other related sources:** Additional reference books (such as dictionaries) are available from Laridian. This is especially useful if you want to study the text or prepare talks on biblical topics.

Your iPAQ is also much smaller and easier to carry around than a printed Bible — especially when you consider all the extra books (such as different translations) that you can get from Laridian. Your iPAQ doesn't get any heavier when you add those extra books, either!

Chapter 17

Playing Around with Your iPAQ

In This Chapter

▶ Playing games on your iPAQ

▶ Finding some new games

*I*f you are one of those people who feels guilty about taking a few minutes now and then to enjoy yourself, you may want to just skip this chapter. But it would probably be better if you didn't because no matter how you look at it, everyone needs the chance to relax and unwind a bit. In fact, I bet that you could be even more productive if you let your hair down and have some fun.

The iPAQ is a surprisingly good video game machine. In fact, your iPAQ can run literally hundreds of games in dozens of genres, so no matter what type of game interests you, you're bound to find at least one that fits your definition of fun. In the limited space that I have available, I show you a few games that I like, but at least this should serve to whet your appetite. Go ahead, have some fun!

I Wanna Play Right Now!

When you really need to play a game, you need it right now. After all, can you predict just when you'll need to spend a few minutes kicking back and taking it easy? That's why your iPAQ comes standard with a couple of games, Jawbreaker and Solitaire, so that you can just get to it and have some fun.

To quickly find the games on your iPAQ, tap the Start button and then choose Programs to open the Programs folder. Tap the Games folder that appears at the top of the Programs folder.

Jawbreaker

Jawbreaker is one of those deceptively simple-looking games that quickly becomes quite addictive. The whole point of the game is to remove the colored balls (jawbreakers) from the screen by tapping groups of balls of one color. Figure 17-1 shows the screen after the first couple of moves in a typical game.

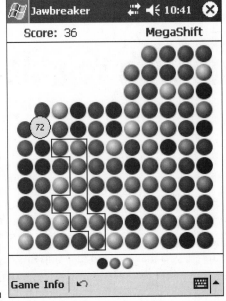

Figure 17-1:
Tap groups
of a single
color to
remove the
balls and
score
points.

The challenge in Jawbreaker is to get the highest possible score by putting together the largest possible grouping of a single color before you tap the group to remove it. Each extra ball that you add to a group multiplies the score because you are awarded points based on this simple formula:

```
group points = number of balls x (number of balls - 1)
```

So, for example, a group of 2 balls is worth 2 points, a group of 3 balls is worth 6 points, and a group of 4 balls is worth 12 points. In the figure, the selected group has 9 balls, so the point value is 9 times 8 or 72.

The strategy for making larger groups of a single color is to remove small groups lower down so that you drop the balls into a position where larger groups of a single color are created. It sounds simple, but you quickly discover just how much of a challenge that can be.

Just to keep things interesting, Jawbreaker includes four different ways to play the game. Choose Game⇨Options to display the Options screen, and then select one of the game play options from the Game Style drop-down list box.

If you let someone else play Jawbreaker on your iPAQ, select the Guest Mode option on the Options screen to prevent their scores from being permanently recorded — you wouldn't want them posting the new high score, after all!

Tapping the Close button in Jawbreaker does not actually close the game. If you want to really stop the game, tap the Start button and choose Settings to display the Settings screen. Tap the System tab and then tap the Memory icon to display the Memory screen. Tap the Running Programs tab and then choose Jawbreaker from the list of running programs. Tap Stop to close Jawbreaker and then tap OK to close the Memory screen. Tap OK to close the Settings screen.

Playing Solitaire

Solitaire is probably the all-time favorite computer game. Sure, many fun games have all sorts of fans, but Solitaire has probably burned up more computer time than virtually any other computer game. One reason for this may simply be that versions of Solitaire are available on almost any type of computer. Solitaire is also installed on every iPAQ right out of the box, so you can play if you want to do so.

Figure 17-2 shows the iPAQ version of Solitaire. To play Solitaire, click the Start button and choose Programs to open the Programs folder. Tap the Games folder to open it and click the Solitaire icon to start a new game.

To choose your game options, choose Tools⇨Options to display the Options screen.

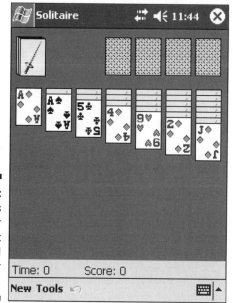

Figure 17-2: Solitaire is another game that you can find on your iPAQ.

Finding More Games to Challenge You

As you may have guessed, the fertile minds of game developers have created more for the iPAQ than just the ones previously mentioned in this chapter. All sorts of games have been developed for the iPAQ.

Downloading iPAQ games

Most iPAQ games are quite small, so downloading them from the Web is one of the best ways to get them. Many iPAQ games are free, but you can also find shareware games and commercial products at various sites. *Shareware* programs come in several varieties, but they all share one common thread: You get the chance to give them a try before you buy them. If you like the game, you send in a small amount of money to register your copy. Registration allows the game to continue to be used after the expiration date (if one exists). It may also add extra features or simply ease your conscience knowing that you aren't stealing the fruits of someone else's work.

Some Web sites offer several varieties of games in a single listing. If you see notations like PPC and HPC (or something similar), the programs that you want are those listed as PPC.

One of the first places to go for iPAQ games to download is the Pocket PC Downloads Web site at `www.microsoft.com/windowsmobile/resources/downloads/pocketpc/default.mspx`. Here you find links to a number of interesting programs.

For freeware and shareware iPAQ games that you can download, one of the best places is the Tucows Web site at `pda.tucows.com/top_section_142.html`.

Looking at some other iPAQ games

The games that you can play on your iPAQ run the gamut from deceptively simple to extremely complex. Some of the best of them are the ones that seem very simple but end up requiring a lot of strategy to do well.

In this section, I look at some really great games that get you itching to play.

Monopoly

Monopoly is one of those classic board games that almost everyone has played at some point when growing up. Who doesn't remember the hours spent wheeling, dealing, and trying to bankrupt your friends and family members as you moved through familiar streets like St. Charles Place and Boardwalk?

All the fun of Monopoly is now available for your iPAQ, as shown in Figure 17-3. This version, from Handmark (www.handmark.com), allows up to four players in any combination of real people and computer-generated opponents.

Figure 17-3: I'll trade you two railroads for Pacific Avenue.

Handmark's version of Monopoly plays very much like the original board game but it removes the possibility for the banker to dip his or her fingers into the till. Just watch out for property auctions — the computer seems to win most auctions by conveniently ignoring competing bids. (However, you can choose Game⇨Rules and then select the Pass Instead of Auction check box to eliminate the auction option if you prefer.)

Tap the tiny Menu tab in the upper-left corner of the board to display a menu when you want to buy or sell houses and hotels, mortgage a property, or set up a trade. Be sure to do this before you tap the dice — otherwise, you have to wait for your next turn before you can act.

Scrabble

Scrabble is another classic board game that has arrived on the iPAQ. It's one of those enjoyably frustrating games — after you begin playing, you just don't want to quit.

Figure 17-4 shows a game of Scrabble in progress. (As Player 1, I'm winning this time.) Just like with Monopoly, you can play against human or computer-generated opponents. Scrabble is available from Handmark (www.handmark.com).

Figure 17-4:
Scrabble
can be quite
addictive on
your iPAQ.

Warfare Incorporated

If classic board games aren't your style, you may want to check out Warfare Incorporated, another of the Handmark games (www.handmark.com). In this game, your objective is to build a mining colony and defend it against a bunch of hostile opponents. You have to mine ore, build your forces, and try to wipe out the enemy without running out of money or allowing your facilities to be destroyed. It's not as easy as it sounds!

Figure 17-5 shows an example screen from Warfare Incorporated.

Pocket Gambler

If you love to play casino games but you can't always do so — either because a casino isn't next door or because it costs too much — check out Pocket Gambler from ZIO (www.ziointeractive.com/games_ppc.html). Figure 17-6 shows the video poker game — one of seven games that are included in the Pocket Gambler package.

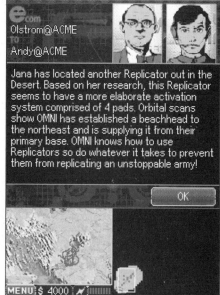

Figure 17-5:
Warfare
Incorporated
pits your
mining
operation
against
ruthless
opponents.

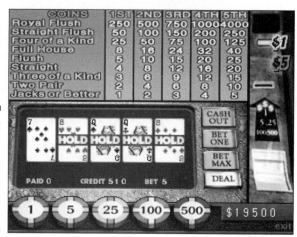

Figure 17-6:
If only I
could find
that cash
out button in
Pocket
Gambler!

Part VI
Working with iPAQ Add-Ons

The 5th Wave   By Rich Tennant

"You can sure do a lot with an iPAQ, but I never thought dressing one up in G.I. Joe clothes and calling it your little desk commander would be one of them."

In this part . . .

You see where to find iPAQ-compatible programs, how to install them, and how to make the ones you want fit into the available space. You discover what you need to make traveling with your iPAQ a truly enjoyable experience by adding the right accessories like a GPS receiver, a translator, or a travel guide to make your iPAQ into a great traveling companion.

Chapter 18

Finding iPAQ Applications

- -

- -

*Y*our iPAQ is pretty handy all by itself, but it can be even more useful with the addition of a few new programs. That's where the versatility of having a real computer that fits into your pocket really shines — your iPAQ isn't limited to performing just one or two dedicated functions. By adding new programs, you can use your iPAQ for virtually unlimited purposes. In fact, almost anything that can be done with a desktop PC can also be done with an iPAQ.

In this chapter, I show you how to get what you want from your iPAQ by finding and installing new applications that are compatible with your iPAQ.

Understanding What Can Run on the iPAQ

Your iPAQ uses an operating system called Windows Mobile 2003. From this name, you may get the impression that any of your Windows programs from your desktop PC can run on your iPAQ; this simply isn't so. Windows Mobile 2003 may be related to the version of Windows that runs on your desktop PC, but the relationship isn't quite close enough to allow you to share your programs.

Here are some important things that you need to know about what can run on your iPAQ:

✔ **For the iPAQ:** If a program is specified as being specifically for the iPAQ, it can almost certainly run on your iPAQ — unless the specifications also indicate that the program is for a specific iPAQ model. Most programs designed for any iPAQ model can also run on other iPAQ models, but this is not always the case. When in doubt, ask the software manufacturer before you buy (or get a trial version if one is available).

✔ **For the Pocket PC 2002:** Most programs that were designed for the Pocket PC 2002 devices also run on Windows Mobile 2003, but a few exceptions do exist. Again, checking with the manufacturer or using a trial version is your safest bet.

✔ **For Windows CE 2.0:** Many programs designed for Windows CE 2.0 also run on the iPAQ, but it's best to try before you buy. Windows CE 2.0 programs swap the positions of the iPAQ's Start button and the program's menu or toolbar, but this change is temporary. After you exit the Windows CE 2.0 program, your iPAQ returns to normal.

✔ **For palm-sized PCs:** Some programs are listed as being for palm-sized PCs. This term could mean many things. For example, it may mean that the program is really for the Palm PC operating system (OS) and is totally incompatible with your iPAQ. Don't buy one of these programs unless you get some assurance that you can get your money back if it doesn't work on your iPAQ.

✔ **For Windows CE HPC or HPC/Pro:** If a program says that it's for Windows CE HPC or HPC/Pro devices, it probably doesn't work on your iPAQ unless it specifically says that it also runs on Pocket PC (PPC) devices. You may even see other variations on this jargon jungle, so always watch for the PPC or iPAQ designation.

One of the most important things to ask for when buying iPAQ software is whether you can try the program to make sure that it works before you plunk down your money. Many iPAQ programs have demo or trial versions that you can check out before buying. If you can't get a trial first, make certain that you can get a refund if the program doesn't work on your iPAQ.

Finding Software on the Web

Most iPAQ software is distributed by way of downloads from the Internet. One of the big reasons for this is that iPAQ software tends to be very compact compared to desktop PC software. An awful lot of functionality can be packed into a very small package when that package is intended for the iPAQ.

The Web sites that distribute iPAQ software tend to fall into two major categories: Web sites that belong to software developers and Web sites that offer software from many different manufacturers. Each has advantages and disadvantages:

✔ **Disadvantage:** A software developer's Web site generally offers only those products produced by that one company, which limits your choices somewhat compared to the more general sites.

✔ **Advantage:** The software developer's Web site may have the most recent updates sooner than the general sites. You may also find *beta* versions that enable you to test features that will appear in upcoming release versions. (Beta software is software that isn't quite ready for prime time — it's a test version that may contain a number of bugs and other gremlins to make life interesting for the testers.)

✔ **Disadvantage:** Sites offering software from a variety of manufacturers can make it a little harder for you if you are looking for software from a specific manufacturer because of the sheer variety of options they offer.

✔ **Advantage:** A Web site that offers software from a variety of manufacturers gives you more choices and often uses a rating system to help you decide which products best suit your needs.

Some great iPAQ software download sites include the following:

✔ www.microsoft.com/windowsmobile/resources/downloads/pocketpc/default.mspx

✔ www.developerone.com

✔ mobile.handango.com/home.jsp?siteId=1

✔ pda.tucows.com/pocketpc.html

✔ www.handmark.com/products/category.php?cat=20

✔ www.pocketgear.com/

Getting down to business

Chapter 17 introduces many different types of games for your iPAQ. Games may be a lot of fun, but playing games doesn't get your work done. If you want to get down to business with your iPAQ, plenty of programs are available to help you do so.

Here's a sample of the types of business-related programs that you can find for the iPAQ:

✔ **Database:** Several developers have filled an important gap in the suite of built-in iPAQ applications by creating database programs. These types of programs can be extremely useful for anyone who needs to keep track of lots of information, such as an inventory listing or the status of rooms in a large convention hotel.

TIP

If you want to use a large database on your iPAQ, the built-in storage memory likely needs to be expanded by using a memory card.

✔ **Unit conversion:** A number of developers have created iPAQ programs that are loaded with different unit conversions, which can be quite useful for anyone working on a large international project or for someone ordering supplies for a building project. They also take the place of pocket reference guides because these programs not only show the conversion factors but also do the math for you.

✔ **Calculator:** You can find applications that turn your iPAQ into a super-sophisticated calculator. These programs come in handy for anyone involved in science or in financial calculations.

✔ **Fax:** Some programs even enable you to send a fax from your iPAQ. Even though e-mail capability is built into the iPAQ, some people don't have e-mail addresses, so sending them a fax may be the only way to quickly get written information into their hands.

Chapter 21 shows some specific examples of some very useful business-related iPAQ programs. Figure 18-1 shows one iPAQ program, eWallet from Ilium Software (www.iliumsoft.com). One difference between programs for your iPAQ and those for your desktop PC is that iPAQ programs tend to be far less expensive, making it much easier to justify adding a handy program that you could really use.

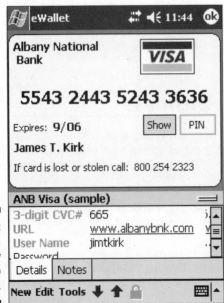

Figure 18-1: eWallet is a very handy addition to your iPAQ.

Adding some utilities

Utility programs aren't the most exciting of iPAQ applications. That's to be expected because most people don't want to put much thought into the inner workings of their iPAQ. Still, the utility programs do have a lot to offer:

- **Taking screen captures:** You may never need to take screen captures of your iPAQ screens, but aren't you glad that someone created that utility so that I can show you the lovely pictures throughout this book?

- **Switching between programs:** Closing down programs on an iPAQ isn't always easy because your iPAQ is supposed to close unneeded programs when something else needs the memory. Still, it's really nice to have a utility program that allows you to easily switch between open programs and to decide for yourself which ones to shut down.

- **Managing memory:** Because memory space is so important on an iPAQ, several utilities have been designed to help you manage memory. Some seek out useless files that can be deleted, and others make it possible to cram more into memory by compressing data into less space.

- **Reading PDF documents:** Because many important documents are only available in Portable Document Format (PDF), you may want to be able to read those types of documents on your iPAQ. Luckily, software has been created for you to do so.

- **Using a scripting utility:** If you often use your iPAQ to perform complicated tasks that require a whole series of precise steps, a *scripting utility* could be quite useful. A scripting utility enables you to create a *script* (or macro) that goes through the whole process for you so that you don't have to keep repeating it yourself.

These are just a few examples of the broad range of useful utility programs that you can find for your iPAQ. Figure 18-2 shows one of these utilities, Custom Convert from Surerange (`www.surerange.com`).

Many utility programs are useful only occasionally. Rather than using up memory on your iPAQ by keeping them loaded all the time, you may want to load them when you need them and then remove them when you're done using them. You can always use ActiveSync to reload these programs from your desktop PC as necessary. Be sure to keep any activation codes handy, though, because some programs require you to re-enter those codes if you reinstall the program.

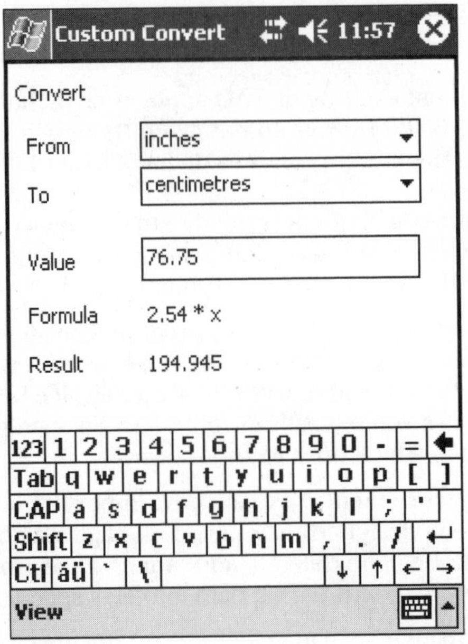

Custom Convert 📶 📢 11:57 ✕

Convert

From | inches ▾

To | centimetres ▾

Value | 76.75

Formula | 2.54 * x

Result | 194.945

123	1	2	3	4	5	6	7	8	9	0	-	=	⬅
Tab	q	w	e	r	t	y	u	i	o	p	[	]
CAP	a	s	d	f	g	h	j	k	l	;	'
Shift	z	x	c	v	b	n	m	,	.	/	↵
Ctl	áü	`	\			↓	↑	←	→

View | ⌨ ▲

Figure 18-2: You can easily convert between all sorts of units with Custom Convert.

Loading Programs You've Downloaded

When it comes to installing new programs on your iPAQ, your iPAQ and your desktop PC really are companions — you generally need your desktop PC to help install programs on your iPAQ. A few exceptions do exist, but most programs must first be loaded onto your desktop PC before they can be added to your iPAQ.

It's a good idea to set up a folder on your desktop PC specifically for any iPAQ programs that you download. That way, you always know where to find them when you want to install or reinstall them.

Here I step through a typical iPAQ program installation so that you know what to expect when you want to add new programs to your iPAQ:

1. **Make sure your iPAQ is connected to your desktop PC and ActiveSync is running.**

2. **Open Windows Explorer on your desktop PC by clicking the Windows Explorer icon and locate the installation program.**

Make note of the location where you save the program when you download it. If you obtained the iPAQ program on CD-ROM or diskette, obviously you can find the installation program there.

3. **Open the installation program by clicking or double-clicking it depending on how your particular PC is set up to run programs.**

   This screen serves one very important purpose — it tells you which program you're trying to install.

4. **Click Next to continue.**

   You now probably have several steps to follow that may include accepting a license agreement, choosing where to store the files on your desktop PC, and choosing where you want the program to appear on your desktop PC's Start menu. Continue through these steps until you see a message similar to the one shown in Figure 18-3.

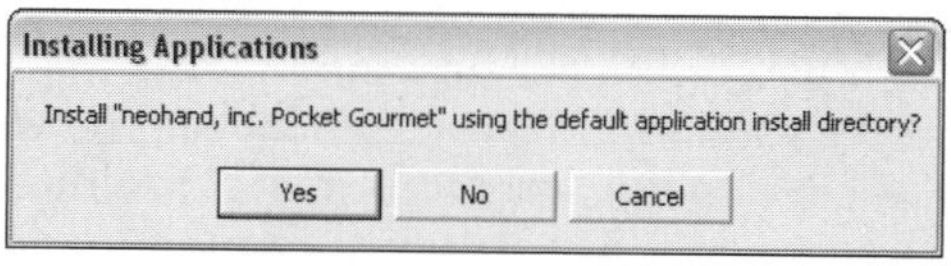

Figure 18-3:
You're ready
to begin the
iPAQ setup.

Installing Applications	☒

Install "neohand, inc. Pocket Gourmet" using the default application install directory?

| Yes | No | Cancel |

5. **In most cases, you want to click Yes to begin installing the program onto your iPAQ.**

   The one exception is if you want to install the program onto a memory storage card. If this is the case, click No and then choose the directory in which you do want to install the program on your iPAQ.

6. **When you see the message shown in Figure 18-4, you're finished with your desktop PC and need to look at your iPAQ's screen to see if you need to do anything there.**

   Typically, nothing is required on your iPAQ, but a few programs make you disconnect your iPAQ and press the reset button.

7. **Tap OK to finish.**

Be sure to read the user's manual, installation notes, or any other documentation that comes with your iPAQ programs. These often contain some excellent tips that help you make the most of the program that you just installed.

Figure 18-4:
Be sure
to look at
your iPAQ's
screen.

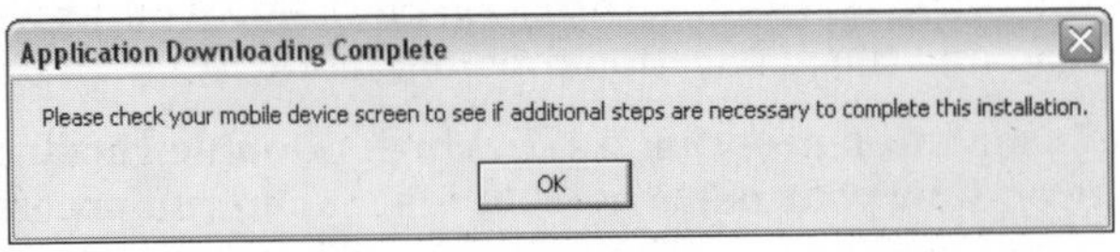

Application Downloading Complete

Please check your mobile device screen to see if additional steps are necessary to complete this installation.

OK

Freeing Up Memory

An old saying claims that you can't be too thin or too rich. When it comes to iPAQs, you can say that you can't have too much memory. Your iPAQ differs in one very fundamental way from your desktop PC: Your iPAQ must store all programs and data in memory at all times. Your desktop PC, on the other hand, can put unused stuff out on a disk somewhere until it's needed.

This difference between your iPAQ and your desktop PC is an important one. It means that you can't simply add new programs whenever you want without making certain that you have enough room for them. On a desktop PC with gigabytes of hard disk space, you'll probably outgrow your desktop PC long before you need to worry about space. On an iPAQ, available space can be an issue almost as soon as you start adding new programs.

Unloading programs you don't need

One of the great things about having your desktop PC and your iPAQ as partners in installing iPAQ software is that you can typically remove programs from your iPAQ and yet still have them available if you later decide to reinstall them. And because you may have to unload some programs when you want to try out new iPAQ software, this can be a real lifesaver!

You can unload programs from your iPAQ in one of two primary ways: Remove them by using just your iPAQ or by using ActiveSync on your desktop PC. Both methods work, so it's really up to you to decide which you prefer. I prefer to use ActiveSync on my desktop PC because that way the desktop system and my iPAQ always agree about which programs are installed.

Unloading programs by using ActiveSync

If you want to remove programs from your iPAQ by working through ActiveSync on your desktop PC, here's what you need to do:

1. **Place your iPAQ in the synchronization cradle and open ActiveSync on your desktop PC if it isn't already open. (See Chapter 5 if you need help with this.)**

   Of course, if you're using a wireless network connection for your iPAQ, you can skip the part about placing it in the synchronization cradle because your network connection is likely much faster than the USB connection — meaning that the wireless connection is a better option for installing and removing most programs.

2. **Choose Tools⇨Add/Remove Programs.**

   ActiveSync examines your iPAQ to see which programs are currently installed and then displays the Add/Remove Programs dialog box (see Figure 18-5).

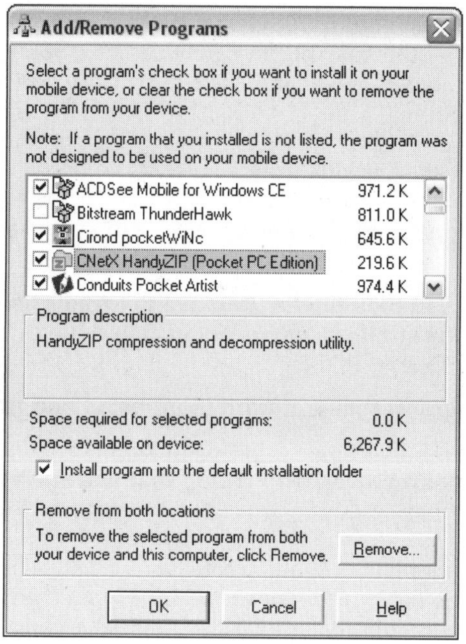

Figure 18-5:
You can add or remove programs from your iPAQ by using ActiveSync on your desktop PC.

3. **Remove the check mark from any programs that you want to uninstall from your iPAQ.**

   You can also add a check mark to any of the listed programs that you want to install.

Don't click the Remove button — doing so removes the program from both your iPAQ and your desktop PC.

4. **Click OK to make the changes.**

Be sure to look at your iPAQ's screen to see if you need to do anything else, like reset your iPAQ.

Using ActiveSync on your desktop PC to remove programs from your iPAQ has another advantage that you may not have considered: By using ActiveSync, you can be sure that you still have the ability to reinstall the program if necessary. If you uninstall a program directly on your iPAQ as shown in the next section, it's possible to remove programs and not be able to reinstall them without first downloading the installation program from the Web.

Unloading programs directly on your iPAQ

If you'd rather work directly on your iPAQ, you can uninstall programs without using your desktop PC — this may be your only choice if you're away from your desk but need to download a large file directly into your iPAQ by using your Internet connection.

Here's how to unload programs directly from your iPAQ:

1. **Tap the Start button on your iPAQ and choose Settings to open the Settings screen.**

2. **Click the System tab and then tap the Remove Programs icon to display the list of programs that are currently installed in your iPAQ's storage memory (see Figure 18-6).**

3. **Select any of the programs that you want to uninstall and then click the Remove button.**

4. **Tap OK when you have removed everything that you don't want and you're finished.**

You've probably noticed that neither using ActiveSync on your desktop PC nor using Remove Programs directly on your iPAQ offers you the option of removing all the programs on your iPAQ. That's because the basic applications on your iPAQ — things like Pocket Word and Pocket Excel — are loaded permanently into your iPAQ's *ROM* (read-only memory). Even though these items are loaded into permanent memory, it's possible to update them with special software that can modify *Flash ROM* — a special type of ROM included in all iPAQ systems specifically so that updates can be made if necessary. See the support pages for your particular iPAQ model at www.hp.com for information on possible updates.

Settings ⇄ ◀€ 12:22 **ok**

Remove Programs

Programs in storage memory:

Microsoft VB Runtimes for PPC
neohand, inc. Pocket Gourmet
Surerange Custom Convert
Ilium Software eWallet [Pocket PC]
Conduits Pocket Player
CNetX HandyZIP (Pocket PC Edition)
ACDSee Mobile for Windows CE
Conduits Pocket Artist
Pocket Speech

Remove

Total storage memory available: 6264k

Adjust memory allocation.

Figure 18-6:
Choose the
programs
that you
want to
remove.

Deleting unneeded files

Of course, programs aren't the only files that can eat up memory space on your iPAQ. It's a sure bet that other unneeded files are wasting space.

You have several ways to remove unneeded files from your iPAQ. For example, if you've loaded a bunch of eBooks into the Microsoft Reader library, you can delete those books when you're done with them by using the tap-and-hold method. You then choose Delete from the pop-up menu, and they're sent off into digital nothingness.

You may think that the Find link on the Memory settings screen offers a good way to find and delete unneeded files. If so, you'd be half right. Sure, you *can* use the find tool to locate files, but you can't delete them when you find them.

A better way to find and delete files is to use the File Explorer, shown in Figure 18-7. Here you can not only locate but also delete files.

To open File Explorer on your iPAQ, click the Start button and choose Programs to open the Programs folder. Then, tap the File Explorer icon.

To view your files sorted by size (or some other sort order), tap the sort list just below the time display and choose the sort order that you prefer. In Figure 18-7 the list is sorted by name.

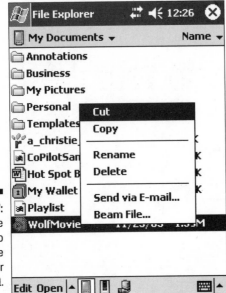

Figure 18-7:
Use File
Explorer to
manage the
files on your
iPAQ.

Using HandyZIP

Almost anyone who uses a PC has encountered *zipped* (compressed) files at some point. By using one of the popular Zip utilities such as WinZip (www. winzip.com) you can compress files so that they take less room and so that they're faster to send via e-mail. Because of the far more limited storage space on an iPAQ, being able to compress your files is even more important than it is on your desktop system.

Unfortunately, the Zip utility that you use on your desktop PC doesn't work on your iPAQ. To work with Zip files on your iPAQ, you need a Zip utility, such as HandyZIP (www.cnetx.com), designed specifically for use on your iPAQ.

Outlook has built-in security features that block certain types of file attachments. If you send an e-mail message containing an attachment that Outlook considers to be potentially dangerous, the recipient can't open or save the attachment — even if the attachment really is safe. One of the best ways to avoid this type of problem is to place the attachment into a Zip file and then send the Zip file as the message attachment. Outlook doesn't block Zip file attachments, so the recipient can open and save your attachment.

Chapter 19

Traveling with Your iPAQ

*I*f you have ever taken a laptop PC along on a trip, you're really going to love traveling with your iPAQ. The much smaller size of the iPAQ means that it's convenient even in situations where lugging along your laptop sounds like medieval torture. By comparison, your iPAQ weighs just a few ounces and can fit into a space smaller than most paperback novels. In this chapter, I show you some of the many ways that your iPAQ can be the perfect traveling companion.

Your iPAQ as a Traveling Companion

Traveling can be lots of fun. Traveling can also be stressful — especially if you don't know where you're going or you can't speak the local language. Your iPAQ is a really great tool for helping you cope with the problems that can make travel less enjoyable than it should be. The past several years have seen some pretty significant advances in the capabilities of the iPAQ and its add-ons to make traveling far more enjoyable.

Using your iPAQ while traveling

Normal life doesn't stop simply because you've hopped onto a plane for some far-off vacation spot. Your iPAQ can help you keep things under control even when you're off on a trip. Here are some things that your iPAQ can do for you while you're traveling:

✔ **Managing e-mail:** Your iPAQ can help manage your e-mail by letting you send and receive e-mail on the go. You can quickly handle the really important messages that demand attention, and the rest can simply wait until you get home.

✔ **Planning ahead:** You can use your iPAQ to check local weather forecasts so that you know what to plan. After all, there's no sense trying to plan a day at the beach if a sudden storm is coming in tomorrow. Maybe that art museum won't be quite as stodgy as you feared.

✔ **Dining out:** If you suddenly get the urge for a great meal, you can use your iPAQ to find restaurant ratings for the area in which you're traveling. Not all of your vacation meals have to come out of a fast food bag, do they?

✔ **Finding fun places:** If the place that you're visiting turns out to be really boring, you can log on to your favorite travel Web site and find out what other destinations are available at bargain prices at the last minute.

✔ **Curing boredom:** If you get really bored, you can whip out your iPAQ and play a couple rounds of Jawbreaker. Playing Jawbreaker is probably more interesting than listening to that salesman tell you everything that you didn't want to know about buying wool socks.

iPAQ travel considerations

Traveling with your iPAQ should be as simple and carefree as possible. If your iPAQ is going to make travel easier and more fun, dealing with problems along the way is about the last thing you want to do. Here are some things to remember to make your iPAQ a better traveling companion:

✔ **Consider your power source:** iPAQs can run only as long as they have power. Because all iPAQs use special built-in batteries, you can't just pop into the local drugstore and get new batteries for your iPAQ. Make certain that you bring your power adapter along so that you can recharge your iPAQ's batteries when necessary.

✔ **Have a foreign outlet adapter:** If you're going to be traveling in a foreign country, you probably need an adapter to plug the iPAQ's AC adapter into a power outlet. These adapters for foreign outlets can be hard to find on the road, so I suggest that you buy the right adapters before you leave.

✔ **Think of alternative power options:** You may want to consider one of the solar panel or spare battery options that I mention in Chapter 20. That way, you can avoid the whole funny electrical outlet mess while you show everyone just how cool you really are.

✔ **Get local Internet access numbers:** Connecting to the Internet while you're on a trip can be a real experience. Research the local access numbers before you go so that you know how to access your ISP. You also need to know what toll-free numbers are available because local access numbers have a tendency to change frequently.

- ✔ **Check Internet access rates:** If you're going to be traveling in a foreign country, check out your Internet access options before you go. Even if you're able to connect easily, make certain that you aren't paying expensive international long distance rates to access the Internet.

- ✔ **Try not to look suspicious:** It's even possible that some authorities may consider your iPAQ or some of its accessories — especially things like GPS receivers — to be spying equipment. You can lose your iPAQ or even be thrown in jail if the authorities are feeling especially hostile. If you're in doubt, check with your travel professional before bringing along your iPAQ. Whatever you do, be prepared to demonstrate that your iPAQ really does work and that it isn't a bomb in disguise.

- ✔ **Protect your iPAQ from theft:** An iPAQ can look pretty attractive to a thief. Be sure to set a system password before you go (see Chapter 3), and don't put your iPAQ down anywhere that it becomes an easy target.

Finding Your Way — Without Asking for Directions

No one really likes to stop and ask for directions. Sure, some people (men and women) make a joke about how members of the opposite sex (again, men *and* women) drive on into oblivion because they refuse to ask for directions, but the ones making that joke probably couldn't tell if a map was upside down or backwards, anyway.

One of the problems with asking for directions is simple — the directions that most people give are usually so poor that no one could follow them even if they wanted to. When people give directions, they tend to forget to include a lot of important details. I don't want to know that I'm supposed to turn by Mrs. Jones' apple tree; I want to know that I need to follow Highway 101 for 2.3 miles and then turn right onto Crosspointe Boulevard. Your iPAQ can help eliminate these directional woes.

Reading maps on your iPAQ

Roadmaps are the standard tool for finding your way around unfamiliar territory. Of course, finding the right maps and keeping track of them while you're traveling just adds additional complication to what should be an enjoyable trip. To cut down the clutter and make things easier, you can download maps onto your iPAQ.

As handy as having roadmaps available on your iPAQ may be, I think that pairing your iPAQ with a GPS receiver (as I discuss in the following section) is a far better way to navigate with your iPAQ. Each of the GPS receivers that I discuss comes with its own set of maps, so you don't have to figure out where to get the ones you need.

Connecting a GPS to your iPAQ

If you've ever been lost while traveling, you're going to love adding a *Global Positioning Satellite* (GPS) receiver to your iPAQ. This innovation has made it possible to always have an accurate fix on your position to within a few feet of your exact location. If you have a GPS and still get lost, you've got to be really trying to get lost!

GPS receivers work by comparing radio signals from a series of satellites that are circling the earth. In order to actually receive these very weak signals, your GPS receiver must be in a position where it can actually "see" the sky directly overhead, which means that a GPS receiver generally doesn't work inside your house, while you're driving through a tunnel, or even in a forest if the canopy of trees overhead is too dense. It also means that when you first try out your GPS unit, you're likely to find the whole experience a little frustrating if you're attempting to get familiar with it in the comfort of your office. Go outside, and your GPS receiver begins to work as soon as it can see the satellites. You can try placing the GPS receiver in a window, too; but don't you need to get some fresh air anyway?

Getting the right GPS receiver

When the first iPAQs became available, owners had few choices in GPS receivers. Recently, though, the number of different options that you can choose from has exploded. This is great because it means that each manufacturer is producing far better hardware and software packages than those that were available even a couple years ago.

Several different GPS receiver manufacturers exist, so you have a number of choices in buying a GPS receiver to team up with your iPAQ. First, you need to decide which type of hardware you want. GPS receivers designed for use with the iPAQ come in three general flavors:

> ✔ Some GPS receivers connect to your iPAQ by using the sync connector at the bottom of your iPAQ. That means that the connection is made through the same connector you use to connect your iPAQ to your desktop PC. These type of GPS receivers require a special cable that is designed for the iPAQ. These GPS receivers also typically include an adapter that plugs into the 12-volt power outlet on your car's dash to power both the GPS receiver and your iPAQ.

✔ A number of CF-slot GPS receivers are also available. These GPS receivers plug into the CompactFlash (CF) expansion slot on the top of your iPAQ so that you can use your iPAQ and the GPS receiver as a single, compact unit. These units are especially handy for use when you're hiking because they don't depend on being powered by your car. Remember, though, that this type of GPS receiver doesn't fit any of the iPAQ models that have a single Secure Digital (SD) expansion slot.

✔ The newest types of GPS receivers are the Bluetooth models. These connect wirelessly to your iPAQ via Bluetooth and leave your expansion slot open so that you can add memory to hold your maps. Typically, these Bluetooth receivers include (or offer as an option) a rechargeable battery so that they can operate for up to six hours between charges. (Isn't that built-in Bluetooth a great capability?)

Each model of GPS receiver seems to offer a different mix of connection and power options. In most cases, you want the ability to power both your iPAQ and the GPS receiver from your car's cigarette lighter, so choose the proper cables (even if they are optional) to allow this. Be sure to see Chapter 20 for additional ways to power your iPAQ on the go.

Although the GPS manufacturers don't really want you to know this, I've found that you can use any of the navigation software with any of the iPAQ-compatible GPS receivers. This doesn't mean, however, that all of the GPS receivers are identical. It simply means that they all adhere to the *NEMA* standard — the means by which GPS receivers transmit data to computers.

The h1930/1935 iPAQ is incompatible with GPS receivers that connect via the sync cable connector. Because this model lacks both a CF slot and built-in Bluetooth capabilities, the only way for it to use a GPS receiver currently is to add an SDIO Bluetooth card such as the one that's available from Socket (www.socketcom.com), and then use a Bluetooth GPS receiver. Unfortunately, this solution does have one drawback: You can only store as many map files as can fit into the internal memory because no expansion slots can be available when the SDIO Bluetooth card is in use.

I take a quick look at several GPS receiver and software packages that you may want to consider. Because I can only show you a very little about each of them in the available space, I strongly urge you to visit the Web sites that I mention to find out more about each of them and see which one best suits your needs.

CoPilot Live Pocket PC 4

ALK Technology's CoPilot Live Pocket PC 4 is an excellent example of the new type of thinking that makes the current generation of GPS packages far more useful along with your iPAQ than were the earlier efforts. As Figure 19-1 shows, the ALK CoPilot GPS receiver is a small Bluetooth-equipped unit that you can place up to 30 feet from your iPAQ (making this just the ticket for back seat drivers, I guess).

Figure 19-1:
The CoPilot GPS receiver is a compact unit that easily fits on your dash.

Just what do I mean by a new type of thinking? Well, if you've ever used a GPS receiver along with your laptop PC, you know that the trip directions can be difficult and dangerous to read while you're driving. Sure, most GPS navigation software has voice prompts, but hearing and understanding those prompts can be really hard — especially if you like to listen to the radio while you're driving. CoPilot Live Pocket PC 4 addresses these problems with a product designed especially for the small screen on your iPAQ. Rather than showing you a lot of minute road details, CoPilot Live Pocket PC 4 concentrates on making your very next move easily understandable. Figure 19-2 shows how the screen typically appears when you're navigating with CoPilot Live Pocket PC 4.

CoPilot Live Pocket PC 4 also incorporates a live vehicle tracking feature that enables you to remotely track the location of a vehicle if it has a wireless Internet connection. You can find out more about this product at www.alk.com.

Earthmate GPS

You've probably noticed that different people often approach the same task from a different perspective. The DeLorme Earthmate GPS and Street Atlas USA 2004 Handheld bundle certainly takes quite a different approach to navigating with your iPAQ than some of the other packages that I tested.

Figure 19-2: CoPilot Live Pocket PC 4 makes it easy to see where to make your next turn.

The first difference with the Earthmate GPS unit (see Figure 19-3) is how many different options it provides. This GPS receiver has the ability to connect to your iPAQ or your laptop PC via Bluetooth, USB, or a serial connection — depending on the optional cables that you buy. It also offers several power options including AAA batteries, a rechargeable battery pack, an adapter for your cigarette lighter, and an AC adapter.

The DeLorme Street Atlas USA 2004 Handheld software also differs considerably from most other mapping software for your iPAQ. DeLorme is certainly one of the leaders in mapping and GPS software for desktop and laptop PCs, and this handheld version reflects that heritage. For example, although Street Atlas USA 2004 Handheld allows you to set up routes directly on your iPAQ, you can also use Street Atlas USA 2004 to set up your route on your desktop system, and then easily export the route and the maps to your iPAQ. You may find that this approach suits your needs quite well because it is generally far easier to set an exact route on your desktop system than on your iPAQ. Figure 19-4 shows an example of starting to navigate with Street Atlas USA 2004 Handheld.

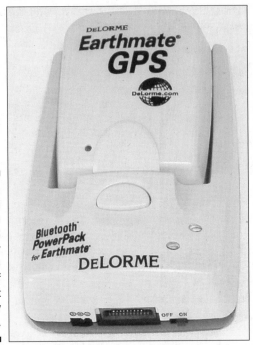

Figure 19-3:
The
Earthmate
GPS
receiver
offers a
multitude of
options to fit
virtually any
need.

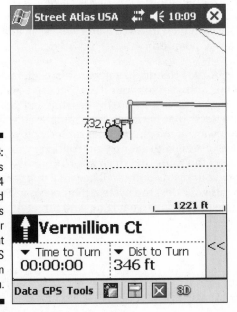

Figure 19-4:
Street Atlas
USA 2004
Handheld
provides
another
excellent
iPAQ GPS
navigation
option.

You can discover more about the Earthmate GPS receiver and the Street Atlas USA 2004 Handheld software at the DeLorme Web site (www.delorme.com).

PocketMap Navigator GPS

PocketMap Navigator GPS from Space Machine (www.spacemachine.net) offers another excellent choice for GPS navigation with your iPAQ. Space Machine offers GPS receivers in Bluetooth, CF, and the *mouse* type of unit that connects directly to the sync port on the bottom of your iPAQ (see Figure 19-5). The mouse type of receiver that I tested is particularly handy for use in your car because a single cable plugs into your cigarette lighter and powers both the GPS receiver and your iPAQ.

The PocketMap Navigator mouse-type GPS receiver doesn't work with the h1930/1935 iPAQ due to an incompatible sync port on that model of iPAQ.

The PocketMap Navigator software offers some of the best voice prompts of any of the navigation software that I tested. (It sounds like Professor Stephen Hawking.) This can be an important factor in helping you safely navigate — especially if you're driving alone. Figure 19-6 shows an example of navigating with the PocketMap Navigator software.

Figure 19-5:
The PocketMap Navigator mouse-type GPS receiver plugs into the bottom of your iPAQ.

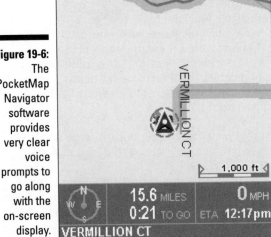

Figure 19-6:
The
PocketMap
Navigator
software
provides
very clear
voice
prompts to
go along
with the
on-screen
display.

TeleType WorldNavigator

The TeleType WorldNavigator (see Figure 19-7) is the only CF-type GPS receiver that I tested for this book. For those iPAQ models with a CF expansion slot, this type of GPS receiver is certainly the most convenient for navigation on foot. With a CF-type GPS receiver, your iPAQ provides the power to the GPS receiver and you have one neat little package.

The TeleType GPS software (shown in Figure 19-8) offers a number of unique features including voice recognition. As the figure shows, this software also provides navigation prompts that are quite easy to see. The maps that are included tend to concentrate on major roads, however, so you may have a little bit of difficulty navigating to smaller roads in some rural areas. You can find out more about the TeleType GPS products at the TeleType Web site (www.teletype.com).

Figure 19-7:
The TeleType WorldNavigator GPS receiver plugs into the CF slot found on some iPAQ models.

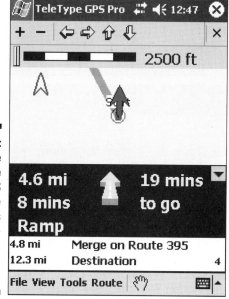

Figure 19-8:
The TeleType GPS software provides large on-screen navigation prompts.

Pharos iGPS

Pharos was one of the earliest providers of GPS receivers and navigation software for the Pocket PC market, and their newest Bluetooth iGPS receiver certainly reflects the progress that they have made. This receiver (shown in Figure 19-9) is by far the coolest-looking Bluetooth GPS receiver anywhere with its clear plastic case and blue light-emitting diode (LED). The Pharos unit is also the only one that comes in a travel case so that you have an easier time keeping everything together.

Figure 19-9:
The Pharos iGPS receiver is the best-looking receiver you can find.

The Pharos Ostia software (see Figure 19-10) offers fairly simple voice prompts (such as "left turn ahead"), easy to read navigation notes, and good road detail. You can find out more about the Pharos products at their Web site (www. pharosgps.com).

Socket GPS Nav Kit

It simply wasn't possible to test every GPS receiver and navigation software combination that's available for your iPAQ, so some units like the Socket GPS Nav Kit had to be left out. Still, you may want to add this unit to those you want to consider. If so, visit the Socket Web site (www.socketcom.com) for the latest details.

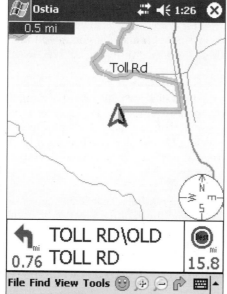

Figure 19-10:
The Pharos
Ostia
software is
easy to
use and
accurate.

Storing your GPS maps

One of the biggest problems with using a GPS receiver with any type of hand-held device is that detailed maps can take a lot of space. And because you probably want the best, most detailed map possible when you're traveling, storage space on your iPAQ is suddenly a big issue. Here are some possible solutions:

✔ Try downloading a map that covers a smaller area or one that has less detail.

✔ You can uninstall pretty much everything else from your iPAQ's built-in storage memory. Of course, this greatly reduces the value of your iPAQ as a traveling companion, and it still may not even give you enough room for some maps.

✔ You can add a memory storage card to your iPAQ and store your maps there. This is by far the best solution, and the only one that I recommend (unless, of course, your GPS receiver is already using the expansion slot). This is an especially good solution with those iPAQ 2002 systems that have two independent expansion slots.

The software user's manual for your GPS receiver has information on the specific procedures necessary to download maps from your desktop PC to your iPAQ.

Using your GPS receiver

You have two ways to use a GPS receiver along with your iPAQ: navigating by latitude and longitude and navigating with maps. If you need to navigate to a specific location by using latitude and longitude, the GPS receiver can show you this in very fine detail.

Use the GPS Info display (see the help files for your brand of mapping software if you need help finding this) to identify a precise location even when a map is unavailable for an area. For example, you can use this display to return to the exact spot on a large lake where you caught all those fish on your last fishing trip, and you don't have to worry about leaving any markers that may tip off other anglers to your favorite hot spot.

One important point to remember (no matter which GPS receiver and navigation software you use) is that manufacturers often release free updates and patches on their Web sites. You should check for these fixes often — especially if you're having any problems making it all work.

Trying to navigate with your iPAQ and a GPS receiver while you're driving can be very dangerous. If possible, have someone else watch the display or make certain that you have a good idea of your route before you begin driving. If your navigation software offers voice prompts, this can also increase the safety factor considerably.

Using your iPAQ as a pilot's companion

If you happen to be a pilot, you certainly can appreciate the compact size and convenience of an iPAQ. Nothing else is quite as cramped as the cockpit of a typical private aircraft. So when it comes to choosing tools to help you plan a trip and find your way, you want something that does a lot for you and doesn't take up too much room — if this doesn't describe an iPAQ, I don't know what does! iPAQs are very popular with private pilots for exactly this reason.

I've discovered a very useful program aimed at iPAQ owners who also happen to be pilots. Although I don't have a lot of room to devote to this, I would like to mention it and then suggest that you visit the manufacturer's Web site for more information. Hahns's Flight Planner (www.hahnsllc.com) offers complete flight-planning functions and even assists you in filing a flight plan. Figure 19-11 shows an example of using the program to obtain a weather briefing.

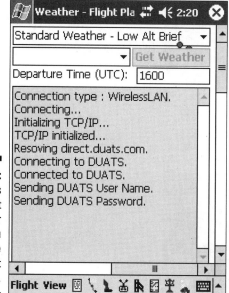

Figure 19-11:
Hahns's
Flight
Planner
helps you
prepare
your flight
plans.

Speaking the Language

One of the most difficult things about visiting foreign countries is being unable to speak the common language.

Aside from learning the languages that are spoken in the areas where you want to travel, getting a language translator that runs on your iPAQ may be one of the best ways to deal with understanding what's going on when you're traveling. Getting a quick translation may also be the key to keeping yourself from going hungry, as Figure 19-12 illustrates.

One product that I've found for translating between languages on the iPAQ is the ECTACO Partner Voice Translator (shown in Figure 19-12). This software is available in versions for many different languages (www.ectaco.com).

Although you can use the ECTACO Partner Voice Translator to translate your spoken phrases into another language, I've found that the results can sometimes be more amusing than accurate. It's generally safer to tap the View button and then choose the phrase you want from the list that appears.

Figure 19-12:
Being able
to translate
foreign
language
into
something
that you can
understand
can come in
handy.

Entertainment Guides

When you're traveling, it's really nice to have a local expert to give you advice about where to find a good meal or other attractions. Unfortunately, it can be pretty hard to find those experts when you need them, and the result could be yet another lousy hotel restaurant meal. With a bit of help, though, your iPAQ can be that expert and you can be spared the rubber chicken. All you need is one of the applications that I mention next.

Vindigo

Vindigo is a service that helps you find all those handy details that make a trip more enjoyable. Want some great German food or the location of the best local art museum? Or maybe you don't want to spend the evening in your hotel room watching TV and would like to find the closest wine bar? Well, Vindigo can help.

Figure 19-13 shows the Vindigo main screen. You simply tap one of the buttons, make a few selections, and you're on the way to having some fun on your trip.

Figure 19-13:
Vindigo gets
you out of
your hotel
room and
into having
some fun.

Vindigo is a subscription-based service. After you set up your favorite cities, Vindigo automatically downloads new information from their Web site (www.vindigo.com). You can sign up for a free 30-day trial to see if Vindigo is for you.

ZAGAT TO GO

ZAGAT TO GO is another option that functions similarly to Vindigo. When you install the ZAGAT TO GO service on your iPAQ, you then have the option to download some of the best-known restaurant guides in the world. Figure 19-14 shows how ZAGAT TO GO displays a listing so that you can find a good meal. You can find out more about subscribing to ZAGAT TO GO at their Web site (www.zagat.com).

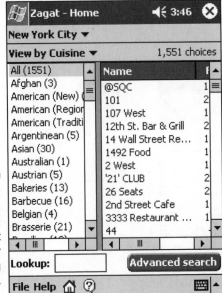

Figure 19-14:
ZAGAT TO
GO is a
great help at
finding your
next dining
experience.

Part VII
The Part of Tens

The 5th Wave   By Rich Tennant

@RICHTENNANT

"Oh wait — this says, 'Lunch Ed from Marketing', not 'Lynch', 'Lunch'."

In this part . . .

I show you the best iPAQ accessories that I've found, along with the best iPAQ business programs. I also reveal some really great utilities that can help you get even more from your iPAQ.

Chapter 20

Ten Great iPAQ Accessories

*I*n case you haven't noticed this already, you can buy a lot of add-ons for your iPAQ. Some of these accessories are really useful, some are a lot of fun, and some defy easy description. One of the benefits of writing a book like this is that I get to try out a lot of these gadgets, and in this chapter I show you some of the best of them.

What Works with Your iPAQ

Before you go out and spend your money on accessories, you need to know which devices actually work with your iPAQ. Nothing is worse than getting excited about some great gadget, buying it, and then finding out that it doesn't work. Here are some guidelines to help you avoid this disappointment:

✔ **Know your expansion slot:** Make certain that you know the type and size of your iPAQ's expansion slot. The most common one is the Secure Digital (SD) slot, but CompactFlash (CF) expansion slots and PC Card expansion slots are also available with some iPAQ models.

✔ **Have the proper connection cables:** iPAQs generally have a serial connection, but you may need to buy a special cable from your iPAQ's manufacturer to connect to standard serial devices (like external modems).

> ✔ **Check the required driver software:** Even if you have the correct cable, some serial devices don't work with an iPAQ. Anything that needs special driver software works only if it includes a driver specifically designed for the iPAQ. Drivers intended for the version of Windows on your desktop PC don't work on your iPAQ.
>
> ✔ **Check the required iPAQ model:** Some devices are designed to work with specific iPAQs. If the package lists specific models but not the particular iPAQ that you own, ask before you buy (and get an assurance that you can return the item if it doesn't work for you). This especially applies to the h1900 series because they seem to have the most compatibility problems.

Adding Storage

Without any question, my favorite iPAQ accessory is additional storage. Because iPAQs store everything in memory, it's easy to use up the available memory when you get carried away with adding new programs, eBooks, music, or whatever to your iPAQ. In fact, that's one of the main hazards of being as versatile as the iPAQ is — users tend to dream up all sorts of great things to do with them.

When you want to add more memory to your iPAQ, you need to get the correct type to fit your particular model. Figure 20-1 shows why this is so. In this case, I placed three different types of memory next to each other so that you can see how they differ in size. The large unit on the left is a PC Card hard drive, the one in the middle is a CF memory card, and the one on the right is an SD memory card. All current iPAQ models have an SD memory slot and a few have a CF slot, but no iPAQ has a PC card slot built-in.

Although all current iPAQ models have at least one built-in expansion slot, many older iPAQ models require an expansion sleeve like the MemPlug from Portable Innovation Technology (www.pitech.com) shown in Figure 20-2. Some expansion sleeves even include PC Card slots.

Two excellent sources of memory cards for your iPAQ are SanDisk (www.sandisk.com) and SimpleTech (www.simpletech.com).

Any expansion card that's inserted into your iPAQ draws a small amount of power, so you may want to remove any cards (when they aren't needed) to maximize battery life. The drain caused by memory cards is extremely low, though, so it might not be worth the risk of losing the card by removing it.

Figure 20-1:
The three types of memory expansion differ greatly in size.

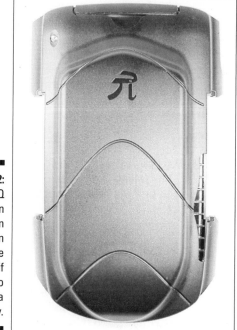

Figure 20-2:
Older iPAQ models often require an expansion sleeve like this one if you want to add extra memory.

Communications Accessories

After you add some memory to your iPAQ, you probably want to add some accessories that help your iPAQ communicate with the outside world. These accessories cover a broad range of abilities, so in the following sections I break them down into some general categories.

Wi-Fi adapters

Wi-Fi is probably the best thing that has ever happened to iPAQs. Wi-Fi gives your iPAQ freedom from all those cables, allows you to find a comfortable spot as you sit back and surf wirelessly, and opens up the whole world of public hotspots for you. These are just some of the reasons why I feel that a Wi-Fi adapter is a must-have accessory for any iPAQ owner whose iPAQ doesn't have built-in Wi-Fi capabilities.

Wi-Fi adapters come in two iPAQ-compatible formats. The most common are the ones that fit a CF slot, but SDIO Wi-Fi adapters also exist. Both types worked well in my testing, but I found the CF Wi-Fi adapters to be a little easier to configure, and they also seemed to offer a bit more range than the SDIO models.

Here are the Wi-Fi adapters that I tested. I can recommend any of them for use with your iPAQ:

- ✔ D-Link DCF-660W Wi-Fi adapter (www.dlink.com)
- ✔ SanDisk SDIO Wi-Fi adapter (www.sandisk.com)
- ✔ SMC SMC2642W Wi-Fi adapter (www.smc.com)
- ✔ Socket SDIO Wi-Fi adapter (www.socketcom.com)

The SDIO port on the h1900 series iPAQs has proven to be somewhat problematic. In fact, Hewlett-Packard (HP) has released a patch for the h1900 in an attempt to correct the problem. You can find out more about this patch and how to apply it at www.socketcom.com/faq/faq.asp?ID=172.

Adding a modem

Modems connect your iPAQ to the Internet so that you can use e-mail and browse your favorite Web sites. Unfortunately, modems do have several disadvantages. Not only are they slow, but you need to find a compatible phone jack and then string a phone cord between your iPAQ and the outlet. In addition, modems do not currently come in SD format, so you can use a modem only if your iPAQ has a CF slot.

Still, at times a modem is your only choice. Socket's 56K CF Modem (www.socketcom.com) is the unit that I have tested and found to work acceptably.

If you have a serial cable for your iPAQ, you can use almost any external modem — you don't need a special iPAQ-compatible external modem. Socket also sells serial adapters for the iPAQ.

Adding a digital phone card

If you already have a digital cell phone, you probably have most of what you need to connect your iPAQ to the Internet wirelessly. Using your cell phone as your iPAQ's wireless Internet connection is an option if a Wi-Fi connection isn't available. You can use the unused airtime from your cell phone for your connection and you probably don't have to pay extra to access the Internet.

Once again, Socket is the best source for digital phone cards, but a recent visit to their Web site seems to indicate that digital phone cards may be on the way out. Several models were listed as discontinued, so if you are interested in this option, it's probably a good idea to act quickly.

Connecting to your network

Your iPAQ normally connects to your desktop PC by using a USB connection, or in some cases by using a Wi-Fi connection. You may find that these types of connections simply aren't convenient in your case because your desktop PC's USB ports are hard to reach or you don't have a wireless network. If so, you can also connect with an Ethernet adapter in your iPAQ to make a network connection. Socket makes a couple different CF Ethernet adapters if you want to try this type of connection.

A network connection is probably faster than either a USB or standard serial connection when you're transferring files. But unless you've added a very large capacity memory card to your iPAQ and you're moving a huge amount of data, this doesn't make much difference.

Adding a Keyboard

Any time you use a PC, you interact with it by inputting information. It doesn't really matter if you're using an iPAQ or a desktop PC — you still need a way to let the computer know what you want it to do.

The iPAQ presents both unique challenges and unique opportunities with regards to input. As a result, some very interesting input accessories have appeared.

Your iPAQ offers two primary means of inputting information. You can tap out words by using the on-screen keyboard or you can write on the screen. Both methods work, of course, but when you need to enter a lot of information, you soon look for another option. That option can be a real keyboard like the one on your desktop PC.

Figure 20-3 shows the Belkin folding wireless keyboard that I prefer to use with the iPAQ. This keyboard uses infrared signals to communicate with your iPAQ, and it folds into a neat little package that's just about the same size as an iPAQ.

Even though the h4350 iPAQ has a built-in keyboard below its screen, you probably find that an external keyboard like the Belkin unit shown in the figure is far easier to use — especially if you're going to be entering lots of text.

Figure 20-3:
The Belkin
wireless
keyboard
makes data
entry on
your iPAQ
much easier.

Digital Cameras

Digital photography has really made a huge impact on the world. Film companies sell far less film than they once did, and the most popular cell phones today are those with built-in digital cameras. It seems only natural, then, to add a digital camera accessory to your iPAQ.

It's time to be honest about this — a digital camera accessory that you add to your iPAQ is really more of a novelty than a replacement for a good quality, standalone digital camera. Sure, the iPAQ add-on is much smaller than any ordinary digital camera, and the ability to snap quick photos with your iPAQ is kind of cool, but just don't expect award winning photos from this type of setup. If you think of the digital camera accessory as being a replacement for one of those disposable snapshot cameras that you buy at the drugstore, you're going to be a whole lot happier.

In writing this book, I tested two digital camera add-ons. I take a quick look at each of them.

FlyCAM-CF

Figure 20-4 shows the LifeView FlyCAM-CF. This unit has a flash, can take still images up to 1280 x 1024 pixels, and can record Audio Video Interleave (AVI) movies at up to 180 x 136 pixels. The lens rotates so that you can use the camera to take ordinary photos or self-portraits.

You can find out more about the LifeView FlyCAM-CF at the LifeView Web site (www.lifeview.com).

Veo Photo Traveler for Pocket PC

Figure 20-5 shows the Veo Photo Traveler for Pocket PC. This camera attachment is a bit simpler than the LifeView FlyCAM-CF. The Veo Photo Traveler for Pocket PC doesn't have a flash and its maximum resolution is 640 x 480 pixels. It does, however, have the ability to record short video segments.

You can find out more about the Veo Photo Traveler for Pocket PC at the Veo Web site (www.veo.com).

Although both of the digital camera accessories that I tested require a CF slot, HP now offers a similar unit that fits the SDIO slot on the iPAQs. Unfortunately, however, the HP digital camera add-on wasn't available for testing.

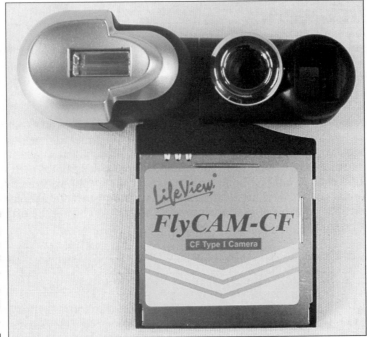

Figure 20-4:
The LifeView
FlyCAM-CF
makes your
iPAQ into
a digital
camera.

Figure 20-5:
The Veo
Photo
Traveler for
Pocket PC
is another
iPAQ digital
camera
add-on.

Powering Your Way to Freedom

This next accessory isn't as cool or neat as some of the ones that I mention earlier in this chapter, but it's still something that no iPAQ user should be without. iPAQs all run on batteries, and they're automatically recharged whenever your iPAQ is placed into the synchronization cradle (or, in the case of models that don't include the cradle, whenever the sync cable is connected). And because iPAQs use very aggressive power management, an iPAQ runs a long time in normal use — anywhere from five to ten hours — on a single charge.

Okay, so your iPAQ runs a long time on one charge, but that doesn't mean that it can run forever. Eventually, the batteries need to be recharged or your iPAQ dies. And because you can't just pop in a fresh set of batteries from the drugstore, you have to bring your iPAQ home and place it into the synchronization cradle for refueling.

Power from your car or laptop

So what does this have to do with a great iPAQ accessory? Simple: You need a second power adapter for your iPAQ so that you can charge up the batteries no matter where you are. Here you have several choices. The most obvious is to get a second AC adapter, but that may not be the best option. You can also get adapters that plug into a cigarette lighter in a car. Alternatively, you might look into getting a special type of cable that plugs into the USB port on any PC and uses the power from the USB port to recharge your iPAQ. This type of cable can also be used to sync your iPAQ with your laptop or desktop system, but even if you only use it to grab some watts from a handy PC, it's still a great idea.

The units that I tested include the following:

- **iBIZ Compaq Ipaq USB Charging/HotSync Kit:** (www.ibizpda.com/pda_accessories/pda_cables.html) This cable is as simple and compact as can be. It has a standard USB plug on one end and a plug for the sync jack on the bottom of your iPAQ on the other. Keep in mind, though, that you need to plug the USB end directly into a desktop or laptop system — a USB hub doesn't work unless it has its own power supply.

- **Belkin USB Sync Charger for iPAQ (Part number F8Q2000):** (www.belkin.com) This unit is similar to the iBIZ cable, but it includes one important extra — a cigarette lighter adapter with a USB jack to provide power from your car. This adapter takes up a bit more room than a simple cable, of course, but it can be a real lifesaver when no PC is available.

✔ **Griffin Mobile 3-in-1 Pocket PC Charger Kit:** (`www.griffinmobile.com`) I call this the boy scout model because when you have the Griffin kit, you're prepared for anything. This kit comes in its own slick little case and has the USB charging cable, a cigarette lighter adapter, and an AC adapter to cover every possible scenario. Note, though, that this kit requires the charging adapter that came hanging off the end of your iPAQ's sync cable because it's a universal type of kit (which also means that you can use it to charge some other devices besides your iPAQ).

Power when you're away from an outlet

Your iPAQ could be a great camping and hiking companion. It's small, it can entertain you, and it can help you navigate so that you don't get lost. There's just one problem — when the battery in your iPAQ runs down, everything stops working. And unless your idea of a great campsite is your own back-yard, finding a place to plug in the iPAQ's power adapter can be a real adventure when you're out camping.

Solar power for your iPAQ

One great solution is right there all around you — use the sun to power your iPAQ. With the help of one of the really cool solar power units that I found, you can sit out at a primitive campground for weeks and still be able to use your iPAQ. Here are the details:

✔ **POCKET-PAL Solar Charger:** (`www.aurorasolar.com`) This solar charger is a small, inexpensive, folding unit that fits into a space even smaller than your iPAQ. In full sunlight, this unit can charge your iPAQ in a couple of hours. It's the perfect companion to an iPAQ with a CF GPS receiver. If you go on a trip, you need to bring along the charging adapter that came with your iPAQ to use the POCKET-PAL.

✔ **iSun Portable Solar Charger:** (`www.icpglobal.com`) This device is similar to the Pocket Pal unit, but it's just a bit larger and slightly more powerful. The iSun unit includes a set of adapter plugs so that you can use it with many different types of equipment. It's unique in that several units can be ganged together for higher output. Figure 20-6 shows how the iSun portable solar charger looks when it's open and ready to power your iPAQ.

✔ **SunCatcher Sport:** (`www.powerexperts.com`) This unit is a bit larger and more expensive than the other two units, but it also has some really nifty features. The SunCatcher Sport uses its solar cells to charge a 1250-ma, 12-volt battery, and this battery powers your iPAQ, cell phone, or whatever else you want to plug into its cigarette lighter jack. The rechargeable battery also means that the Sun Catcher Sport can do something that few solar cells can do — it can power your equipment even when the sun isn't out! Remember, though, that you need a 12-volt power cord that powers your iPAQ from the cigarette lighter to use the SunCatcher Sport.

With one of these solar power units, you can travel anywhere and never worry about finding the right electrical outlet to power your iPAQ. Nor do you have to trail along several miles of extension cord when you go hiking or camping.

Figure 20-6:
The iSun
Portable
Solar
Charger can
help power
your iPAQ
when no
outlet is
in sight.

Extra batteries

Solar power for your iPAQ is a great idea, but what if you need to keep going for a long time and can't depend on having enough sun to give you the power that you need? In that case, you may want to rely on some external battery packs to get you through. I tested two of these that you may want to consider.

At the convenient end of the spectrum is the HP iPAQ Auxiliary Battery from Innergy (`www.pwrplant.com/PDA.html`) shown in Figure 20-7. This unit is built into a Targus leather case that can hold your iPAQ, and the unit is designed to last about double the normal battery life. (Note, however, that this battery pack is designed as a spare fuel tank for your iPAQ rather than as a battery charger — the iPAQ's charging light doesn't come on when this battery pack is attached.)

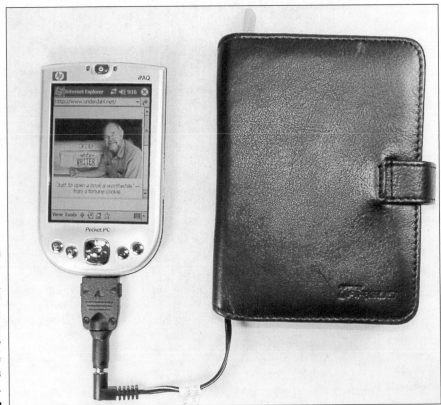

Figure 20-7:
The HP iPAQ Auxiliary Battery is a convenient way to double your iPAQ's battery life.

If you're thinking of considerably more extreme conditions, Innergy offers some really heavy-duty options, too. Figure 20-8 shows Innergy's Force 10 battery pack, which is designed to keep your iPAQ running for days. This is a serious battery pack that comes in its own backpack — it's not what you'd call a lightweight!

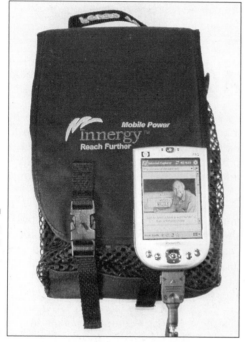

Figure 20-8:
The Force 10 battery pack is designed for really extreme needs.

Emergency power packs

Have you ever considered that batteries must be made by Murphy and company? How else could you possibly explain the fact that batteries always pick the absolute worst time to die. For example, suppose that you're using your iPAQ to give an important presentation to some potentially very big customers — can you imagine a worse time for your iPAQ's batteries to go dead? And, of course, that is precisely the one time when you also forget to bring the iPAQ's power adapter.

One excellent way around this potential mess is to bring along some emergency power in the form of one of the INSTANT POWER Chargers from INSTANT POWER (www.instant-power.com). These ingenious devices contain a special type of battery — known as a *zinc-air battery* — which remains fresh and ready to use for years. Zinc-air batteries are activated by opening the package and allowing air to enter the battery pack. Until they're opened, the battery simply sits there without going flat.

Each INSTANT POWER Charger has a disposable PowerCartridge that you can replace after it's used up. The PowerCartridge is good for about three complete recharges of your iPAQ, and can be resealed to store any unused capacity for up to three months.

Cases for Your iPAQ

Your iPAQ probably came with a simple little leather or vinyl case to protect its screen when you slip it into your pocket. You've probably noticed, however, that although the case HP may have provided does protect your iPAQ, it really leaves something to be desired in terms of utility and convenience. If so, you may want to consider getting something that was designed with your needs in mind.

Cases to fit your iPAQ come in all sorts of different styles. HP provides minimalist cases; some hard shell metal cases are designed to protect your iPAQ from extreme conditions; and certain large, more elaborate cases can hold your iPAQ, a cell phone, and even a quick change of clothes (if you pack light).

I know of a few great sources for cases to fit your iPAQ:

- **MARWARE:** (www.marware.com) This company makes several styles of cases. Their cases tend to take a minimalist approach to pack the best protection into the smallest size. I particularly like their SportSuit models that can be fastened to your belt.

- **Officeonthegogo:** (www.officeonthegogo.com) On this site, you can find the PDAPak — a case that has quite a few different pockets and compartments so that you can bring along your iPAQ, your cell phone, and any other assorted gadgets that you may need. The PDAPak also has a number of optional strap configurations, so you're sure to find a comfortable way to carry whatever load you happen to pack in there.

- **Seiko Instruments:** (www.siibusinessproducts.com) The Seiko SmartPad is an iPAQ case with a unique twist that no one else can match. The SmartPad includes a digital pen that you can use to draw on an ordinary pad of paper. Almost magically, whatever you draw on the paper instantly appears on your iPAQ's screen. If you want the coolest iPAQ accessory around, the Seiko SmartPad is for you.

Mobile Mounts for More Convenience

If you've ever tried to use your iPAQ to help navigate while you were driving, you no doubt realize that holding your iPAQ in one hand while you drive with the other hand is not the best idea ever. Not only is it pretty difficult to do, but it's also pretty hard to explain when you run into the back end of a patrol car.

Some iPAQ-compatible GPS receiver kits include a vent mount kit in the package. Use this to mount the receiver on your air-conditioning vent so that it doesn't slide around on your dashboard.

The following are two sources of mobile mounts for your iPAQ:

- **Pharos:** (www.pharosgps.com) The PDA Holder is a clever little device that clips to the air conditioning vent on your car's dashboard or sticks to your windshield with a suction cup (depending on the model that you buy). This holder has two powerful magnets in the mount and a small metal plate that sticks onto the back of your iPAQ. All of your iPAQ's ports remain usable when it's sitting on the MagnaHolder, and the magnet holds your iPAQ securely while allowing you to easily remove your iPAQ when you park your car.

- **Arkon Resources:** (www.arkon.com) This company makes a number of different mounts that can clip to your dash or stick to your windshield by using suction cups. The various Arkon mobile mounts use a unique system of spring-loaded, movable padded jaws to hold your iPAQ, and they even include a handy stylus so that you don't have to try getting the one out of your iPAQ. If Arkon doesn't have a mobile mount that works in your vehicle, maybe it's finally time to replace that horse-drawn cart.

Using Your iPAQ as a Radio

This next iPAQ accessory fits into a very specialized niche. The iBIZ pocketRADIO (www.ibizpda.com) adds an FM radio tuner to your iPAQ (see Figure 20-9). Sure, this probably makes your iPAQ into the most expensive pocket radio ever, but it really is a handy add-on — especially when you want a little respite from the noise around you. The included ear bud earphones do a pretty good job of blocking outside sounds, and by using the ear buds you don't bother any of your neighbors. By the way, you need an iPAQ with a CF slot to use the iBIZ pocketRADIO.

Figure 20-9:
The iBIZ
pocket-
RADIO
allows you
to listen to
your favorite
radio sta-
tion with
your iPAQ.

Controlling Your Life

If you don't need this next accessory for your iPAQ, I'm sure that you know someone who really does. The Griffin Mobile Total Remote (www. griffinmobile.com) turns your iPAQ in a super remote control that can replace virtually every infrared remote that currently clutters your family room. Just think — no more pile of remote controls that no one knows how to use.

Total Remote consists of two things: a powerful infrared transmitter module that plugs into the headphone jack on your iPAQ, and a software application that you can configure to control all sorts of devices from TVs to stereos. You can even program a single tap to execute a whole series of commands.

The Total Remote plugs into a standard 3.5mm (1/8") headphone jack. You can use it with iPAQ models that have a 2.5mm jack (like the h1930/1935) by using the adapter that comes packed with those models.

Connecting Your iPAQ to a Big Screen Display

Your iPAQ's screen is simply too small to use when you want to give a presentation to a group of people. Not even the people in the front row could read your PowerPoint slide show (although for some of the PowerPoint shows I've seen, that might be considered a blessing). If you're going to show what's on your iPAQ's screen to a crowd, you really need a bigger display.

Well, you *could* pass your iPAQ around the room, but that doesn't make for a very lively show, does it? Besides, what happens when the guy in the fifth row decides that he wants to see what else this neat little gadget can do? There goes your show.

A much better idea than trying to make everyone crowd around your iPAQ is to send the show to something larger. The problem, of course, is that your iPAQ doesn't seem to have any way to connect to a bigger display. But as you have no doubt guessed, I've found ways to correct this little problem.

Two different manufacturers make cards that fit your iPAQ and allow it to output to a large display:

✔ **Margi:** (www.margi.com) The Presenter-to-Go is a handy little unit that can display output from your iPAQ on a large screen monitor or through a digital projector. The Presenter-to-Go comes with a business card-sized infrared remote so that you can control the display from several feet away. The Presenter-to-Go is available in both CF and SD form factors, so you can find one to fit your iPAQ.

✔ **Colorgraphic:** (www.colorgraphic.net) The Voyager VGA CF works very much like the Presenter-to-Go, although the Voyager VGA CF can also be connected to a TV set for those times when a large monitor or digital projector is unavailable. You do, however, need an iPAQ with a CF slot to use the Voyager VGA CF.

If you want to display content from your iPAQ on your monitor, but don't want to spend a bunch of money on a piece of hardware, you might want to consider downloading a copy of Remote Display Control for Pocket PC. This free download, which you can find at www.microsoft.com/windowsmobile/resources/downloads/pocketpc/powertoys.mspx, is one of the Microsoft PowerToys for the iPAQ. With the Remote Display Control, you can zoom the iPAQ display on your monitor up to three times normal size — although zooming doesn't increase the resolution of the display so things might get a bit blurry when you zoom in.

Chapter 21

Ten Great iPAQ Business Programs

*Y*our iPAQ is the most capable computer that has ever been able to fit neatly into a pocket. Because your iPAQ is a real computer (and not just a PDA), you can easily add new capabilities simply by installing some new programs, and that makes the iPAQ an ideal business tool.

In this chapter, I show you some of the great business-oriented programs that you can add to your iPAQ. It's virtually impossible to choose the ten best business programs for your iPAQ, though, so you should consider this chapter to be a quick sampler rather than a list of my favorites. To be honest, it's the individual nature of the way that different people use their iPAQ that makes this all so interesting. You may prefer some other choices rather than the ones that I show here, but this gives you a place to start.

ACDSee Mobile

Many types of businesses use images for a number of different reasons. A real estate agent might want to show customers views of interesting homes; a sales person might want to carry along product images; and an artist might want to keep samples of their work handy. In each of these cases, an iPAQ can be a very convenient way to carry along a great assortment of digital images — especially if you add the right software.

It's true that some iPAQ models include image-viewing applications, but none of these built-in programs can match the sheer versatility of a program like ACDSee Mobile from ACD Systems (www.acdsystems.com). This program (shown in Figure 21-1) allows you to find and view all the images on your iPAQ, display those images singly or as a part of a slide show, and zoom in to the images to examine small details. In addition, ACDSee Mobile easily handles a wide range of image formats.

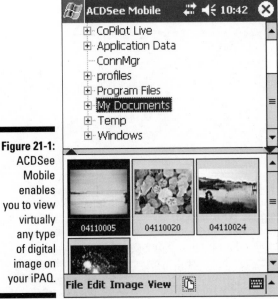

Figure 21-1: ACDSee Mobile enables you to view virtually any type of digital image on your iPAQ.

Developer One Agenda Fusion

If you use your iPAQ to help you keep track of a busy schedule, you probably wish that you could see a bit more of your schedule at a quick glance. The Developer One Agenda Fusion (www.developerone.com) makes this and a number of other scheduling tasks far easier.

Figure 21-2 shows just one example of how Agenda Fusion improves your scheduling options. Here, I'm able to view my agenda for today and also see what tasks I have on the schedule for the rest of the week. In addition to simply showing your schedule, Agenda Fusion can help you manage your contacts, set alarms, and generally make keeping track of a busy life a whole lot easier.

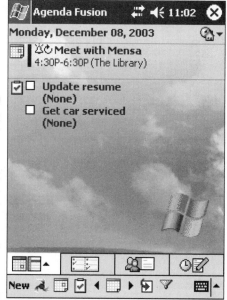

Figure 21-2:
Developer
One Agenda
Fusion
makes it
easier to
control my
schedule
by showing
more of
what's
planned.

Handmark PDAStreetFinder

If you often travel for business, you know that having good maps and the locations of hotels and restaurants can be very important. You probably also know that it can sometimes be difficult to find addresses in a strange city. A good travel guide can be a real lifesaver. That's where a program like the Handmark PDAStreetFinder (www.handmark.com) shown in Figure 21-3 shines.

Handmark PDAStreetFinder has a very easy-to-use desktop application that includes the ratings and descriptions from the *Mobile Travel Guide*. After you select the area that you want to see, you can easily export both the map and selected listings to your iPAQ.

Ilium eWallet

You probably have a wallet full of credit cards, a driver's license, and various other pieces of identification that you need for doing business. If you've ever lost your wallet, you know the danger of keeping all your valuable information in one place. That's where a program like Ilium's eWallet comes in handy (www.iliumsoft.com). As Figure 21-4 shows, you can safely store all sorts of important information in eWallet.

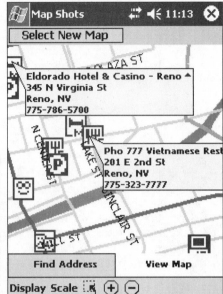

Figure 21-3:
Handmark
PDAStreet-
Finder
combines
good maps
with a travel
guide.

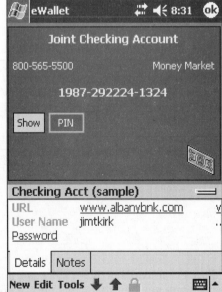

Figure 21-4:
Ilium
eWallet
provides
secure
storage
for your
important
pieces of ID.

You may be wondering how storing credit card numbers and identification documents in eWallet protects all that sensitive information. After all, what happens if someone steals your iPAQ? Will they be able to go on a giant shopping spree with your credit cards? Well, rest assured. The information that you store in eWallet is password protected, and unless you put your password on a sticky note stuck to your iPAQ, your credit card numbers are safe.

Ilium Keep Track

When maintaining financial records, it can be difficult to keep track of every transaction — especially if you find yourself short on cash and need to make a quick withdrawal at an ATM or if you use your debit card to buy some gas. It's even harder to remember all these things if you transfer funds over the phone because you probably don't have any printed receipt to remind you later.

That's where Ilium's Keep Track (see Figure 21-5) really shines (www.iliumsoft.com). This handy little program makes quick work of keeping a record of all those transactions so that you don't get any nasty surprises when you go to balance your checkbook.

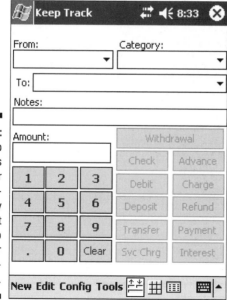

Figure 21-5: Ilium Keep Track limits the number of rude surprises by making it easy to track your bank transactions.

Ilium ListPro

The idea behind a list is really simple, but that doesn't change the fact that lists are awfully handy. For example, Figure 21-6 shows how a building contractor might use Ilium ListPro to make certain that all the necessary materials were ordered for a jobsite.

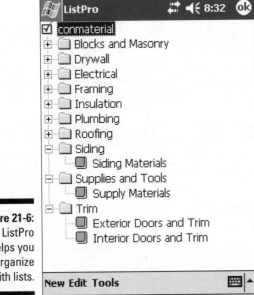

Figure 21-6:
Ilium ListPro
helps you
organize
with lists.

One very handy feature of ListPro is that you can download a whole bunch of free lists from the Ilium Web site (www.iliumsoft.com) so that you don't have to create all your lists from scratch.

Pocket Quicken

Pocket Quicken (see Figure 21-7) from LandWare (www.landware.com) is an absolute essential for any people who use their iPAQs for business purposes and use Quicken on their desktop PCs. This program provides seamless, two-way financial data exchanges between your iPAQ and the version of Quicken on your desktop system. (Microsoft Money for Pocket PC can only import Quicken data — it can't have a two-way exchange.)

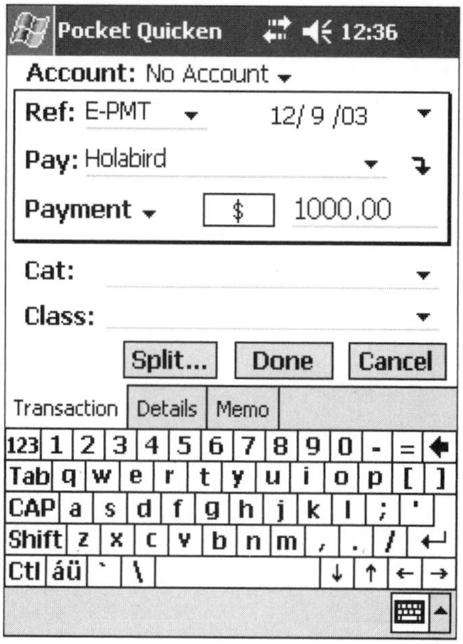

Figure 21-7:
If you use
Quicken,
you should
have Pocket
Quicken on
your iPAQ.

Microsoft Money

If you prefer to use Microsoft Money on your desktop system, you would no doubt prefer Microsoft Money for Pocket PC (see Figure 21-8) on your iPAQ. In either case, the essential point to remember is that the desktop application and the application on your iPAQ must match if you want to automatically share information back and forth between the two.

You can probably find a copy of Microsoft Money for Pocket PC on the Microsoft Money CD, or you can download it for free from the Windows Mobile Web site (www.microsoft.com/windowsmobile/resources/downloads/pocketpc/money.mspx).

EZ-Expense

Although Pocket Quicken and Microsoft Money for Pocket PC are obvious choices for users of the associated desktop applications, EZ-Expense (see Figure 21-9) from Soft Pocket Solutions (www.softpocketsolutions.com) may be a better choice if you use a different method of tracking your business expenses (such as an Excel spreadsheet or a corporate accounting system). Although both of the other two programs are designed to work with a specific desktop accounting package, EZ-Expense allows you to export the data from your iPAQ as an Excel file.

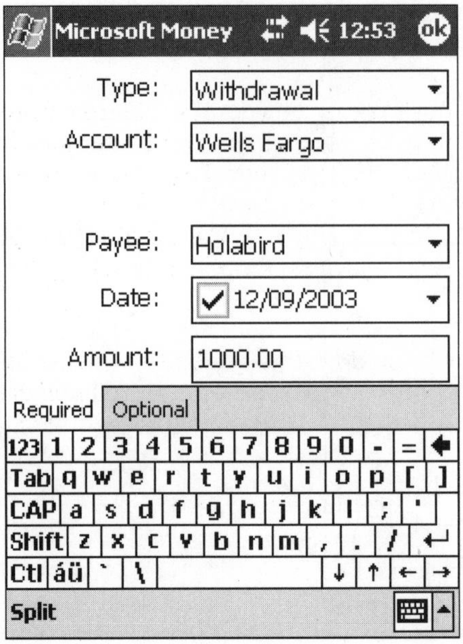

Figure 21-8:
If you use
Microsoft
Money, you
should have
Microsoft
Money for
Pocket PC
on your
iPAQ.

Figure 21-8:
If you use
Microsoft
Money, you
should have
Microsoft
Money for
Pocket PC
on your
iPAQ.

Microsoft Money ⇄ ◀€ 12:53 ok

Type:	Withdrawal ▼
Account:	Wells Fargo ▼
Payee:	Holabird ▼
Date:	✓ 12/09/2003 ▼
Amount:	1000.00

Required | Optional

```
123 1 2 3 4 5 6 7 8 9 0 - = �backspace
Tab q w e r t y u i o p [ ]
CAP a s d f g h j k l ; '
Shift z x c v b n m , . / ↵
Ctl áü ` \              ↓ ↑ ← →
```
Split

Figure 21-9:
EZ-Expense
is an excel-
lent expense
manager for
iPAQ users
who don't
use Quicken
or Money.

EZ-Expense ⇄ ◀€ 1:31

New Expense Report

Title: [   ]

City: [   ]

Business Purpose:
[   ]

Week Ending: 12/ 9 /03 ▼

Cash Advance: 0.00 ▼

Status: ☐ Submitted
☐ Reimbursed

Main | Advanced

✓ ✗ ❓

TeleType GPS Pro

The final program that I mention here is considerably different from the others in this chapter, but bringing it up serves to give you a better idea of just how many divergent business-related functions your iPAQ can perform given the right application. In Chapter 19, I show you how you could use a GPS receiver along with your iPAQ to help you find your way. But the TeleType GPS Pro software can also serve a very useful business purpose in tracking the location of company vehicles.

Real-time tracking requires a live connection (such as a wireless Internet connection). You can find out more about the necessary equipment at the TeleType Web site (www.teletype.com/pages/tracking.html).

Chapter 22

Ten Great Ways to Have Fun with Your iPAQ

Sure, you bought your iPAQ as a business tool, but that doesn't mean you can't have some fun with it, too. Your iPAQ is a real computer, and that means it's quite capable of serving many different purposes. At least one (or ten) of those purposes should be getting a bit of enjoyment.

In this chapter, I present a sampler of ten different ways to enjoy your iPAQ. You can choose which of them suits your lifestyle the best.

Pocket Gourmet

Everyone has to eat, of course, but some people get a lot of enjoyment out of great food experiences. If you're one of those people who really likes to eat, though, you know that sometimes dining out can be a bit more of an experience than you planned on — especially if you aren't an expert on every little esoteric term that might be used on a menu.

That's where a program like Pocket Gourmet from neohand (www.neohand.com) can really help. This program has a menu assistant that describes exactly what those strange terms mean (see Figure 22-1). Pocket Gourmet also has a feature that enables you to make notes about restaurants so that you can remember why you don't want to go back to Billy Bob's Sushi and Bait Shack. Pocket Gourmet also has a tip calculator.

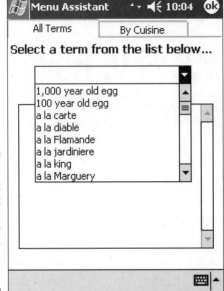

Figure 22-1:
With Pocket
Gourmet
helping,
you know
exactly
what you're
eating.

Pocket Vineyard

To many people, nothing is better than pairing the right wine with a good meal. Sometimes, though, choosing the proper wine can be somewhat intimidating. Your iPAQ can once again come to the rescue when you install Pocket Vineyard from neohand (www.neohand.com).

As Figure 22-2 shows, Pocket Vineyard acts as your personal wine steward. You can check to see what you can expect from a particular vintage (and this is broken down into very specific locales), see definitions of various wine-related terms, and even get recommendations for the types of wines to consider with specific types of food.

Monopoly

Is there anyone who didn't spend hours playing Monopoly when they were growing up? It's hard to imagine that such a person exists because the game has always been so popular. With the iPAQ version of Monopoly from Handmark (www.handmark.com) shown in Figure 22-3, you can relive those days any time you want.

Figure 22-2:
With Pocket Vineyard, you can be an expert at selecting the proper wine.

Figure 22-3:
Monopoly brings out the capitalist in anyone.

Tetris

Tetris is one of those maddening games that can easily get you hooked. It's a classic computer game, and you can get a copy for your iPAQ in the Tetris Classic Game Pak from Handmark (www.handmark.com). Figure 22-4 shows how the game appears shortly after it begins.

Be sure to choose Tools➪Buttons so that you can find out how to control the game — Tetris is played with the buttons on the front of your iPAQ rather than with the stylus.

Figure 22-4:
Tetris is a classic computer game that originated in Russia.

Pocket Gambler

Pocket Gambler from ZIO (www.ziointeractive.com) is one of those rare programs that can easily pay for itself by keeping you from gambling with real money. It does so by letting you play any of seven different casino games on your iPAQ (see Figure 22-5), and you never have to worry about emptying your bank account.

As the figure shows, Pocket Gambler switches your iPAQ into landscape mode and uses the entire screen for game play. This program offers some of the best graphics that I've seen on an iPAQ. I only wish that I could make it pay my winnings!

Figure 22-5:
Get your gambling itch scratched by Pocket Gambler.

Scrabble

If you prefer a slightly more intellectual pursuit, Scrabble from Handmark may be your game. This game requires you to make words by placing tiles on the board (see Figure 22-6). Unlike the actual board game, though, there's no risk of losing the game tiles when one player gets frustrated and tosses the board across the room.

Figure 22-6:
Scrabble makes you look for the right word.

You can play Scrabble against another human player by passing your iPAQ back and forth, but if they have their own PDA, you can choose the option to beam the game before play begins. Scrabble runs on any Pocket PC (not just iPAQs) as well as on Palms.

Pocket Player

It's time to shift focus in a different direction. The Pocket Player from Conduits (www.conduits.com) is an excellent alternative to the Windows Media Player that comes on your iPAQ. Pocket Player (shown in Figure 22-7) offers some very interesting features that you can't find in Windows Media Player. My favorite feature is the graphic equalizer that enables you to tailor the playback to suit your needs. For example, you can boost the middle frequencies to bring out the words in a vocal that you're having trouble understanding. Or, you can cut those same frequencies to hide the vocals if you want to use your iPAQ for karaoke.

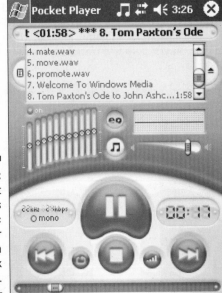

Figure 22-7:
Pocket Player has a graphic equalizer and a playback display.

Pocket Artist

I'd guess that most graphic artists probably prefer to work on a screen that's somewhat larger than the one on an iPAQ. But even so, at times being able to modify an image directly on your iPAQ could be awfully handy (or just plain fun). For example, Figure 22-8 shows an image that's open in Conduits Pocket Artist (`www.conduits.com`). I don't know about you, but I have a whole bunch of ideas for thought balloons that I'd like to add to that picture!

The Conduits Web site offers free 30-day trial versions of a number of programs that you may want to try on your iPAQ.

Figure 22-8:
Pocket Artist puts graphics drawing and editing tools into your pocket.

Vindigo

My iPAQ can without a doubt help me enjoy traveling. With a service like Vindigo (see Figure 22-9), I can find the best places to eat, shop, and visit when I'm on the road. And because Vindigo is a service, the information is constantly being updated so I'm not likely to waste my time trying to find that cool-sounding restaurant that closed a month ago but is still listed in the local phone directory.

Figure 22-9:
Vindigo
makes
sure that I
have fun
while I'm
traveling.

You can discover more about Vindigo and view a demo at their Web site (www.vindigo.com).

PocketChess

This final entry in the "have fun with your iPAQ" category is a bit different from the other applications that I mention in this chapter. PocketChess is a part of the Handmark Tetris Classic Game Pak (www.handmark.com) but somehow it seems like a world apart from something as frantic as Tetris. PocketChess demands serious contemplation if you want to have a satisfying game — especially if you set your iPAQ's skill level high enough in the program's settings.

Figure 22-10 shows the beginning of a game of PocketChess. You can play against your iPAQ, against a human opponent, or if you're a real sadist, you can have your iPAQ play both sides.

Figure 22-10:
PocketChess
keeps you
challenged
and makes
you think.

Chapter 23

Ten Great iPAQ Utilities

*Y*ou might be excused if you think of utilities as the "miscellaneous" category of iPAQ applications. These types of programs fulfill a rather broad range of functions — some of which may have you wondering if they're anything that you would ever find a use for. Well, that's okay; the point of this chapter is really just to give you some ideas about how capable your iPAQ can be given a bit of imagination. So sit back, enjoy, and see what your iPAQ can do with the addition of the proper utility program.

Airscanner Mobile AntiVirus Pro

It's an unfortunate fact that computer viruses not only exist but can be a great danger to your data. The sick people who create these viruses don't really care if they cause you great damage or that you've never done anything to them; all they care about is being evil.

Airscanner Mobile AntiVirus Pro (see Figure 23-1) is a program that's designed to protect your iPAQ from various types of threats including viruses and *Trojan horses* — programs that aren't what they claim to be and often cause damage.

You can download Airscanner Mobile AntiVirus Pro from Airscanner's Web site (www.airscanner.com). It's currently free for non-commercial use. Corporate, educational, government, and small business/home office users must purchase an annual license within 30 days of installing it.

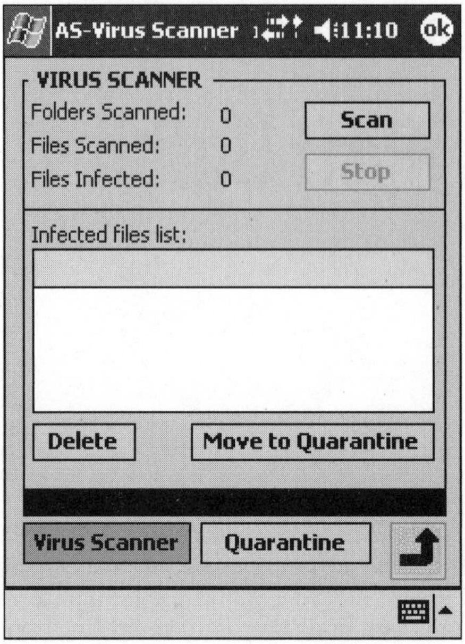

Figure 23-1:
Airscanner
Mobile
AntiVirus
Pro helps
protect
your iPAQ.

Symantec AntiVirus for Handhelds

I would like to mention another antivirus option that you may want to consider. Symantec AntiVirus for Handhelds (see Figure 23-2) is an antivirus application for your iPAQ that comes from one of the big names in PC protection.

If you really depend on the data that you store on your iPAQ, you may be a bit more comfortable with Symantec's antivirus solution because it offers both automatic protection and the Symantec LiveUpdate feature. However, you do have to weigh these features against the higher cost and the fact that Symantec AntiVirus for Handhelds is sold on a yearly subscription basis. You can check out the Symantec Web site at www.symantec.com.

pocketWiNc

The next utility to look at is pocketWiNc from Cirond (www.cirond.com). This is by far the best tool for helping you find and connect to Wi-Fi access points and hotspots. With Wi-Fi capabilities either built into or available through a Wi-Fi adapter card for any iPAQ, pocketWiNc gives you far more information than the so-called "zero configuration utility" that's built into Windows Mobile 2003 (see Figure 23-3). Sure, the built-in utility often tells you if a Wi-Fi signal is available, but it doesn't tell you important information about what type (if any) of security is in use. Without this information, you can waste time trying to connect to a site that's not really available for your use. pocketWiNc has a free trial version, and you need to pay to continue using it after the trial expires.

Figure 23-2:
Symantec
AntiVirus for
Handhelds
is an option
that auto-
matically
protects
your iPAQ.

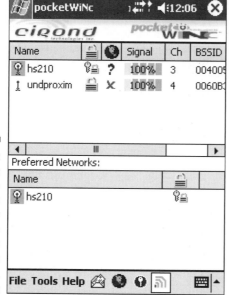

Figure 23-3:
With
pocket-
WiNc, you
can identify
Wi-Fi con-
nections
that you can
actually use.

Nevo Remote Control

Nevo is a remote control program that's available on some iPAQ models. It's designed to replace the pile of remotes (the ones that likely clutter your coffee table) by allowing you to use one device — your iPAQ — to control everything. You simply add the devices (like your TV or stereo) that are in each room, and then use your iPAQ in place of the remotes for those devices (see Figure 23-4).

You can download updates and a user manual from the Nevo Web site (www. mynevo.com). Unfortunately, you cannot add Nevo if your iPAQ doesn't already include it.

Nevo appears on the Start menu if it is installed on your iPAQ, but it does not appear in the Programs folder.

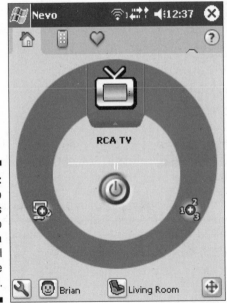

Figure 23-4: Nevo enables your iPAQ to become a universal remote control.

Total Remote

Okay, so you think that Nevo sounds like a great idea, but you don't find it when you tap the Start button on your iPAQ — what are you supposed to do? Are you doomed to be buried under a mound of orphan remote controls or is there hope for the poor iPAQ user who lacks Nevo?

Actually, in some ways you might be better off if your iPAQ doesn't include Nevo because then you won't feel bad about buying a copy of Total Remote from Griffin Mobile (www.griffinmobile.com). As Figure 23-5 shows, Total Remote turns your iPAQ into an extremely capable remote control that has all the controls you need. What the figure cannot show is that Total Remote can learn new commands and you can even program a series of commands that execute with a single tap.

Figure 23-5:
Total Remote can replace your tower of half-dead remote controls with your iPAQ.

Total Remote has another feature that really puts it into a class of its own. The package includes a high-powered infrared radiation module that can control devices like your TV from up to 100 feet away. Imagine the fun that you could have by programming in the codes for your neighbor's TV!

PHM Registry Editor

PHM Registry Editor is one of those programs that no one would mistake for anything other than a utility. It's a serious tool that enables you to do things that are otherwise nearly impossible to do, such as examining and modifying the Registry in your iPAQ (see Figure 23-6).

This isn't a tool for the faint of heart: Modifying the Registry incorrectly can do serious damage. In fact, it's possible to mess up so severely that your only choice is to do a hard reset (which conveniently wipes out all your data and any programs that you installed).

If you're willing to accept the responsibility of using PHM Registry Editor wisely (or at least not blaming anyone else if you mess up), you can find out more about the program at `www.phm.lu/Products/PocketPC/RegEdit/`. The author of the program, Philippe Majerus, provides free downloads at this Web site.

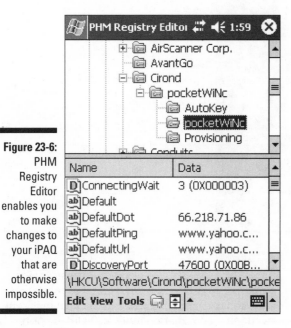

Figure 23-6:
PHM
Registry
Editor
enables you
to make
changes to
your iPAQ
that are
otherwise
impossible.

vxUtil

vxUtil is another of those pure utility programs (and another of the free ones). It includes a number of very useful functions that can help you figure out what is going wrong when you are experiencing networking problems. Figure 23-7 gives you an idea of all the different features that are available in this program.

You can download a free copy of the vxUtil program from the Cambridge Computer Corporation Web site (`www.cam.com/vxutil_pers.html`).

Use the Info function in vxUtil to determine the current IP address of your iPAQ and various other related pieces of information.

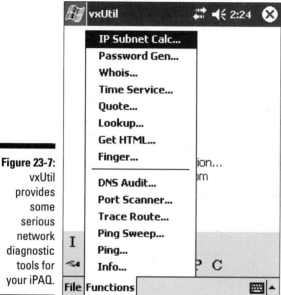

Figure 23-7:
vxUtil
provides
some
serious
network
diagnostic
tools for
your iPAQ.

X-Lite

X-Lite from Xten (www.xten.com/index.php?menu=products&smenu=xlite&ssmenu=download) is another free utility that may be of interest to many iPAQ users. X-Lite (see Figure 23-8) is a program that enables you to make free calls over broadband Internet connections. (This is also known as VOIP — voice-over IP.) This free utility works in conjunction with the free service called Free World Dialup (www.pulver.com/fwd/).

Currently, you are limited to calling other Free World Dialup users, but there's no reason why your friends and relatives can't sign up, too. Just think: You could call a friend halfway around the world while you sit in that Wi-Fi–enabled coffee shop, and it wouldn't cost you a dime!

Be sure to download the Auto-Config "Free World Dialup" version of X-Lite. That way, you don't have to deal with the somewhat confusing configuration options that are necessary to set up your account.

Figure 23-8:
X-Lite
allows you
to make free
calls over
the Internet
from your
iPAQ.

Pocket Slides

Pocket Slides from Conduits (www.conduits.com) is a program that enables you to display PowerPoint presentations on your iPAQ. So what's the big deal about that, you ask? Well, a couple of things make it a big deal (and an extremely useful utility to have on your iPAQ). First, no version of PowerPoint exists for the iPAQ, so you need a third-party program like Pocket Slides to even show your PowerPoint presentation. Second, although other PowerPoint viewers do exist for you iPAQ, Pocket Slides has the added feature of allowing you to modify your presentation right on your iPAQ. Third — and this is a big one — Pocket Slides can handle huge PowerPoint presentations that every other iPAQ PowerPoint viewer I tested simply chokes on. For example, Figure 23-9 shows one of 631 slides in a 225MB PowerPoint slideshow that I created for a Holabird American auction (www.holabird.org). No other PowerPoint application for the iPAQ could load this slideshow because of its size.

Pocket Slides is completely compatible with the Margi Presenter-to-Go (www.margi.com). The combination of these two utilities enables you to bring along your PowerPoint presentation without lugging a laptop and without worrying about whether you can find a compatible PC.

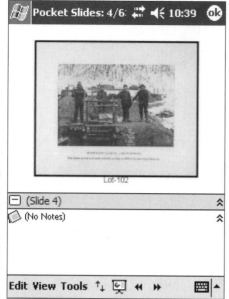

Figure 23-9:
Pocket
Slides is the
best iPAQ
PowerPoint
utility that
I've found.

Really huge Pocket Slides presentations like the one that I did for the auction don't need to be transferred to a storage card by using ActiveSync. You can save time by transferring the file directly to the storage card by using something like a SanDisk card reader (www.sandisk.com).

Adobe Acrobat Reader

Adobe Acrobat is one of the most popular document formats for one very good reason: Documents that are in the PDF format can be viewed on virtually any type of computer (if it has a version of the Acrobat Reader) and still retain their original appearance. (PDF stands for Portable Document Format.) The Adobe Acrobat Reader for Pocket PC (see Figure 23-10) is a free utility that enables your iPAQ to view PDF documents.

You can download the Acrobat Reader from the Adobe Web site (www.adobe.com). Be sure to download the version that's listed as being for the iPAQ. (Don't worry that Windows Mobile 2003 isn't listed; the version that's available works just fine.)

Figure 23-10:
Adobe
Acrobat
Reader
brings PDF
documents
to your
iPAQ's
screen.

Index